His Road Trip 2

a continuing…

Aspiring Adventure

Across America

By Lugene Hessler Hammond

Published by WebPowerPros, Inc.,
POBox 51654, Myrtle Beach, SC 29579
Copyright 2017 by Lugene Hessler Hammond

www.HisRoadTrip.com

Thanks for purchasing our little book. Funds from this sale will enable us to continue our ministry and keep us on the road for Him.

www.MotorHomeMinistry.com, a ministry for connecting the Bible to kids and parents.

Printed in the United States of America

ISBN 978-0-692-93204-9

Unless otherwise indicated. Bible quotations are taken from:

Most Bible quotations are taken from the New International Version (NIV) Holy Bible, New International Version®, NIV® Copyright ©1973, 1978, 1984, 2011 by Biblica, Inc.® Used by permission. All rights reserved worldwide.

Introduction Bible quotations are taken from the Holman Christian Standard Bible (HCSB) Copyright © 1999, 2000, 2002, 2003, 2009 by Holman Bible Publishers, Nashville Tennessee. All rights reserved.

This book is dedicated to our
wonderful, amazing, smart, talented, and beautiful daughter,

Diana

We share a lifetime of memories that include
ringlets to bad haircuts
Cabbage Patch to Barbie to Madame Alexander
Homemade outfits to prom dresses
Spelling tests to math—lots of math
Girl Scout Cookies to Girl Scout Camp to
Girl Scout Silver Award
Princess crowns to messy rooms
Bob Ross to art supplies to art exhibits to art degree
OPK's (Other People's Kids) to root beer floats
to Interns and Chairman of the Board
Trips to school to trips to Japan and Italy
Emergency rooms, broken bones, seizures,
kidney stones, and stitches
One crazy dog
Lots of love   Lots of laughter   Lots of tears

I've always said that you have a lot of your dad in you, but
just enough of me to make you really special.

Because your momma loves you.
You are my world. Forever.

and especially dedicated to
my Lord and Savior, Jesus Christ,
who makes All things possible.

To God be all the glory!

PREFACE

Decades ago, when I worked for a home health aide agency, I attended a workshop entitled, "Who you are is where you were when." Huh? I had no idea what all of this was about, but it turned out to be something I would never forget. The presenters emphasized that the elderly and their quirks that we dealt with on a day-to-day basis had all lived through some very stressful times in America's history, times that we would never be able to comprehend. The effects The Great Depression and the World Wars had on economic and socialistic times would be forever engrained within them as individuals. And those effects were different for each and every one of them. For instance, the lasting effects of the Great Depression on a 12-year-old child would be much different than its effects on a 25-year-old in need a job to support his family.

Hence, it is all about where you were when.

When I wrote my first book, I felt it necessary to present a detailed history of our lives leading up to our embarking on a personal mission named Motorhome Ministry. No one could truly appreciate the personal importance of doing such a thing, unless they could understand what life experiences had brought us to this point.

And especially our faith experiences.

As I did in my first book, I will apologize in advance for the number of times I will use the words *wow, amazing, beautiful, breathtaking, awesome, terrific, spectacular, remarkable, stupendous,* and other such superlatives. Even these words do not do justice to God's beautiful creations.

There are Bible verses throughout this book. As Christians, the Bible is our instruction manual and I feel these scriptures bring our story to life.

One important note as you read this book, when I refer to Him with a capital "H", I'm referring to my Holy Father God above, our Lord and Savior, Jesus Christ. Anybody else, is just a plain him.

To bring this book to life, we've uploaded thousands of beautiful photos, in date order, on our web site www.HisRoadTrip.com. You will find some of the most amazing scenery, architecture, historic landmarks, flowers and plants, and wildlife across North America. There are some blurry ones, many of which were taken through a bug-specked windshield at highway speeds. We chose not to delete these, because they still help to tell our story.

There's another thing that needs explaining before you begin reading my journal entries: we have named our navigation electronics. Frick was our first, our Garmin. He was okay in the days that he was the best technology available, and we always keep him on standby, in the motorhome cockpit.

Then there's Frack, my iPhone Google Maps app. I really like Frack, but he does have his limitations. And Frick and Frack used to argue relentlessly. That's why my husband insisted we needed yet another app.

Frank is our Sygic program designed for truckers. He's really got some terrific options, when they work. Larry, my husband of 40+ years, set it up to know that we are indeed a big rig, and supplied it with our length, our height, our width, and our weight. Frank contemplates our destination from our origin and finds the perfect route, taking into consideration all the parameters described above. Or sometimes, he just screws up. And when he does, he screws up BIG time.

And then, of course, there always Suri. You know her. Apple Computer's AI (Artificial Intelligent) alter ego.

I talk a lot about getting a "stamp in my Passport." Well, it's not the same Passport I'd present to Homeland Security when I travel. It's a Centennial Passport issued by the National Park Service in 2016, in celebration of their 100th Anniversary. Each Park has their own set of rubber stamps with old-fashioned ink pads, so that you can stamp where you've visited. Mine is so full in certain regions, that I had to add pages in the back!

There are also references to doing a "shop." We have done work based on an app named "Easy Shift." They offer a set sum of money for going into a place of business, answering a few or many questions regarding certain products, and taking some pictures. We have searched for shops available in an area where we were visiting, reviewed the basics of the shop versus the amount of cash it pays, then decided whether or not to reserve it. Some were shops about cookie and cracker brands. Some were about beer brands and how the store has them on display. The toughest ones (but pay well) were about wine—label names and types—but they were hard. Stores usually have wine displays all over! The cash we earned appeared in our checking account, usually the next day. We found it a great way to make some extra cash, when we had the time to spare.

I pray this book will encourage you to not only go out and see this beautiful land that we have the freedom to roam without restraint, but to also encourage you to seek His amazing grace and enjoy a greater personal relationship with our Lord and Savior, Jesus Christ.

> Psalm 19:14
> May the words of my mouth and the meditation of my heart
> be pleasing in your sight, O Lord,
> my Rock and my Redeemer.

BACKGROUND

Larry and I grew up in a then-small suburb of Cincinnati, met in high school band class, graduated, and were married in 1973. I worked 2 jobs while Larry attended college and worked full time. A new job for Larry moved us to Winston-Salem, North Carolina, where we bought our first new car, our first house, and had our first baby. When Diana was born in 1976, I was terribly homesick, and we moved back to Ohio late that year. We purchased my childhood home and Diana's brother Bobby arrived in 1979. We were close to friends and family. We were active in a wonderful church. Life was good.

I've enjoyed a personal relationship with my Heavenly Father since I was a small child. Larry did not. Some would have said that we were unequally yoked from the start. But we did okay.

Several years later, another job opportunity took us to Louisville, Kentucky, then quickly on to Indianapolis, Indiana. By Christmas, 1985, the kids were doing great in school, Larry and I both had great jobs, we loved our house, the neighborhood, and our church was only a mile away. Everything was perfect. Until disaster struck.

On New Year's Eve, our new best neighbors, Jim and Jill would arrive at any minute. We had agreed earlier to spend the celebration here at our house, with all four of our kids. They would cut through a couple of back yards to get here, and we would play games, watch movies, and stuff our faces until midnight. It would keep us all off the roads. We would be safe against the world.

Our friends would be arriving soon, so I sent the kids off to tidy their rooms, telling them, "I don't want our new friends to think we live like heathens!" Excited about the upcoming evening, they scooted off quickly. Diana skipped her way back to the kitchen after about 5 minutes, proud that her room didn't need much work. I sent her back to check on her brother. Larry and I will never forget her words, as she ran back: "Bobby had an accident and I think he's dead."

Why on earth would she say such a thing?

Larry and I rushed back to Bobby's bedroom. He had received a bicycle lock chain for Christmas and had been "locking up" all sorts of things earlier that week. We found him hanging from the chain on his bunkbed, not breathing. I ran to call 911.

Larry, alone then with Bobby: *I ran into the room, carefully removed him from the chain, then started to give him CPR and mouth to mouth. As I was desperately trying to bring him back to life, God spoke to me directly for the very first time in my life. I heard Him say clearly, "He's okay. He's with Me. Let him go." I didn't hear this through my ears or thought it through my mind it was just there. Loud and clear. A strong presence was with me. But I just kept on going. I couldn't stop! I had to be in control! I stopped only when the first responders poured into the room and took over. I felt emotionally broken, almost to the point of collapsing.*

I phoned for our new friends to come quickly, as something terrible had happened. Without question, they arrived in minutes. The ambulance and police had already arrived. Other neighbors were out on the street, wondering what could be happening to the new folks in their quiet little neighborhood.

The paramedics quickly loaded Bobby into the ambulance, and leaving Diana with our friends, we were quickly whisked away in a police car. The officer driving was male; his partner a woman. I was sitting right behind her in the patrol car, with Larry to my left. As uncomfortable as it must have been, she reached over the high bench seat to firmly hold my hand the entire ride downtown. My other hand was holding onto Larry's. No one spoke.

Traffic was horrible, as expected. There was no easy way to get to the hospital district in downtown Indianapolis. The ambulance eventually radioed the cruiser and asked that we run ahead of them with lights and sirens, to cut a path in the traffic. Both sets of blue and red lights pulsated against the close buildings. There were sirens, white lights, and traffic lights. We would race up the block, screech to a stop in the middle of the intersection, wait for the ambulance to catch up, then speed ahead to the next light, over and over again. It was total and complete mayhem.

While we had followed the ambulance, I could see everything through the glass windows in the back. I was glad when we pulled ahead of them. I no longer had to witness their futile efforts.

So, while sitting and holding hands, my mind is racing, shooting questions one after another: "Where's my Mom and Dad? I've got to call them. Oh, they're in Florida, at a campground. What campground? It's late and the campground office might be closed. Maybe I can call the local police. Where are they in Florida? I need to call Larry's Mom and Dad to tell them. No. I'll call my sister-in-law and let her and her husband drive over to tell my in-laws. What if he dies? What if he lives and needs special care? OH, MY GOD, WHAT IF?"

And my world stopped. All the flashing lights, all the sirens, all the traffic and holiday lights, all the mayhem. My mind was completely still. Then God explained that this was no one's fault, no accident. Everything was going according to His plan. I had indeed called upon the Lord with a plea and He had immediately answered. That was different, and He had my complete attention.

> Jeremiah 29:11
> "For I know the plans I have for you," declares the Lord,
> "Plans to prosper you and not to harm you,
> plans to give you hope and a future."

Larry didn't share with me his experience with God's words until years later, but I knew at that very moment God had already called Bobby home to be with Him. I knew the doctors would not be able to revive him. At the hospital, they worked on him for another hour or so, to no avail.

Sweet Bobby, full of smiles and giggles, who had been stealing Baby Jesus out of the manger scene just a few days ago, was gone. He was only six years old.

The next few months were agonizing. After such a loss, I immediately began taking Diana to counseling, and I participated, as well. Larry claimed that "men don't talk about touchy-feely emotions with other men." Nope. Forget it.

With that said, Diana and I did pretty well in working through our grief together, but Larry did not. And the greatest problem was that Larry was angry with God.

But God had others plans to convince him. Christmas, 1986 quickly arrived.

Larry: *"Christmas is almost here again Dad, get out the decorations," my 10-year old daughter, Diana insisted. When I'd put away the Christmas things last year, we'd just buried Bobby. My wife had carefully packed each item in its labeled box and I'd lugged everything out to the storage shed. I didn't want to face those sad memories again. But Diana wanted Christmas as usual, with the tree and all the trimmings. She was absolutely right. Life goes on. I steeled myself and headed out to the shed. It was a crisp, clear, windless day, with the sun high in the sky, but the beauty was lost on me. I thought I would never again enjoy Christmas.*

How can I, without all of us here together?

I yanked open the shed door and a cold wind swooshed out. A sheet of paper floated toward me, slowly coming to rest at my feet. Then the air was still once more. I bent down to pick up the paper— a handmade Christmas card. How did this get here? I wondered. We had a special box for cards we'd saved, cards whose messages were worth reading year after year. We cherished those. Especially this one from last year, the one I held in my hands. As I reread his penciled message, I could hear Bobby's voice see his face on Christmas morning.

His card read...from first grade 1986:

"Have a Merry Christmas Mommy and Daddy. Happy New Year." Love, Bobby

Bobby would always be with us, and one day we'd be with him."[1]

HE would always be with us, too.

I was pale as I went inside and recounted this incident to Lugene. I started to question in my mind. What? Why did this happen? This would be the second encounter with God, and a turning point in my faith.

> Psalm 91:11
> For He will command his angels
> concerning you to guard you in all ways.

---

[1] This story was submitted by Larry Hammond to Angels on Earth, A Guidepost Publication, printed and published in Nov/Dec 2000 Christmas issue.

Within months, we could see the people closest to us undergoing changes in their lies—amazing changes. We had been the only members of our extended families that regularly attended church. Over the months and years, one by one, family members began to attend church, accept Christ, and were baptized. A marriage was saved. New children were born. One began singing praise in churches. A few played in praise bands. One became a minister. One is a church secretary, another works for the church. One is studying to become a missionary. A couple created and ran ministries for the poor, the elderly, and those with special needs.

God had assured me that He had a plan, and that Bobby's death was part of the plan. I had accepted His assurance and although I grieved, I sat back and patiently waited for His plan to be revealed.

I am happy to say that, as this story continues, you will learn of many other lives that are changed daily, even to this very day. And, God willing, every tomorrow ahead. Every day of every one of our lives is spent in service of Jesus and bringing new souls to Christ.

John 16:20
Very truly I tell you, you will weep and mourn
while the world rejoices. You will grieve,
but your grief will turn to joy.

God is good. All the time.

By 1988, still struggling with his relationship with God, Larry decided that his corporate life had no meaning for him anymore. We sold our home in Indianapolis and moved to Gatlinburg, Tennessee to open a little gourmet popcorn and candy store. There were some lean years, but Diana especially flourished, away from the constant reminders of the tragedy that occurred there in our home.

By 1995, we moved to Myrtle Beach, South Carolina to open a larger store at a new entertainment complex called Broadway at the Beach. Diana started college at Coastal Carolina University and we all nearly worked ourselves to death. Diana graduated in 2000.

We learned in 2004 that our landlords had no intention of renewing the lease for our store. By the time it expired in 2005, we had gone tens of thousands of dollars in debt to build another store close by, but there just wasn't enough foot traffic to make it successful. In the meantime, Larry had been afflicted with an autoimmune disorder that no doctor or specialist could figure out. He was much too sick to work, and that left everything up to me and Diana. The store died a slow and painful death, until we closed it in September 2006.

Along with Larry's mother and sister, Lisa, we fell in love with Langston Baptist Church in nearby Conway. It was the largest church we had ever attended. We were encouraged to join a Sunday School class, and it was the best decision we ever made. I had quit going to Sunday School when I graduated high school, and I taught for a while after that. I always considered Sunday School was for school kids. I was so wrong.

The study of God's word is a very important thing, and should be done daily. There was an average of 30-40 members in that class and they welcomed us with open arms. We got to know them well. We prayed for one another, rejoiced with them in good times, and interceded in their troubled times. We had pot lucks once a month and a grand but silly Christmas party every year. Once we were comfortable in there, other relationships began to form.

Ever since junior high, I've been a back-row Alto. I love to sing in large groups, but you will never hear me sing solo. Langston had 60+ in their adult choir and I loved being a part of their back row.

Going on a mission trip is what first caught Larry's eye. Another member of our Sunday School class had taken a group the year before and she planned to take another. Larry jumped right in. It was something he'd never done before and he loved it so much, that he went each year for 6 more years. It pushed him to the limit of his poor health, but he loved it.

As time went on, we both participated in seasonal dramas, I assisted with the children's choir, and Larry was voted in as a Deacon. There were programs to help the poor, benevolence meals to prepare, special evangelism events, special choirs, and the need for golf cart drivers for the crowds that attended. We enjoyed every minute of service.

During that same time, Langston decided to sponsor nearby Waccamaw Elementary School for a Good News Club. A national program of Child Evangelism Fellowship, it was difficult to find volunteers. It took place after school, but still during the typical workday. Being disabled, and not on a schedule, Larry showed up to see if he could help.

The Club invited kindergarteners through fifth graders. I will never forget when he came to my office after his first Club. I was sitting in my desk chair. He stood close to me, looked down and said, "I don't think the kids like me." I looked up at him and checked him up and down. Larry's a big man, 6' 3" and at that time, weighed over 300 pounds. That day he had chosen to dress all in black. I replied, "Well, looking up at you from this angle, dressed all in black, you look pretty scary to me, too." It was agreed that he would wear something less imposing the next week, and he wore a comically-illustrated jungle animal shirt. It made all the difference.

They loved him and he loved them! He volunteered with the same club for 6 years, until we went on the road for Him.

Also during that time, I began to keep the books for our county Baptist Association. The woman I worked with, Diane, had led Larry's mission team to Guatemala. They went there to accompany a team of doctors and dentists through Medical Missions Ministries, based in Guatemala City, Guatemala. She had since then become a local leader for Operation Christmas Child and enjoyed it so much. During her annual recruitment, she invited me to become a member of her team. Those couple of years as a full-time volunteer introduced me to an amazing group of people who accomplish amazing things. The millions they reach worldwide are kids who would not otherwise hear the Gospel. You should participate, too. Check out samaritanspurse.org, Operation Christmas Child.

I'd known for years that my primary gift was the gift of service. I was always happiest when I was serving others. Larry had come to realize, over these past 10 years, that Evangelism was his primary gift. He also realized that offering up his life in such service gave him amazing fulfillment, too. God was finally getting through to his heart.

And if that hadn't been enough, one night he paid a visit to Heaven. All the precious details are in the original *His Road Trip.* He choked to death in his sleep, and awoke pain-free in Heaven. But God motioned for him to go back; it wasn't yet his time. When he awoke, struggling for breath, he considered what he had seen. Not an earthly word had been spoken to him, but he knew without a doubt that God had bigger plans for him. It would still be another couple of years before that life mission would be revealed, but that encounter brought him so much closer to God. His anger was finally gone. That burden lifted, it was time to get to work on his personal relationship with God.

We continued to struggle in the years that followed. The real estate market collapsed and the home we loved so much was breaking us financially. Larry couldn't work, that was a fact. Finding a permanent, decent job in the fluctuating tourist job market of Myrtle Beach was next to impossible, much less for this 60'ish grey-haired woman, who'd been self-employed the last 2 decades. I was a little short on job references. Something had to give.

By now, Larry had a much clearer idea of what God wanted him to do. He wanted us to sell everything and commit our lives in service to Him. Larry's impression was to do this on the road. We found a motorhome to lease, and gave our house back to the mortgage company. Anything that couldn't fit in the motorhome was either sold or given to charity.

But I had told Larry that hitting the road without some money in the bank was just plain foolish. I have always trusted the Lord to take care of me, but what if this mission of his was not a mission of His? I was adamant: we would not leave with an empty bank account.

By November 2014, I was finally working full-time. We were living in Myrtle Beach, in that rig when disaster eventually struck.

It was October 20, 2015. We were beginning our long drive to the 2015 Spyder Rally in Fontana Village, North Carolina. We were the sponsors, and our Rally the previous year had been a great success. There were over 1,000 people pre-registered this year, and others were free to drop in as they wished. We were so excited.

We were still in our home county, when we realized I had failed to secure the bathroom door and with every bump and turn, it banged open, then banged closed. I am a firm seatbelt advocate. My car doesn't move without my seat belt buckled. I reasoned that we were on an open stretch of highway we were quite familiar with. There wouldn't be another stop light—or car—for miles. I unlatched my seatbelt and ran to the back to secure the door.

I was back in less than 8 seconds, but a moped had appeared out of nowhere and yanked right in front of Larry, who slammed on the brakes to spare the life of the kamikaze driver. In a heartbeat, I had been thrown head-first into the windshield and fallen to the floor. Long story short, after 2 ambulance rides, 2 hospital emergency rooms, and lots of tests, it was confirmed I had fractured my C-2. I just know it hurt like hell.

I called Diana at work, to explain what had happened. She needed to go with her dad to Fontana—there was absolutely no way Larry could handle such a crowd on his own. Her new boss was admirably cooperative and in a few hours, they were repacked and on their way, the windshield reinforced with clear tape.

I spent 5 days in the hospital, with the neurosurgeon's promise that if I keep the cervical collar on, it will heal itself in 3 months.

Well, 3 months later, tests revealed that not only had the fracture not healed together, it had actually separated. I would need immediate surgery.

After that surgery was performed, the pain was unbearable. But even more unbearable was the news the neurosurgeon brought later that evening: we will have to operate again. So, 3 days later, on Valentine's Day, 2016, he did.

Even birthing 2 babies, I had never known that level of pain. It's amazing how much physical strength is required to hold up your own head. I couldn't return to work for weeks, as the pain was so bad. Financial woes continued to worsen.

A couple of weeks after the accident, I received a telephone call from an attorney in Charleston. He made the 3-hour trip to explain that I might have settlement options available that we may not be aware of. At the end of the meeting, I asked him how he had learned about me. He had seen the Go Fund Me page on Facebook that my dear supervisor had set up for me. What an angel she was.

In short, God had turned that 8-second trip into something life-changing in more than one way. He used that painful event to provide for all our needs—we now had cash in the bank to hit the road for Motorhome Ministry. My one and only concern had been addressed in a mighty way.

We said goodbyes to our church family and left Myrtle Beach on March 30, 2016. The rest, as they say, is history.

Proverbs 16:3
Commit your activities to the Lord, and your plans will be achieved.

"The greatest legacy one can pass on to
one's children and grandchildren
is not money
or other material things accumulated in one's life,
but rather a legacy of character and faith."

--Billy Graham--

AND THE JOURNEY CONTINUES...

SEPTEMBER 1

Larry drove our Ford Escape to Canyonlands National Park today, which is just down the road from the Arches National Park. The Visitor Center is miles into the park. They even had their own viewpoint which was fantastic, where you could walk to the edge of a massive canyon. Larry went as close as he could to get some good pictures. I was more cautious and stayed back. We again viewed the park movie and got the Passport stamped. We drove to some overlooks and followed a large tour group in a bus at every viewing point. The rock formations and the canyons are amazing, beyond any description in words.

Imagine a level rock floor that extends for miles in every direction. Then, somebody pulls a plug and the bottoms fall out at random locations, causing great slot canyons to form. The colors were so awesome—there were red, pink, and purples with the green Colorado river twisting like a snake at the bottom. Then you look in another direction, it looked like somebody randomly blobbed Playdough, creating huge, miles-wide buttes, an isolated hill with steep sides, and a flat top (similar to but narrower than a mesa).

The National Park Services explains that, "Canyonlands National Park preserves 337,598 acres of colorful canyons, mesas, buttes, fins, arches, and spires in the heart of southeast Utah's high desert. Water and gravity have been the prime architects of this land, sculpting layers of rock into the rugged landscape you see today".[2] It was indescribably fascinating.

There are 14 hikes listed on the National Park Service website, from .3 miles to overnight treks of nearly 22 miles. I can't

---

[2] nps.gov

begin to imagine what those trekkers were privy to see. I will never know for myself, that's for sure, but that's okay.

The only green trees or grasses you find in this area follow the Colorado River, and then in great abundance, quite a contrast to the otherwise barren landscape.

We returned to the motorhome for a quick nap in the cool. A tasty Stouffers for supper, then off to the hot tub until rain threatened. It was mesmerizing to watch as the sun set, the rays and shadows creeping up the sides of the cliffs. Despite the elevations all around us, we saw two beautiful rainbows before rain became imminent.

> Genesis 9:16
> Whenever the rainbow appears in the clouds,
> I will see it and remember the everlasting covenant
> between God and all living creatures
> of every kind on the earth."

We tried to watch a movie but the DVD player needed cleaning. We finally gave up and went to bed. I love to sleep with the sound of rain on the roof.

SEPTEMBER 2

Finally, we enjoyed a day of rest. Well, maybe not rest, but at least a chance to catch up on mundane things. I defrosted the freezer and reconciled the business checking account. We drove into town. I got a much-needed haircut and we had a great time at the Moab Brewery for supper.

Later that evening, we enjoyed another dip in the hot tub. I had an interesting conversation with a very outspoken Aussie woman who loudly proclaimed that I was a complete and total idiot for even considering voting for Trump. Why would she even care about America's politicians and campaigns? Go figure. Idiot or not, it will be my choice.

Oh, well. To each her own. Thank you, Lord for another fine day. This place has surely been touched by the hand of God.

Psalm 95:4-5
In his hand are the depths of the earth,
and the mountain peaks belong to him.
[5] The sea is his, for he made it,
and his hands formed the dry land.

SEPTEMBER 3

Today we drove the motorhome to Capitol Reef National Park, in Fruita, Utah. We're back on US191 north to I-70 again, back the way we came into Moab. We headed west this time on I-70, then took UT24 to the southwest. Again, everywhere along the barren land of the desert, were iconic red rock formations. Each one was totally different from the next in shape, size, and slightly in color. We passed some hills that clearly had copper in them. You know that ugly green that aging copper makes? That was the color of the middle of the hills.

"Settlement came late to south-central Utah; the Capitol Reef area wasn't charted by credible explorers until 1872. In the last half of that decade, Latter Day Saints (Mormon) settlers moved into the high plateau lands west of Capitol Reef and established communities based on short-season farming and grazing."[3]

---

[3]nps.gov

> Isaiah 35:1-2
> The desert and the parched land will be glad;
> the wilderness will rejoice and blossom.
> Like the crocus, [2] it will burst into bloom; it will rejoice
> greatly and shout for joy.
> The glory of Lebanon will be given to it,
> the splendor of Carmel and Sharon;
> they will see the glory of the LORD, the splendor of our God.

The settlement itself was small. The campground was busy, with families and lots of kids. There were active orchards just up the road, but not much was in season at the time. From Google maps, this oasis looks like a little green patch in the middle of the brown desert of southern Utah. There was water nearby, for sure.

We drove our car from the campground to the Visitor Center, and we saw the park movie and got the Passport stamped. We drove on to the nearby settlement which had a store, a barn, a blacksmith, and orchard. We were delighted to find a small house that offered goodies for sale, especially fresh baked goods. We made our selections and had to stand in a long line to pay. We bought their last pan of homemade glazed cinnamon rolls and two small pies. Larry chose an apple pie and I got a mixed berry. They were each a little bigger than a pot pie and incredibly delicious!

What we desperately needed was a bag of ice. There are no utilities here and Larry just won't drink Diet Coke without plenty of ice. We thought there would be some at that little house, but they only had baked goods, honeys, and goodies in jars. With directions, we had to drive ten miles each way to get that silly bag of ice. But at least the drive was scenic and we were amazed at its changes, in every direction that we turned.

Considering that much of Utah is desert, this truly was an oasis for those who came. With water nearby, they had a great but limited growing season. They could provide for themselves. The Mormons did well in choosing this place in which to settle.

Back at the campground with ice now, we stayed near the motorhome for the much of the afternoon. We did take a drive into the park later that afternoon on US24 west, then a back road called Scenic Drive, that ended at Capital Dome. The road took us through a lot of stretches with signs warning of washouts from flash floods. There must be an awful lot of water that comes gushing down the trenches from the mountains when it storms, but today they were all bone dry. Most of these stretches had been repaved with concrete; I guess the water had washed out the asphalt too many times to count.

Later, Larry set up the camera and tripod and took some remarkable photos of the sunset and the red rocks cliffs. He kept taking pictures well into the darkness, when the stars, planets, a crescent moon, and the Milky Way were in their full splendor. There were no city lights to spoil the show.

We were surrounded by kids, but no one was touching the packets. Larry decided to go speak to the dad that had five kids camped nearby. He asked if they would like some activity packets about Jesus for their kids. "No, we're okay" was his only response. I think they were Mormons.

But the group behind us was a totally different song. The first thing I had noticed was that there were two young girls in wheelchairs with the group. They were friendly, and would wave at me energetically every time I came and went. What if they're not coming because they can't move their wheelchairs across the grass, I wondered. I grabbed some packets and walked the short distance to their site.

They eagerly greeted me again. I made some small conversation and introduced myself. I asked them if they knew Jesus. Oh, yes was the overwhelming reply. I asked if they would enjoy a book and other things about Jesus and they most definitely did.

One young lady seemed hesitant to ask, but then politely explained that there were other children with them, and could they each have one, too? I asked for a head count and returned to the motorhome for more. Everyone was delighted and smiling widely when I left. The youngest was tearing into his and went straight to the crayons. Yes, Lord. I rejoice that they know you.

Deuteronomy 4:9
Only be careful, and watch yourselves closely
so that you do not forget the things your eyes have seen
or let them fade from your heart as long as you live.
Teach them to your children and to their children after them.

SEPTEMBER 4

We drove on to Bryce, Utah on US24 west again to UT62 south. The winding and narrow roads took us through some open canyons.

We were excited to see Big Horn Sheep on a cliff above us, out in the middle of nowhere. We arrived with the hope that we could check into the National Park campground a day early, but they were full. We had passed a campground called Ruby's Inn RV Park on the way into town, and went back to inquire about space there.

They apologetically explained that a big RV group was arriving that very day. The only place available for our big rig was in the employee campground across the road. It had everything the campground had, except trees. It was a huge site and it was sure okay with us. This scenery all around is beautiful; full of wide open spaces. You could see for miles in every direction.

We wandered around just a bit today, and concluded that summer has finally come and gone. It was only in the 60's here today and it's going down into the 30's tonight. The propane furnace will be working hard this week.

We spent part of the afternoon stuffing kid's packets, as the kids at Capitol Reef had just about cleaned us out. We keep all our packet supplies below in the "basement," a storage compartment below our main living area. We got everything out, spread piles all over the kitchen and made about 25 packets. Then put it all away. It's a good time, knowing that this work is in God's name.

For supper, I fixed this great little dip from scratch. I named it "Erin's Chicken Stuff", because I got the recipe from a young woman at church, named Erin, of course. (recipe in the Back of the Book). She brought it to a Deacon's Wives event and everybody loved it. You serve it up with those Scoop chips. It was the first-time Larry had tasted it, and he loved it. I'm sure we will have it again.

SEPTEMBER 5

We packed up everything just to move a few miles up the road to Bryce Canyon National Park Campground, that Larry rated a 4.

The National Park Service calls Bryce Canyon "A Forest of Stone. There is no place like Bryce Canyon. Hoodoos (odd-shaped pillars of rock left standing from the forces of erosion) can be found on every continent, but here is the largest collection of hoodoos in the world! Words and descriptions fail. Photographs do not do it justice. An imagination of wonder will serve you when visiting Bryce Canyon National Park."[4]

We had to look up "Hoodoo" while we were there, as we had never heard the term before, and had no clue what it was.

There was also a very narrow hiking trail around the rim, about halfway down the cliffs. It was definitely not a place for old folks like Larry and me to go. You would have to be part goat to make that trip!

Once we set up, we just could not get the satellite to work. I spent an hour on the phone—again—and we finally managed to get it working. We had no choice but to use the manual dish and tripod because the roof-mounted dish couldn't get a clear path through the trees. Per Larry, we just had to get FOX News! We were closer to the election and the debates were priceless. You just never know what was going to come out of Trump's mouth.

Proverbs 21:23
Those who guard their mouths and their tongues
keep themselves from calamity.

We headed to the Visitor Center to enjoy their park movie and collect another Passport stamp. We drove through part of the park and made plans for tomorrow. There, we found some huge solar panels that followed the sun throughout the day, which we learned was used to provide electric for the Visitor Center. There was technology at its finest, out here in the middle of nowhere.

We enjoyed a great meal at a local restaurant, Bryce Canyon Pines Restaurant out UT12, about 5 miles away. Back at the

[4]nps.gov

motorhome, we watched some Rizzoli and Isles on DVD before some more FOX News. Sigh. I get so sick of this political mud-slinging. Can't we all just act like adults? Then, considering there was nothing else to do when generator hours were over, we went to bed.

Deuteronomy 8:9
a land where bread will not be scarce and
you will lack nothing; a land where the rocks are iron
and you can dig copper out of the hills.

SEPTEMBER 6

The park smells of pine. It's a clean, natural scent that reminds me of Christmas, wherever I am. The air feels good as it fills my lungs.

Isaiah 44:14
He cut down cedars, or perhaps took a cypress or oak.
He let it grow among the trees of the forest,
or planted a pine, and the rain made it grow.

This morning we drove the eighteen-mile south road and enjoyed the indescribable vistas of hoodoos. We drove to the end first and then backtracked, hoping we could bypass the traffic.

The end of the road was at Yovimpa Point, where you could see for miles. The formations were in different colors: some were the classic red for this area, but others seemed white in contrast, where others were shades in between. It was breathtaking.

For another stop, the National Park Service describes, "The viewpoint at Inspiration Point consists of three levels that provide varied spectacular perspective of the main amphitheater. From here, visitors look toward the Silent City (near Sunset Point) with its many rows of seemingly frozen hoodoos set against the backdrop of Boat Mesa. All who look out from this point are bound to be inspired, considering the intricacies of the hoodoos and their formation through the erosion of the Claron Formation."[5] In layman's terms? WOW!

Larry was determined to climb to the upper overlook at Inspiration Point. It was a long, steep, and difficult walk that took him half an hour. His poor weakened legs sure paid the price, but the view, he said was worth it. He could see jeeps and four-wheelers on trails down in the canyon, and said they looked like Matchbox toys!

We could see the beautiful red Natural Bridge from the parking lot, which held plenty of family cars, all here for the view. But one car stood way out: A blazing, shining and waxed, sport-striped orange and white Corvette with a license plate that read SCAREZM. Now that was something you don't see every day, either.

After eating lunch in our own "sports" car, the Ford escape, we drove back to the motorhome for a rest. The afternoon was cool and sunny, with FOX News providing background noise.

After supper, we went back out and headed for Sunset Point to well, watch the Sunset. On the way, we were delighted to stop and take photos of 4 deer who were peacefully grazing as the day cooled.

Proverbs 5:19 A loving doe, a graceful deer—

[5]nps.gov

> may her breasts satisfy you always,
> may you ever be intoxicated with her love.

The sign at Sunset Point proclaims that the elevation is 8,000 feet. If you Google "sunset point Bryce", there are hundreds of photos that will illustrate the indescribable beauty of this place. We took plenty of pics as the landscape changed with every passing minute of the sunset, then traveled on to the Ponderosa Canyon.

The sign at Ponderosa Point states 8,904 feet in elevation. We set our chairs outside, bundled up, and waited for the stars to arrive. As the sky darkened, I began to point out constellations to Larry. I don't know many, but I easily found the ones Diana had taught me from her college classes: The Big Dipper, Cassiopeia, The Seven Sisters, Orion. We could see Venus in line with the small, dim waxing crescent of the moon.

The Milky Way, in all its colors, was awesome, despite we had no equipment to view it other than the telephoto lens on the camera. We craned our necks to the heavens above and marveled at the works of a mighty God. We were alone and felt we were on top of the world. Or so we thought. Until we heard noises.

> Psalm 89:6
> For who in the skies above can compare with the LORD?
> Who is like the LORD among the heavenly beings?

Wait, what was that? Chatter? Then louder voices. Maybe 3 people? And sure enough, out of the pitch-black trees they all came. They had been hiking and were confused as to exactly where they had come up off the trail. After we explained our location, it became clear that they'd planned to come out in the daylight, and definitely someplace else. That someplace was where they had parked their car.

They laughingly asked if they could bum a ride to their car. We felt really sorry for them, but we explained that our car barely had room in it for the two of us. It was filled with a cooler, a gas grill, two bikes and a crate full of tow dolly straps and chains. We were so sorry.

I think we were more upset about the situation than they were. Even without flashlights, they laughed and admitted they'd better start walking, and off they went, into the pitch-black night. We didn't even have a flashlight to give them. God go with them.

We spotted a lot more deer on the way back down to the campground, but it was too dark to take pictures. It had been a wonderful day of discovery and delight. Thank you, Lord for an absolutely amazing day.

> Psalm 148:3
> Praise him, sun and moon; praise him, all you shining stars.

SEPTEMBER 7

Today was a much slower day and I decided to clean the fridge, which is no simple task in this motorhome. It's small compared to home refrigerators, but so is my kitchen. So, when you take everything out, there's just no place to park everything. When you fill up the counter, then try to wash the produce bin, there's nowhere to drain it. The challenge is real, my friends.

While I'm busy with that, Larry cannot find his computer mouse, and the world as we know it has come to a screeching halt. It's a wireless mouse and he had looked everywhere! We all tell kids that something can't just disappear, but apparently, this mouse did. Fortunately, he had an old corded one to serve in such a pinch.

For supper, we decided to grill skewers of shrimp and pineapple, glazed with sweet and sour sauce. Yummy!

These past few days we had been eyeing a stack of wood that previous campers had left on our site. We decided to put it to good use tonight, before we leave in the morning. Larry started a blazing fire that we enjoyed all evening, then left it to smolder in the ring when we went to bed. There was plenty of cedar in the stack and it smelled delightful. We even roasted marshmallows. What a wonderful way to spend our last night here. God is good.

P.S. I found the mouse later, in the trash can. It had slid off the top of the printer, right into the can. Now, what it was doing on the top of the printer to begin with, I cannot say, as it was not my mouse. See, I knew it didn't just disappear!

SEPTEMBER 8

We set out in the rig this morning for Zion National Park, only a couple of hours away. The Bible mentions Zion as the City of David. I suppose this is why someone long ago had chosen to name it Zion, because it is beautiful.

We pulled into Zion Canyon Campground in Springdale, Utah, that Larry rated a 4. The route we took was RT12 west, but then we couldn't take US89 south. Going south would have saved us an hour's drive, but there was one little problem: a tunnel too short for us. The tunnel is considered eleven feet, and we are at least thirteen. Some say that we could fit down the middle with an escort, but why ask for trouble, or waste everyone's time, just to try and fail?

The National Park Service posts this on their site: "The Zion-Mount Carmel Tunnel. If your vehicle is 11'4" (3.4m) tall or taller or 7'10" (2.4m) wide or wider, including mirrors, awnings, and jacks, you will need a tunnel permit. Construction of the 1.1-mile Zion-Mount Carmel Tunnel began in the late 1920's and was completed in 1930."[6].

We had to take US89 north (the other way) to UT20 west to I-15 south, UT17 to UT9 into Springdale, Utah.

The elevation was 3,930 feet in the canyon floor, along the Virgin River, and mountains around the park were as high as 6,744 feet. Our campsite was right along the river, which was moving slowly. We should be fine, because no rain is forecast during our stay.

When we registered, we learned that the FedEx man had already delivered our replacement satellite dish. Once we were set up, Larry headed to the top of the rig and I passed him up tools in a bucket on a string. Teamwork!

We had stopped for groceries on the way, so I grilled a fresh T-bone and nuked a fresh ear of corn that was still in the shuck. Everyone should fix corn that way, it's so juicy! Four minutes in the microwave, husk and all. Supper was delish.

Larry and I suited up after dinner and walked the short distance to the pool. He stuck one toe in and declared, "No way." I figured a cool pool was better than no pool, so I spent a little while in there, while he just sat and watched. When we went to watch TV, the satellite worked great.

> Psalm 48:2
> Beautiful in its loftiness, the joy of the whole earth,
> like the heights of Zaphon is Mount Zion, the city of the Great King.

[6]nps.gov/zion/planyourvisit/the-zion-mount-carmel-tunnel.htm

SEPTEMBER 9

The City of Springdale, Utah borders Zion National Park. Due to the great number of folks who visit and the frailty of the park, passenger cars are not allowed within the park boundaries.

The National Park Service operates free shuttle service both in the city as well as in the Park itself. They have made it simple to catch the shuttle at stops on the main street of town, and be delivered right to the Park's main Visitor Center. From that point, you catch another shuttle to various destinations within the Park.

We stopped at the Visitor Center as well as the natural history museum there We watched the park movies and got the Passport stamped. As with the other National Parks we'd visited, American Indians were here long before the rest of us. Then Mormons had settled here as well, traveling from Salt Lake City.

We caught the bus that took us to The Narrows, a gorge and hiking area inside the park. The path was paved and about six feet wide. I could touch the canyon wall with my right hand as we walked by, sometimes forced to duck my head to miss an overhang. The view to our left was the winding Virgin River. We walked the foot trail to its very end, about a mile. My back was really giving me trouble and I had prepared by wearing my brace. It helped a great deal, but I still had to stop to rest frequently. Larry's legs however, were killing him.

Despite his pain, Larry decided to walk a bit further on river stones, into the Virgin River just a bit, to peer into the narrow canyon. Not me, I sure didn't want to slip on a rock and go down. Dozens of hikers passed us on the trail, outfitted with matching rental water shoes and walking sticks. They had prepared to go far beyond where I stopped. They were going to hike the 16 miles and is very tiring because it is in the river itself. Larry returned and told me that the canyon walls continued to be very steep, about 1,000 feet tall and only about 30 feet wide, a very narrow passage carved by the Virgin River.

If you were to view this area from above, most of what you would see is red rock and sheer cliffs. The only green you would see is comprised of the trees, flowers, cactus, and the creeping plants which can grow only on the perimeter of the River, their only source of water.

We stopped to sit and rest at the end of the trail. In that open area of the River, we spotted a young boy out in the water, with his father watching from a rock nearby. He was rolling in the mud, and was covered from head to toe in it. The kid was a mess, but he was having a heyday! His sister was staring at him, as we were, amazed at the muddy mess he was. His dad just seemed to smile.

We enjoyed many sights on the mile-long trip out as well as the walk back. The shade was a blessing, as it was quite hot today. There were little waterfalls and all sorts of creeping mosses and flowers clinging to the rock. We saw several "weeping walls", walls of rock from which water weeps, not flows. At one point we stopped, and were quickly joined by a couple of squirrels. They were very brave and came close, hoping for something to eat.

By the time we walked out, we were both hot and in pain. We took the shuttle back to the lodge to enjoy a cool lunch of chicken salad and chips. Larry had to have his Diet Coke, but I was thirsty only for water, and I drank lots of it. We caught the shuttle back to the campground.

Just as we stepped off the shuttle, Larry said one of us just had to go to the Post Office down the road to pick up our general delivery package. I protested loudly, because he wanted me to go. I was dead on my feet, but he finally convinced me that I was hurting less than he was, and we did need that package. I didn't know exactly where the Post Office was and Larry insisted it was only a "couple of blocks away." Yeah, right.

MapQuest later clarified that I had walked nearly a quarter mile, and I grumbled aloud the whole way down. But the surprise was on me. Even though it was a Friday, the little Post Office was open only very limited hours, and had been locked up long ago. They would open tomorrow morning, but for only three hours.

I hadn't taken my wallet, my phone, or any water. I was exhausted, thirsty, and in tremendous pain. I wanted to sit down in the middle of the road and cry until someone came by and offered me a ride back to the campground. But I couldn't. I started back UP the hill. And it was literally quite a hill. But God knew my needs and someone had installed several park benches, right by the sidewalk. Strange, I hadn't noticed any of them on the way down. One of the benches sat amid a carefully-planted patch of lavender. The smell was so amazing, I almost forgot my pain while I rested those few minutes. When I finally managed to get to our motorhome in the far back of the campground, I was nearly sick with pain from the day's activity. I firmly announced that Larry was going to the Post Office tomorrow. He did, and rode his bike.

Supper was nuked Stouffers, with lots of water and a pain pill. We watched a movie, but I have no clue what it was. Thank you, Lord for granting me the strength and tenacity to do all that was expected of me today.

Psalm 38:7

> My back is filled with searing pain;
> there is no health in my body.

> 1 Chronicles 4:10
> Jabez cried out to the God of Israel,
> "Oh, that you would bless me and enlarge my territory!
> Let your hand be with me, and keep me from harm so that I
> will be free from pain." And God granted his request.

SEPTEMBER 10

When I read my journal entry for today, it made me laugh. I had written, "Oh, my God. I cannot walk today!" We both overdid it big time yesterday. And, even though today turned out to be a very pleasant 100-degree day, we stayed in anyway. One hundred degrees that's pleasant, you ask? Believe me, it's all in the humidity, or the lack thereof.

But Larry had to get to the Post Office. Despite my warnings, he rode his bike. Sure, the way down was easy, but he had a bit of trouble on the way back up, to say the least. The package he picked up was the replacement motor for the steps, and was none too light. He installed the motor as soon as he got back, and twenty minutes later, the steps worked! We can finally put that hammer back where it belongs. Hallelujah!

My body wouldn't tolerate much work today, so I kept my tasks small. For afternoon entertainment, I put *Independence Day* in the DVD player and knitted while I watched it for the thirtieth time.

I'd had chicken in the Crock Pot all afternoon, so for supper we had BBQ chicken on the grill with fresh corn on the cob. Yum.

We both went to bed early; two old farts who needed to recuperate from our 2.2-mile trek at the river yesterday, and my more than half-mile trek to the Post Office. Thank you, Lord, for a much-needed day of rest.

SEPTEMBER 11

Today, once again is September 11. I cannot believe it's been fifteen years since those horrifying attacks changed our world forever. I think everyone will always remember exactly where they were, and how they heard the news. Speechless. Breathless. Unbelieving. Weeping. Sick. Larry and I didn't even go in to work that day; we entrusted the store to a few of our employees while we stayed glued to the television. And as the hours ticked away, they announced more and more bad news. Let us never forget the heroes that lost their lives that day; and they were all heroes. Except the cowards—I believe God has appointed a very special level of hell for each of the cowards.

> Isaiah 9:10
> The bricks have fallen down,
> but we will rebuild with dressed stone;
> the fig trees have been felled,
> but we will replace them with cedars.

We left early today in the motorhome, for a short day of travel. We took UT9 west, to Hurricane, Utah then UT59 east, to Arizona. We picked up AZ389 east then US89 north and east, then back into Utah then into Arizona again, south, then east to Lake

Powell, into Page, Arizona. We were in and out of both states all day long. Most of the drive was through barren desert with very little vegetation, but occasionally, we would drive over a small creek or a dry river bed.

We had reservations at the Wahweap Campground, which Larry rated a 7. The campground is part of the Glen Canyon National Recreation Area, which is absolutely beautiful. Lake Powell is a huge reservoir on the Colorado River, straddling the border between Utah and Arizona. The water is an amazing color of deep blue, and dotted with boats. I believe the brown landscape of the desert causes it to look even bluer than it already is. They report over two million people visit every year; I'm sure glad we came during their off-season.

Once set up, we took the car to explore the area. Our first stop was at the Glen Canyon Dam that backs up the Colorado River. It's a large concrete dam, which at first glance, reminded us of the Hoover Dam near Las Vegas. It generates electricity, but we were amazed to learn that its primary purpose is the main water storage basin serving Colorado, Utah, Wyoming, New Mexico, Arizona, Nevada, and as far away as California. Initial construction began in 1956 and was completed in 1963, but it took eleven more years of precipitation for Lake Powell to fill to a depth of 3,700 feet.

The highlight of the day was the most amazing, and within the top ten places we visited on our adventure: a slot canyon tour of Antelope Canyon, about seven miles East of Page. When we arrived, we wondered where the canyon was? The parking lot was dirt, on a level piece of ground. It is on the Navajo Indiana Reservation, and you pay a usage fee to enter the parking area.

After seeing something like the Grand Canyon, where was this one? We soon learned that, "a slot canyon is a narrow canyon, formed by the wear of water rushing through rock. A slot canyon is significantly deeper than it is wide. Some slot canyons can measure less than three feet across at the top but drop more than one hundred feet to the floor of the canyon."[7]

We purchased our tickets and were assigned to a group of ten people. When they called us to begin, BooBoo introduced himself as the guide in charge of our group. It turned out that the other eight people in the group were all Japanese, and they had brought their own interpreter. We had BooBoo all to ourselves. He was a pleasant young man, a Navajo who was born and raised right here in Page. He spent a lot of personal time with us, and we tipped him well.

He led us to a small crack in the dirt lot, then down a set of very narrow and steep steel steps. He continuously warned us to watch our step. Once we were down in the bottom, we couldn't believe our eyes. It's not just about the canyon, it's about the sunlight that comes through the slot in the ground above and shines on the limestone. The walls are smooth, and the passage of water has created all sorts of swirls and sways. The sunlight creates beautiful colors of tan, pink, red, and purple, that all seem to dance on the limestone.

It's as though the walls became incandescent in the light. It's like God's been down here, finger painting. BooBoo told us that the Antelope is 225 yards long and has various widths from five feet to twenty or more. Larry took probably one hundred pictures down there. Even though we were impressed by the colors, the photos are even more beautiful. It's as though the camera could see things that the naked eye could not. BooBoo even showed us a view currently used by Windows 7 as a screensaver. I'd highly recommend your

[7]en.wikipedia.org/wiki/Slot_canyon

looking at the photos online, because you just can't begin to imagine these views in your own mind.

At sunset, the place to be is at the Horseshoe Canyon, about five miles south of Page, on US89 south. We parked the car and walked the mile out to the cliff over the Canyon. I had my back brace on, but on this walk, it seemed to have transferred all the pain to my hips. It was bad. I unashamedly admit: I whined.

It's so frustrating, at our age, you finally get the time to really explore the world, and your body just won't cooperate! But I know that Larry and I are blessed to be able to take this trip at all, much less with the overall good health that we have. Thank you, Lord!

The view of the Horseshoe Canyon in the Colorado River is absolutely amazing! We were standing one thousand feet above the Colorado river, that beautiful green-blue water snaking through the canyon and the setting of the sun casts ever-changing shadows onto the canyon walls.

Larry was a nervous wreck the entire time we were there. There were no barriers or signs warning the idiot public they could easily fall over the cliff to their death. Duh. Everyone was right up to the edge, taking selfies or setting up their tripods for the sunset.

Larry was convinced that someone was going to fall to their death at any moment. He wouldn't even let me get close enough to see the Horseshoe for myself, he said I could see his photos later. When you're standing 1,000 feet above the canyon, on the edge, you have no way to know how that ledge is being held onto the canyon wall. You could be standing on solid rock, or a protrusion that has hundreds of feet of nothing holding it up, because of erosion. You get what I mean, standing on air or rock, you really don't know. Even I had to walk away from them. Stupid, stupid people.

But I could clearly watch the sunset from where I was, and it alone was worth the walk. It was beautiful. Sunsets have become are our favorite part of the day.

> Luke 4:40-42
> At sunset, the people brought to Jesus all who had various kinds of sickness, and laying his hands on each one, he healed them.

SEPTEMBER 12

We'd seen everything there was to be seen at Lake Powell, but I was feeling poorly. I've had chronic sinus problems for most of my life, and being in the desert had made absolutely no difference. Larry drove us into Page, to an Urgent Care. The doctor probably doesn't see all that many folks off-season, and he was in no hurry to finish with me. He stood and talked to me as though he was presenting the Sinus 101 lecture at the University. Blah, blah, blah. I'm thinking, "This is not my first sinus infection. Just give me a script—let's go."

Finally finished, we drove to the local Walmart to get the prescription filled, did some grocery shopping, then completed a shop to earn some cash.

We saw a Verizon store, and decided to go in to ask about changes on our account. We have a complicated account. We have my iPhone 5, and it had fulfilled my two-year contract. We have the Jetpack that supplies internet for the motorhome. Larry's phone was paid for, and he had gotten a new iPhone 6 not long after my accident, by absolutely necessity. One day, when I was in too much pain to continue at work, he came to pick me up. He was kibitzing with me about making a call on his cell while he drove, and I didn't want to do it. I was so sick from the pain and just wanted to be left alone. I finally took the phone—it was plugged in and recharging—and did what he said, so he would hush up.

Now, you must understand that the only place we have to keep our phones in the Escape is in the cup holders between the seats. Finished with the task, I blindly pitched it between the seats—blindly because I couldn't see the holders to my side, because of my cervical collar. Only problem was, I had an open cup of ice water in there, which I never do. The new phone was instantly fried. Caput. Dead.

He had to buy a whole new phone, and we would be paying on both phones now, as well as the extra number we had to buy to cover the new phone. The poor guy was absolutely no help whatsoever. "You need to call Verizon." Yeah, thanks. Bye.

It was a quiet afternoon and peaceful evening, there on Lake Powell. The sunset was again beautiful, but we enjoyed this one from our campground site. There was no hike today. Thank you, Lord for another beautiful day.

SEPTEMBER 13

It was time to pack up and drive to Mesa Verde National Park. I was excited that we would soon be seeing the infamous Cliff Palace that I have read about in books.

We set out on AZ98 east, through the barren desert, then US160 east on the state line of Arizona and Utah near Monument Valley. When we watched *Forrest Gump* recently, we saw something we thought we recognized. Do you remember the scene where Forrest had been running and running and one day, he decided he doesn't want to run anymore? We're convinced that was filmed on US160, right where we traveled today. We took photos of this stretch of highway, if you want to check them out. Let us know what you think.

Just before we were to enter Colorado again, we stopped at the Four Corners. The Four Corners is a region of the United States consisting of the southwestern corner of Colorado, southeastern corner of Utah, northeastern corner of Arizona, and northwestern corner of New Mexico. It's the only place in the United States where four states intersect at one point, known as a quadripoint.

The monument is on a Navajo reservation, and they charge $10 per vehicle to park, then you can walk to view the monument for free. An original concrete marker was erected in 1912, but was later updated to granite with a large round and flat brass marker, which illustrates the four states and their center.

We took photos of each other, standing on the marker. Then others offered to take our photo together, then couple after couple asked us to take theirs. We were happy to do so. There were Navajo souvenir booths all around, selling their handmade wares.

After our visit, we continued to drive US491 northeast into Colorado. We could see storms off in the distance, but we had sunshine all day. We took US160 east into Mesa Verde National Park campground in Mesa Verde, Colorado, which Larry rated a 3.

"It's known for its well-preserved Ancestral Puebloan cliff dwellings, notably the huge Cliff Palace. The Chapin Mesa Archeological Museum has exhibits on the ancient Native American culture. Mesa Top Loop Road winds past archaeological sites and overlooks, including Sun Point Overlook with panoramic canyon views. Petroglyph Point Trail has several rock carvings.[8]"

[8]nps.gov/meve/index.htm

I had been worried about the temperature, but once again, God had gone before us. Here we were with no utilities, and we had just left 100-degree weather in Arizona. But weather tonight will be 35 degrees. Who needs air conditioning? We'll just crank up the propane furnace.

The campground was rustic but well-kept. We would be totally self-contained this week. But as the day progressed, it became clear that something was wrong with the water pump. The water was coming out of faucets in spurts and spits, with lots of air mixed in. Larry took the water pump apart and it all seemed fine. But it had to be the pump.

After a few phone calls, he found an RV repair center in the town of Cortez, Colorado, and they had the same model number of pump in stock. So, we drove the trip, paid triple the price that we should have, and Larry worked until dark to install the pump. Simple, right? Not at all. The problem was still there.

We slept well, and it was a good thing. The devil had much more of the same planned for tomorrow.

SEPTEMBER 14

The day was an absolute disaster, a day of the devil trying to have his way with us. Over time on the road, Larry has become quite the handyman. His understanding of all things mechanical, electrical, hydraulic, plumbing—is really something. My dad would be so proud of him! That's what made this plumbing problem so much worse—he simply could not figure out why the system was doing what it was doing, especially with a brand-new pump. It was sucking air, just like the old pump. And after checking each and every part of the assembly, there was simply no obvious explanation.

Hour after hour, the entire day went this way. We had very little internet to assist us in troubleshooting, and sometimes, we had none at all. Larry inspected every inch of water line and every valve in the rig, and finally narrowed it down to one valve that just had to be at fault. It had the manufacturer's name stamped into the brass, but Google made it clear the company was out of business.

We took the valve downtown and neither the local plumber or the hardware store had anything like it. But at least the nice man at the hardware store offered a suggestion: he sold us a bottle of CLR (Calcium Lime Rust), and explained it would clean out any junk in the valve. Larry cleaned the valve back at the campground, but the problem was still there. It was apparent the valve wasn't closing all the way, and that's where the air was sneaking into the system. This particular valve is the one we would use to introduce antifreeze for winterization and storage, if we ever did store it.

Larry was thinking outside the box when he scrounged up a 95-cent water hose spigot cap and covered the intake to the valve. Bingo! Finally, the problem was solved by very unconventional means. We still have the spare water pump and most of the bottle of CLR, so hopefully the next water problem will be quickly, easily, and inexpensively solved.

Philippians 4:6
Do not be anxious about anything,
but in every situation, by prayer and petition,
with thanksgiving,
present your requests to God.

The day had been a total frustrating waste, but the evening made up for it. With no lights throughout the park, the rising full moon was a breathtaking sight to behold. We sat quietly, enjoyed the night sounds, the smell of other campers' fires, and marveled at God's reassuring presence.

We heard rustling in the nearby trees and knew they were elk, as we had seen them earlier in the day. Life is good. Sometimes we just have to take a deep breath and remember how truly blessed we are. We are more blessed than most, for sure.

SEPTEMBER 15

Now that the water pump was fixed, today was free to enjoy the park. We showered (thank you, Jesus) and drove to the Visitor Center. We watched the park movie and received the stamp for my Passport. You were required to have tickets for a ranger-led tour through Cliff Palace, so we chose ours for a time later that afternoon. We drove the main road through the park, which ascended to a high ridge or mesa that extended the length of the park. We drove south for twenty miles to the dwelling areas and enjoyed amazing views from the overlooks. You could see for miles.

Our first stop was a museum called Chapin Mesa, a very interesting education museum. It was an adobe-style building with large timber supports. From there, we drove on to Cliff Palace to meet up with the ranger to begin our tour.

The meeting area overlooked a magnificent array of ancient structures that had been built under a natural stone ledge. We followed the ranger down a narrow pathway through a gate and over the tops of some large rocks. The path was narrow and steep in places. He let us rest in the shade, under a deep ledge, while he told us lots of stories about the Ancestral Puebloans, or Ancient Ones. You may have also heard them called Anasazi.

While we listened, we could get a closer look at the structure beneath the cliff. There were mud rooms and walls, doors, windows, balconies, fire pits, ceremonial fire rings, and ladders. It seems they built all of this for protection from other tribes living near them.

I can certainly attest to the fact it was very hard to get to this place, even with steps, being on the side of a mesa and under a cliff. Besides, they could see anyone approaching for miles, from this elevated vantage point.

When he was finished speaking, he led us all down several rustic wooden ladders to the dwelling itself. They were certainly not original, considering the Anasazi disappeared about 900 years ago. It was amazing to view it all up close, as the ranger continued to explain what each structure was and what purpose it served in everyday life.

While everyone was quietly walking throughout the area, I asked our friendly ranger if he had ever read Nevada Barr's book, *Ill Wind*, which he had. It's a fictional read about this very place in this very park. I am a great fan of author Nevada Barr, who has been a ranger in the National Park System. She's announced the upcoming release of her 19th fictional who-done-it, her star character being one cranky Ranger Anna Pigeon, each written to take place in different National Parks you've all heard of. They're a great read and best if read in order. Check out www.nevadabarr.com.

Larry had been telling me all afternoon to, "Be careful." I know he was concerned, but I've had my collar off for quite some time now. I joked back that every time he said that to me, he owed me a beer—by the time we left, he owed me three. That's enough for the next few months! To get back up top, we had to pull ourselves up three stories' worth of rustic ladders, then crawl out through the small rock opening. From the street, we must have looked like puppies being born. We had taken water to drink, but ours was long gone. On the way back to the car, I spied a public drinking fountain; I was quick to drink plenty and throw just as much on myself.

Back at the motorhome, after that tough, hot afternoon, I took a well-deserved nap. When darkness came, we nuked supper and watched a DVD with the power of the generator. I'm glad no one was camped close to us, because we wouldn't want to disturb anyone with that noisy generator. It had been another beautiful day of breathtaking discoveries.

SEPTEMBER 16

Today was a driving day, via US160 east, that would take us to Durango, Colorado. Everything was great, until we arrived at Alpen Rose RV Park in Durango, Colorado, that Larry rated a 4.

I was inside setting up and Larry was outside, as usual. When he pulled the main electric cord out to hook up the electric, he saw that the plug was completely melted. How it had continued to work at Wahweap, we'll never know. The head must be replaced completely—again—before we can use it. We have a secondary power cord, but 30amp doesn't power much.

We Googled to find Tarpley RV, a dealer and repair place in Durango, so we headed there quickly to get the large cord fixed. We told them that we'd fixed the plug once already, so we wanted them to test the continuity of the cord first, before repairing it. If the cord tested bad, we would simply buy a new one. If it was just the head, then please repair it. We left it with the promise that it would be ready for us to pick up before they closed for the day.

With time to kill, we did a few shops for cash, then went to watch the movie, *Snowden* at the small Gaslight Theater. Durango is such a quaint and lovely town for wandering. It reminds me of Gatlinburg, Tennessee, where we lived for seven years in the late eighties and early nineties.

Durango is host to a large Labor Day motorcycle rally each year, which draws over 30,000 bikers. It was a busy town in the old west and it's famous for its historic buildings, like the Strater Hotel.

The historic Durango and Silverton Train still runs to this day. "Durango, Colorado was founded by the Denver & Rio Grande Railway in 1879. The railroad arrived in Durango on August 5, 1881 and construction on the line to Silverton began in the fall of the same year. By July of 1882, the tracks to Silverton were completed, and the train began hauling both freight and passengers.

"The line was constructed to haul silver & gold ore from Southwest Colorado's San Juan Mountains, but passengers soon realized it was the view that was truly precious.

"This historic train has been in continuous operation between Durango and Silverton since 1882, carrying passengers behind vintage steam locomotives and rolling stock indigenous to the line."[9] The train passed right by our campground, blaring its whistles, full of waving tourists.

We were impressed that the town was so clean and beautifully decorated ~~with flowering hanging pots~~ throughout the

[9]durangotrain.com

town. The nearby Animas River was a busy place, with kayakers and men fly-fishing along the banks. We passed deer grazing on the side of the road, without a care. Beauty was everywhere.

We were in a valley along the river, so mountains were all around us. Late in the afternoon, we returned to the RV place, where they had replaced the electrical plug. The repairman was gone already, so we could only assume that he'd followed our instructions and that main cord tested okay. We paid for his service and left. It was fixed.

We chose to eat at the Fiesta Mexicana Family Restaurant. FYI: Durango has more restaurants per capita than Denver. The food was great. It was my opportunity to collect my first beer bet. And since I only drink one at a time, the credit on my tab will last a while.

> 1 Timothy 5:23
> Stop drinking only water, and use a little wine
> because of your stomach and your frequent illnesses.

Back at the motorhome, we connected to the electric and all seemed well. We watched a bit of cable, but we were beat. Early to bed. It had been another great day of discovery.

SEPTEMBER 17

After running around everywhere yesterday, today was much quieter. We drove into Old Durango and walked around. We found a bagel shop and shared a nicely toasted bagel with cream cheese. I washed it down with a large, hot, and sweet coffee, while Larry stuck to Diet Coke. With all afternoon to spare, we decided to see the movie *Sully*, starring Tom Hanks. The movie was fantastic. The effects totally convinced you that you were there, on the flight, in heightened fear as every moment passed. The movie provided a storyline that was much different than the point of view the news covered. And, as always, Tom was terrific.

I've mentioned before my love for white Bratwurst. Today I found a new *Lay's* potato chip flavor, *Grilled Bratwurst*. They were lightly flavored and spot on.

We went back to the motorhome for supper and a quiet evening. Thank you, Lord, for a peaceful, restful, and safe day.

SEPTEMBER 18

Today would be a long driving day as we headed to Santa Fe, New Mexico. It was a four-hour drive on US550 south, then I-25 northeast. We chose to pass right by the Aztec ruins because we were concerned about parking. But when you've seen Mesa Verde, you've already seen the best.

The Chaco Culture National Park, another ruins site was several miles out on a bumpy dirt road. Our dependable Allstays app had some reviews that were not very encouraging for motorhomes the size of ours—especially with tow vehicles—to see these places, so we kept to the main roads, anxious to get to Santa Fe.

We wanted to stay at a place called Trailer Ranch, but they were full. We headed to Santa Fe Skies RV Park and they had room for a while, and Larry rated it a 7. The place was further out of the city, but it was nice, perched on the top of a hill.

It had been a long drive, so we set up, ate supper, and watched a bit of TV before going to bed. We were beat. Thank you, Lord, for yet another safe day of travel.

SEPTEMBER 19

We were planning to be in Santa Fe for a few days. Santa Fe Skies is a nice and well-tended campground, but in a different way than most we have been in. Nice campgrounds tend to plant palm trees and blooming bushes for landscaping, in an attempt to create the illusion of an oasis in the desert. This place has taken every effort to plant cacti, succulents, and blooming plants common to the region, but in a structured and manicured way. I liked it very much, staying here in this au natural setting. And the view from our site was lovely.

We hopped in the car to explore the local area. One of the highlights of the day was The Loretto Chapel, built in 1610. It has a staircase to the choir loft that has absolutely no support, and defies engineering logic. Some think it's being held up by God. According to the Chapel's website, "two mysteries surround the spiral staircase in the Loretto Chapel: the identity of its builder and the physics of its construction. When the Loretto Chapel was completed in 1878, there was no way to access the choir loft twenty-two feet above. Carpenters were called in to address the problem, but they all concluded access to the loft would have to be via ladder, as a staircase would interfere with the interior space of the small Chapel.

"Legend says that to find a solution to the seating problem, the Sisters of the Chapel made a novena to St. Joseph, the patron saint of carpenters. On the ninth and final day of prayer, a man appeared at the Chapel with a donkey and a toolbox, looking for work. Months later, the elegant circular staircase was completed, and the carpenter disappeared without pay or thanks. After searching for the man (an ad even ran in the local newspaper) and finding no trace of him, some concluded that he was St. Joseph himself, having come in answer to the sisters' prayers.

"The stairway's carpenter, whoever he was, built a magnificent structure. The design was innovative for the time and some of the design considerations still perplex experts today. The staircase has two 360-degree turns and no visible means of support. Also, the staircase was built without nails—only wooden pegs.

Questions also surround the number of stair risers relative to the height of the choir loft and about the types of wood and other materials used in the stairway's construction. Over the years, many have flocked to the Loretto Chapel to see the Miraculous Staircase. The staircase has been the subject of many articles, TV specials, and movies including, *Unsolved Mysteries* and the television movie titled *The Staircase,*[10] the 1998 movie starred William Petersen, Barbara Hershey, and Diane Ladd. We were amazed at the beautiful staircase and it does indeed, defy explanation.

We continued to stroll the historic streets of Santa Fe, which were full of shops and restaurants. We noticed that much of the city's architecture is done in stucco adobe style, painted in tans or browns to blend in with the surrounding desert colors.

We drove beyond the city to check out the Buffalo Thunder Casino. We walked the floor, but found no signs of Bingo. Larry wasn't interested in anything else, so we quickly left. Our long drive back offered us some shops though, so we earned some extra cash this afternoon, instead of spending it.

---

[10] lorettochapel.com/staircase.html

Back at the motorhome, we had a late supper, watched the news, enjoyed a beautiful sunset, then headed to bed. I'm not feeling my best, and I'm going to assume it's these higher elevations taking their toll on me once again.

SEPTEMBER 20

Although we enjoyed our time at Santa Fe Skies, Trailer Ranch now had a site for us. It's also in Santa Fe, but down in the busyness of town. Larry rated it a 7.

I felt real sickly this morning. I experienced some weird shortness of breath, which I never have. Out of curiosity, I took my blood pressure and it was extremely high, also which I never have. It was such a short distance to get to Trailer Ranch, that Larry decided it was best for me to just follow him in the car, instead of taking all the time to hook it all up on the tow dolly. I had to get my act together, at least for a little while.

Once we arrived and set up, I ate something small for lunch. My pulse was loudly irregular and I felt nauseous. Altitude sickness again? Perhaps. We are over 7,000 feet here. I was good for nothing that day, so I rested.

SEPTEMBER 21

I was feeling a tad better this morning, so we headed out in the car for some exploring. We headed first to Los Alamos, New Mexico. We drove up US285 north then on NM502 west. The route took us through some barren lands and canyons, to a mountain-top ridge. Located there is the Los Alamos National Laboratory, established in 1943 for the Manhattan Project. Yes, the atomic bomb. In the

1940's, the town was an isolated mud hole in the desert when scientists came there to secretly develop the bombs. This lab was designated as Site Y for the single purpose to design and build an atomic bomb. It took just twenty months.

On July 16, 1945, the world's first bomb was detonated 200 miles south of Los Alamos. We visited the Bradbury Science Museum, a National Historic site and learned all about "Little Boy" and "Fat Man", the two bombs dropped on Hiroshima and Nagasaki, Japan, respectively, to end World War II. They have replicas of both and they are remarkably small for the power they held. We learned about the atomic age and the Lab's continued research there.

I was surprised to learn of the number of women that helped achieve this goal. Each of these scientists left their families for months on end, without being able to tell them where they were or what they were doing. Even their mail was delivered to a PO Box back in Santa Fe. What a huge personal sacrifice these people made to put an end to the war.

Standing so close to the "bombs" was a somber and sobering moment. It was amazing to know that something the size of a Volkswagen, could kill nearly a quarter-million people, either by direct hit or as a deadly result of radiation poisoning. I am not a historian of any means, but I think it was the only way to convey the statement, "Enough is enough", so that the war would end. After that, the rest of the world knew what tools we held to defend our liberty and the liberty of others.

> Deuteronomy 29:23
> The whole land will be a burning waste of salt and sulfur—
> nothing planted, nothing sprouting,
> no vegetation growing on it.
> It will be like the destruction of

> Sodom and Gomorrah, Admah and Zeboyim,
> which the LORD overthrew in fierce anger.

SEPTEMBER 22

Today we were forecast to have thunderstorms most of the day, so it would not be a good day to be sightseers. We had already seen everything we really wanted to see, so we decided that today would be a work day. We found some shops to do for cash, and we quickly accomplished those. Except for the store shop that required finding their wine offerings all over the store—and I mean they were tucked in everywhere.

Larry decided that we needed to clean the carpet in the motorhome. One of the grocery stores where we completed a shop has those Rug Doctor machines for rent, so we checked one out and returned to the motorhome. The rest of the afternoon, into early evening, is self-explanatory. I would much rather pay someone $$ to clean it than to get back on my old hands and painful knees to do that ever again. And getting up with my back? Larry won't admit it, but I will: I'm just too durn old to be doing this kind of stuff. So is he.

I made him take me out to dinner for several reasons: 1. we had to return the cleaner anyway, 2. the carpet was wet, and 3. I simply refused to cook, after all that work. Let's go.

On to Tomasita's, a lively and packed restaurant. We were told by the campground owners about this place. "This is the place to go-to for enchiladas, sopapillas, flautas, & more Southwestern favorites amid a festive décor in the area", they said. This was the first time we learned about the red and green chili peppers after we have been seeing them all over town. We saw strings of these peppers hanging from stores outside and inside. There are also locals roasting them by the roadsides.

Well, Tomasita's has them on the menu as a Salsa choice. The difference between RED and GREEN chilies is in the stage when it has been harvested, green chilies are a stage before the chili ripens to a red color. "Which is hotter" we ask? You must try them both. We found out that chilis get hotter as they ripen (that is, as they turn from green to red). Many chili varieties are picked and sold in stores while still unripe and green (e.g. jalapeño, serrano, poblano), but you will occasionally see ripe, red ones in stores as well. We can personally attest the red is hotter!

SEPTEMBER 23

We traveled from Santa Fe to Albuquerque via I-25 southwest then I-40 west right to American RV Park, which Larry gave a rating of 7. This campground has a terrific view of the city of Albuquerque. Plus, you can see five dormant volcanos as well. After check-in, we rested a little before heading out to explore. We came to Albuquerque to attend the 2016 Balloon Fiesta. Our daughter, Diana was going to fly out here from Myrtle Beach to join us for a week of traveling.

With the rest of the day free, we took the car and traveled south through the desert to a place called a Very Large Array (VLA). We took I-25 to Socorro, New Mexico, then headed west on US60, a very deserted highway through small towns. I would say "One Horse Towns," but I didn't see any horses, either, nor any stop lights. It took us several hours to get there, way out in the middle of nowhere.

The Karl G. Jansky VLA is a radio astronomy observatory. When we came over a ridge, these huge satellite dishes suddenly appeared on the flat landscape. Larry asked aloud, "ET, where are you?" We parked at the Visitor Center and learned all about these massive antennas.

"The simply-named Very Large Array, one of the world's premier astronomical radio observatories, consists of 27 radio antennas in a Y-shaped configuration on the Plains of San Agustin fifty miles west of Socorro, New Mexico. Each antenna is 25 meters (82 feet) in diameter. The data from the antennas is combined electronically to give the resolution of an antenna 36km (22 miles) across, with the sensitivity of a dish 130 meters (422 feet) in diameter.[11] We left the Visitor Center and easily walked to one of the nearby antennas. As we stood below it, we marveled that it had to stand at least ten stories high, and we could actually hear the buzz coming from the active electronics.

The scientists can take the radio waves from deep space through each of the antennas, combine them and get a computer generated "image" of the cosmos. The array is searching the heavens for life on other planets. Is there life way out there in the heavens? The Bible doesn't tell us either way, we just know that He created the heavens and the earth.

> Genesis 1:1
> In the beginning God created the heavens and the earth.

Did you know the 1997 movie *Contact* with Jodi Foster was filmed here at the VLA? They had posters of the film and photos of her and the crew during the filming. Kids from a local school were even in the movie. Believe it or not, this "Sci-Fi" movie is actually

---

[11]vla.nrao.edu/

about Faith and the unseen. How do you believe in something that you cannot see, that you cannot touch, or cannot prove to exist?

Larry tells a story to explain to kids about the presence of the Holy Spirit. "What makes a tree move?" he asks. They answer, "The wind." "How do you know it's the wind? You can't see it, or feel it, or touch it, or not even smell it. How can you prove that it exists? It is the same about God—He is just there—He is everywhere."

Jodi Foster's character, scientist Dr. Ellie Arroway goes through the movie not believing in a Higher Being. Then she experiences something amazing. By the end of the movie, she's asked to testify under oath, to explain what she saw. "Because I can't. I...had an experience...I can't prove it, I can't even explain it, but everything that I know as a human being, everything that I am tells me that it was real! I was given something wonderful, something that changed me forever...A vision...of the universe, that tells us, undeniably, how tiny, and insignificant and how...rare, and precious we all are! A vision that tells us that we belong to something that is greater than ourselves, that we are *not*, that none of us are alone! I wish...I...could share that...I wish, that everyone, if only for one...moment, could feel...that awe, and humility, and hope. But...That continues to be my wish."

And there was a pair of simple lines repeated several times in the movie. One person asks, "...do you think there's people on other planets?" The other responds, "I don't know. But I guess I'd say if it is just us...it sure seems like an awful waste of space." Yes, indeed. An awful waste of space.

We were leaving down the long gravel driveway, back to the highway. Just when we thought we'd seen it all, we spotted two people and a small truck pulled over on the left side of the access road. They carried a red, London-type telephone booth, and set it on the ground. We slowed the car to rubberneck, and could appreciate the satellite dishes providing an amazing backdrop for the phone booth. We assumed it was a photoshoot for some type of communications company. I wonder if we'll ever see the finished shoot? (I have searched for it on Google, but haven't found it to date.)

It was a very long drive back to Albuquerque. It was a full day to say the least. We enjoyed the hot tub at the campground in the evening.

Months later, as I'm writing about this day, I must mention that we recently had the opportunity to see the movie *Contact* again. It was fun to see exactly what we'd personally seen this day. I first saw it many years ago, and was so wrapped up in the science of it all, that I failed to appreciate the real message of the movie. The scientist, Dr. Arroway, couldn't find a place for God in the science, but finally, through the science, she found God. If you get a chance, be sure to watch it. Then you'll understand exactly what I'm talking about.

SEPTEMBER 24

We went to the visitor center for the Petroglyph National Monument and learned all about writings and carvings on rocks. They were made between 1300 A.D. and 1600 A.D. The monument is over 7,236 acres just outside Albuquerque, New Mexico. We didn't do any hiking because the hikes were up mountains, through the desert, in the heat. We claim the old fart exemption, and leave the paths clear for the young at heart. We did walk a short distance to one overlook, where we could view a great number of the petroglyphs through the telephoto camera lens. It was an interesting place to visit.

> Job 19:23-24
> "Oh, that my words were recorded,
> that they were written on a scroll,
> [24] that they were inscribed with an iron tool on lead,
> or engraved in rock forever!

We drove down to the old city, just west of downtown and parked the car along the street. We have 2 fold-up bikes, and we always keep them in the back of the car. We set up the bikes and hit the streets. Our first stop was the Albuquerque Museum, formerly known as the Albuquerque Museum of Art and History, just off the famous Route 66. In fact, the museum has a wing devoted to the unusual art you could find along this route. The Museum is in a very modern building that tells the story of the history of Albuquerque, which sits along the Rio Grande. Our route through the southwest in the weeks to come will take us across the Rio Grande many times.

After we walked the entire museum, I treated myself to a Route 66 T-shirt in the gift shop. We rode the bikes to Hacienda del Rio Restaurant, where we enjoyed a delicious traditional Mexican meal. As always, we left behind our packet of seeds and a Motorhome Ministry brochure. We can only hope and pray that our waitress might read this book. Perhaps those seeds and brochure touched her in a mighty way, that she hadn't already, that she's given her heart to Jesus.

> Galatians 2:20
> I have been crucified with Christ
> and I no longer live, but Christ lives in me.
> The life I now live in the body,
> I live by faith in the Son of God,

> who loved me and gave himself for me.

Our faith in God leads us to do these works. How these small works help to complete what He is doing in the big plan, we will not know this side of Heaven. We pray these works are pleasing to Him.

We biked around the old city before returning to the car. The weather had been perfect and the exertion of the ride did both of us some good. We were in bed early, as the fresh air had done us in.

SEPTEMBER 25 AND SEPTEMBER 26

I didn't write down one memorable thing about these two days in my journal; not one single thing.

They must have been days of sleeping late, cleaning and laundry, watching TV, and eating good food. And you know what? That's not so bad at all.

Thank you, Lord for days of rest.

SEPTEMBER 27

The only note I made in my journal today is that Diana called with the news that she has completed the closing of her very first home! There had been plenty of obstacles to overcome these last few months, but now the place is finally hers. She was so relieved that all the dickering was over. She had told me just a few days ago, that she would believe it was hers only after she held the keys in her sweaty, little hands. We were so excited for her and wished we could be there to help.

On the other hand, she didn't know whether to be more excited about the house, or the fact that she would see us in only three more days. What a historic week this will turn out to be!

SEPTEMBER 28

Another day of nothing notable. I know that once Diana arrives, our days will be whirlwinds, to say the least. She has prepared a list of everything on her bucket list for the southwest. She, much like me, has no sense of geography, so I'm sure we won't be able to get to them all. But we will do the best we can. And we will have a wonderful time. God be with us.

SEPTEMBER 29

Today was an anniversary, of sorts. Today marks six months on the road for Motorhome Ministry. In looking back, I was so broken, ill, and full of pain when we left on this mission. Today I can rejoice that I am healed, and I thank God, every day that He enabled this endeavor for His glory.

We drove downtown to attend the RV show at the convention center. They had one exceptional motorhome that would be anyone's dream RV, but with a price tag of $400,000+, it will never be mine. It was way too much spit and polish for my taste, anyway. It was like a mansion on wheels. No, thank you very much.

The outside of the convention center had dozens of large mosaic murals made from colorful tiles, each depicting Indian life. They were absolutely beautiful. Albuquerque has a lot of artistic paintings and statues all around their city. I'll make a point to bring Diana back to see these.

We completed a half-dozen shops today; it's always good to earn a little extra cash. I don't know if practice makes perfect, but now that we've done a few, they do seem to go a lot quicker now.

We enjoyed another yummy Stouffers, and watched TV. The storms that should have passed through earlier this evening, continued well past bedtime. Oh, how I love to hear rain on the roof of the motorhome.

Sleep comes with a smile on my face...Diana arrives tomorrow!

SEPTEMBER 30

We went to the cinema to see *Deepwater Horizon* with Mark Wahlberg. It was amazing. I don't particularly care for movies that I just sit back and watch as an observer, but I do love movies that bring me right into the middle of the fray. And this movie really brought me in. The news covered the oil spill and the wildlife and coastline that it affected. This movie covers everything that happened on the rig itself, the people who were working, and what their jobs entailed. It showed you some of the personal relationships at the time of the disaster, how some died there and the others who lived to tell about it. It was outstanding.

> Job 30:24
> Surely no one lays a hand on a broken man
> when he cries for help in his distress.

We were so excited about Diana arriving today that we were good for nothing. We had the whole day free, because Diana's flight was suffering from weather delays, and wouldn't arrive until after midnight. I kept tidying around the motorhome, and made sure all the laundry was caught up. We headed out in the afternoon to complete some shops, just to have something to do.

Her flight finally arrived after midnight. We were all exhausted, and the drive to the motorhome was short. I collected plenty of hugs, then we all went straight to bed.

Diana writes: *I was so excited to finally see my parents, oh, how I'd missed them. I used to spend every waking moment every day for years with them, between home and at work. It would have its ups and downs, like any family would have. BUT, to be without them...I'll never take it for granted again. I truly had missed them.*

I was in the beginnings of purchasing a home, so I had to be sure that most of the documents were signed before I left or it would have been a disaster. The devil had already reared his ugly head, making delays and problems for the closing of the house. I sat on one of the flights and read a 72-page mortgage document, then made sure to sign on the dotted lines, so that when I arrived in New Mexico, I would FedEx the document straight to the Banker, so the closing preparations could begin.

Little did I know, however, that the devil had followed me on this trip. No sir, you are NOT going to ruin this vacation.

Goodnight, sweet princess. We have the next nine days to catch up on everything else.

OCTOBER 1

The next morning, while getting packed up to go to the Balloon Fiesta, we enjoyed a surprise visitor on our camp site. There in all its glory was a tarantula, a very large, black and brown, hairy, and poisonous spider. We gave it a wide berth, took some pics, and just watched it do its tippy-toe crawl. Larry announced they could jump, too, and Diana and I both took another few steps back. I would have died straightaway, if it had jumped on me or if it had made its giant presence known to me inside the motorhome.

It was a short drive to The Balloon Fiesta RV City. It was a makeshift city full of RV's in a desert field, outside of Albuquerque. We had no hookups or services—a true boondoggle park! We had made reservations for this a year ago! It was acres full of motorhomes, fifth-wheels, trailers, campers, and vans—anything you could sleep in. The space they assigned us was right on the main drag of this huge, dry, graveled lot. Without electric, of course, the windows stayed open day and night. Every single time an RV would drive by, or the shuttles would go past, a cloud of dust came right through the screens, into the motorhome. There were folks driving through and popping gravel all hours of the day and night, right outside the windows.

At the check-in, we received a bag full of Balloon Fiesta Gifts which included brochures relative to the area, a flashlight, Fiesta pins, pens, and a cup, all in a printed bag. Larry got on top of the roof of the motorhome and took some great photos, to capture just how many RV's were there. A lot had flags or banners flying in the wind, antennas, and satellites up, all at different heights above their rigs.

Larry put our Motorhome Ministry banner out along the side of the motorhome and the free kid packets off the side mirror, so people coming by could grab one. And, to God's glory, we gave out dozens. We took Diana out to dinner in the old city before the evening festivities got going. We strolled the shops and bought matching dark grey t-shirts for the Balloon Fiesta. We chose not to buy the pricey "official" ones, but we received so many compliments on how nice and colorful our shirts were!

We came back to the motorhome to discover that the driver's side windshield was cracked, big time! How could this have happened in the short time we were gone? We all stood there, throwing out ideas. We wondered if someone had failed to negotiate the turn correctly and hit us? No, there was no other damage. A rock hit it? No, the fracture seemed to originate down low, by the seal.

We called the insurance company, took necessary photos before it got dark, and made an appointment for a replacement while we camped in Las Vegas, Nevada next week. The representative said it was probably a stress crack, common to motorhomes over time. Until repairs could be done, Larry and Diana got to work and taped up the glass with clear tape. None of the fractures were in his line-of-sight, but the tape would obscure his view in the rear-view mirror just a bit. It would have to do.

After he made the makeshift repairs, we grabbed the shuttle to the main park to watch the Balloon Twilight Twinkle Glow. Hundreds of hot air balloons are tethered to the ground. On cue, they all flare their propane burners to create an amazing glow in their balloons, all at the same time. All this is happening just feet above your head, for as far as you can see.

Diana adds: *bucket list item checked off! Now to be able to ride in one. I looked into flying in a hot air balloon during the festival, but prices were well above $400! I found a Groupon for a flight in Vegas for around $150; maybe we'll be able to fulfill that bucket list item when we get to Vegas.*

The sound is hard to describe; their burners sounded like a thousand blowtorches. There were all kinds of shapes, sizes, patterns, colors, brands, and characters. Many bore assorted patterns of brilliant, beautiful colors, some had names like Star Wars characters Darth Vader and Yoda, Humpty Dumpty was there (still in one piece), as well as Smokey Bear, and the Wells Fargo Stagecoach, just to name a few. There was a huge green frog with twelve large toes, a fish sporting a monocle and a top hat, a flying pink pig, a purple dragon, a penguin, a lady bug, and dozens and dozens more.

After the Glow, came the After-Glow fireworks and laser show. We walked around the carnival-style grounds and shared a funnel cake for a snack. Booths of all kinds were lined up on both sides of the main walking area, selling t-shirts, food, souvenirs, sponsors' tents, TV news crews and personalities. We stopped at the Canon sponsor booth, and had a free picture taken. It showed the three of us standing in a hot air balloon basket. Of course, it was just a basket and a backdrop, but it looked really cool. When we posted it on Facebook, our friends were convinced that we had all gone up in a balloon.

There were hordes of people. It was like crowds from a state fair, theme park, and concert, all in one. When the fireworks were over, we tried to get the shuttle back to the campground, but everyone else had the same idea, and the lines were long. We started to walk, but between Larry's cane and my back brace, a kind worker with a golf cart offered to take us as far as the campground gate. Praise Jesus, indeed. He knows our every need.

Philippians 4:19
And my God will meet all your needs
according to the riches of his glory in Christ Jesus.

OCTOBER 2

Neither Diana nor I are early risers, but we were willing to get up at 5am to witness the Mass Ascension. We each showered and dressed, ate quickly, and caught the shuttle back to the grounds. By first light, the balloon teams were already hard at work. A few balloons were high in the dark morning sky, and you could easily see the fire glow from their burners. These balloons were to test the drift and winds aloft, and report the conditions back to the other balloon pilots.

Promptly at 7am, the sponsor Phillips 66 balloon began to rise, and from the bottom of the basket hung a large American Flag. Over the loudspeakers came some undecipherable chatter, but what became clear was the singing of the National Anthem, as the sun showed itself on a crisp, but beautiful morning. As we sang along with others from around the world, it was patriotism at its best.

Some of the ground crews were already busy inflating their balloons, which indeed takes a "crew". They use powerful fans to begin to inflate the balloons. Once filled with regular air, they begin short bursts of hot flames from the burners to expand the air, which pitches the balloon upright. They will keep it tied down, until it's their turn to ascend.

The Ascension began. First, one balloon from over there, then two from opposite ends of the field. One after another, as the pink sky of dawn turned to a bright blue; one after another, they continued. As some took off, others had disappeared high into the sky. Eventually, at any given moment, there had to have been a hundred balloons aloft. The final balloon left the ground at 9:30am. We had been there two and one-half hours, standing in sheer and utter amazement at this breathtaking sight. Yeah, it was well worth rolling out of bed at 5am.

We slowly walked back toward the entrance to the park, up a slight hill, to visit the Balloon Museum. From one of the viewing windows, we could see that balloons still filled the sky above the building. The Museum was everything you needed or wanted to know about hot air balloons, featuring exhibits, photographs, art, pins from decades of events, and an educational movie. This had been the experience of a lifetime. And the three of us enjoyed it together.

We walked back to the motorhome, at a small lunch and catnapped for a couple of hours. We set out to complete a few shops for some extra cash, then treated ourselves to frozen P.F. Chang's for supper. Before bed, we began to prepare for our departure in the morning. Diana and I watched some NCIS on DVD, then came sleep. Exhausted, sun-and wind-burned, blessed sleep.

> 2 Samuel 22:11
> He mounted the cherubim and flew;
> he soared on the wings of the wind

OCTOBER 3

We packed up our dirty, dusty motorhome, loaded the tow vehicle on the dolly, buckled in, and headed west on I-40 toward Las Vegas, shattered windshield and all. Larry spent nearly the whole day in the captain's seat, and Diana and I had a great time, taking photos of everything we saw.

We stopped off at the Petrified Forest National Park and Painted Desert. We stopped at the Visitor Center, got another stamp in my Passport, and as always, watched the park movie. We drove through the park with the motorhome, to get a firsthand look at the beautiful Painted Desert.

We pulled over at a few of the vista lots, and enjoyed the fantastic views. There was petrified wood all over, but you're not allowed to take any from the Park. We stopped at a trading post outside of the park and they were giving away small pieces for free.

Diana jokes: *And I got my picture taken with a Dinosaur!*

The Park is in Navajo and Apache areas of Arizona with a history of Indian settlements. We took the Petrified Forest Road southwest to US180 west, then back on I-40 west. I-40 in this area runs parallel to the Old Route 66, and it's dotted with tourist traps and railways, amidst the mountainous desert. Diana kept busy taking photos out of the couch window, while safely buckled in.

On the way, we detoured to Winslow, Arizona, right off I-40, because Diana had it on her bucket list. Remember the words of the old Eagles song, *Take it Easy?* "Well, I'm a 'standing on a corner in Winslow, Arizona and such a fine sight to see, it's a girl, my Lord, in a flatbed Ford, slowin' down to take a look at me." Well, we stood right there, on that corner in Winslow, Arizona, and the flatbed Ford was still there! We wandered through the corner shops and took lots of photos of the area and of us on the special corner. And guess what song was playing on the speakers?

Diana: *Dad was not amused; he just stayed in the RV. He complained when we took so long and how small the city road was for him to "just be parked" and waiting on us.*

Yeah, like there was such a traffic jam because of the rig!

Back at the I-40 exit, we decided to eat at Denny's. The hostess quickly sat us in a booth and we waited. And waited. Other wait staff glanced at us sitting there while they worked their tables, but no one said a word to us. After a good fifteen minutes of invisibility, we stormed out. Denny's got a call to their customer service center. They didn't seem to be interested in our bad experience. The representative just said they will notify the district manager and offered no apologies. If their corporate office is this uncaring, I guess it trickles down to their restaurants.

So, we just drove some more, and finally arrived at Meteor Crater RV Park, in Winslow, Arizona, which Larry rated a 4. We had planned to see the crater in the morning, but we discovered that the entrance fee was far too steep for the three of us go look at a large hole in the ground. We checked online, and there were much better photos taken from the air, not standing by the rim. It was a good campground, for a night of full services, close to I-40. We ate a small supper and managed twelve hours of sleep. Diana and I were blessed to see the Milky Way before bed.

Diana complained: *It was also freezing that night. Welcome to the desert.*

It had been yet another amazing day.

OCTOBER 4

Today we arrived at Grand Canyon Camper Village in Tusayan, Arizona, which Larry rated a 2. It was a sad, old, little RV park, but it did have full services. We had tried to get reservations in the South Rim Campground of the National Park, but it was full. We could have gotten a place in the North Rim Campground, but that involved another 250-mile trip up and 250 miles back, despite it was only 10 miles away as the crow flies. We surely didn't have time for that, so we stayed in this private campground instead.

The next statement is the beginning of another huge deed by the devil: we plugged in, but there was no electric. Larry unplugged and plugged in our power cord again. Still no electric. Considering the campground was old, Larry grabbed his electric meter to test the electric from the pole. He confirmed that it was hot with current.

We had already had the cord repaired twice, and tested for continuity by a professional. He spent the next hour trying to figure out what was wrong. Larry finally traced it down to a faulty transfer switch, which he knew, without a doubt, he did not have the expertise nor the parts to repair.

I called the campground office and they gave me two telephone numbers to call. I prayed that God would provide us a Christian who would make our repairs quickly and for a fair price. One was local, but the old woman who answered the phone explained that her husband had recently retired. I whined, but she was unmoved. When I called the second number, a man named Rex answered the phone. Although his company, Neighborhood RV Service was out of Boulder City, NV, he just happened to be less than one mile away, eating lunch after completing an earlier call. He said he would be right there, and within like two minutes, he was!

So, here we sit, in the heat, with a broken windshield, and no power. Per our request, he tested the power cord first, and once again, it tested good. After a while, he said the transfer switch had suffered a surge, which had blown the switches, which had blown the converter and the battery charger, as well.

We were dead in the water, and he explained that he couldn't fix any of it until the next day. Thank the Lord there was no problem with our propane, so at least our refrigerator worked and we would have hot water in the morning. We chose to eat in a restaurant in town, more for their air conditioning than their food, which was very good.

Lord, stay with us and protect us. And please provide Rex with everything he needs to make full repairs tomorrow.

> Psalm 121:7-8
> The Lord will keep you from all harm,
> He will watch over your life
> The Lord will watch over your coming and going
> Both now and forevermore.

Psalm 91

Whoever dwells in the shelter of the Most High
will rest in the shadow of the Almighty.
2 I will say of the LORD,
"He is my refuge and my fortress, my God, in whom I trust."
3 Surely, he will save you from the fowler's snare
and from the deadly pestilence.
4 He will cover you with his feathers,
and under his wings you will find refuge;
his faithfulness will be your shield and rampart.
5 You will not fear the terror of night, nor the arrow that flies by day,
6 nor the pestilence that stalks in the darkness,
nor the plague that destroys at midday.
7 A thousand may fall at your side, ten thousand at your right hand,
but it will not come near you.
8 You will only observe with your eyes
and see the punishment of the wicked.
9 If you say, "The LORD is my refuge,"
and you make the Most High your dwelling,
10 no harm will overtake you, no disaster will come near your tent.
11 For he will command his angels concerning you
to guard you in all your ways;
12 they will lift you up in their hands,
so that you will not strike your foot against a stone.
13 You will tread on the lion and the cobra;
you will trample the great lion and the serpent.
14 "Because he loves me," says the LORD, "I will rescue him;
I will protect him, for he acknowledges my name.
15 He will call on me, and I will answer him;
I will be with him in trouble,
I will deliver him and honor him.
16 With long life I will satisfy him
and show him my salvation."

OCTOBER 5

We spoke to Rex early this morning, to make sure that he was on his way. We agreed he knew what to do, so there was no need for us to hang around all day. We hid the key in a secret place and off we went to explore the Grand Canyon. Diana would be able to check off another item on her Bucket List today.

We were on the South Canyon Rim, and it was spectacular. The views were amazing and breathtaking. There were lots of tourists there, and we were once again a minority of English speakers.

Diana observes: *There is no argument, while gazing upon the massive creation of the Grand Canyon, as to whether or not there is a God. All I could do is stand there and gaze in awe. No words or pictures could ever describe the natural beauty of this place.*

"The Grand Canyon has unique combinations of geologic color and erosional forms decorate a canyon that is 277 river miles (446km) long, up to 18 miles (29km) wide, and a mile (1.6km) deep. Grand Canyon overwhelms our senses through its immense size."[12]

What an understatement. At the Visitor Center, I got another stamp for my Passport. Their park movie was shown on a huge 3-D world globe. It was the first such movie we'd ever seen. From the visitor center, we could watch folks hiking down into the canyon, some with pack mules.

There was also a train that brought tourists from a nearby town, but most of the passengers were employees that worked in the park. We drove the park road, Route 64 east to Watch Tower to

[12]nps.gov/grca/index.htm

view the canyon from places like Yaki Point, Grandview Point, Moran Point, Lipan Point, and Navajo Point. Each point revealed another different view of the spectacular canyon. At Watch Tower, Larry and Diana climbed the stairs, to ascend to the top of the round stone tower.

While we were there, we observed art students and teachers working hard to restore all the Indian murals inside. The views were great from where I was, but Larry and Diana raved about the views they enjoyed from the top of the tower.

Diana: *The park was renovating the inside of the tower, but there were hieroglyphics on every inch inside, including the walls, ceilings, floors, and stairs. Many of the designs were Kopi Indian and very detailed. It was amazing to think those images had been there for hundreds of years. The stairs were very narrow and there was only one way up and down. Surprisingly, everyone seemed to pass without getting angry at each other or falling.*

On one of the stone walls was a plaque that overlooked the Canyon. It was from Psalms 66:4: "All the earth worships thee; they sing praises to thee, sing praises to thy name."

The view from the top was awesome. It was an unobstructed view of the canyon viewed from above.

"The Desert View Watchtower, also known as the Indian Watchtower at Desert View, is a 70-foot (21 m)-high stone building located on the South Rim of the Grand Canyon within Grand Canyon National Park in Arizona, United States. The tower is located at Desert View, more than 20 miles (32 km) to the east of the main developed area at Grand Canyon Village, toward the east entrance to the park. The four-story structure, completed in 1932, was designed by American architect Mary Colter, an employee of the Fred Harvey Company who also created and designed many other buildings in the Grand Canyon vicinity including Hermit's Rest and the Lookout Studio. The interior contains murals by Fred Kabotie."[13]

> Romans 1:20
> For since the creation of the world
> God's invisible qualities—
> his eternal power and divine nature—
> have been clearly seen,
> being understood from what has been made,
> so that people are without excuse.

We had given our insurance information to Rex yesterday, and he had been dealing with them now for two days straight, while we were being tourists in the park. He was finishing up when we returned to the motorhome, and he had quite a humongous bill waiting for us.

We had given him a deposit yesterday of $500, a down payment on the parts he had to purchase. His bill for parts and services today was an additional $2,366.03. We made sure to get copies of everything, as this will all have to be sent to our warranty insurance company. But Rex needed to be paid in full up front. Well, that sure took a bite out of the checking account, but at least we had power and air conditioning! But, as I attempted to use the washer later, we sadly realized that the surge had fried it, too. I called the customer repair line and a service rep determined that the main circuit board had blown. He would send me the part, then we would have to get a certified installer dispatched when we reached Las Vegas.

---

[13]en.wikipedia.org/wiki/Desert_View_Watchtower

Here we were, trying to show Diana a good time, and everything seemed to go wrong. The electric was fixed, the windshield was broken, the washer/dryer was out of commission, but hey—the steps still worked! While we gave the air conditioning a chance to cool down the motorhome, we enjoyed a wonderful Mexican supper at Plaza Bonita, nearby on the main street. It was a delightful little restaurant with colorful chairs and tables. We do love Mexican food.

God was still good. He led Rex to us. Larry took the opportunity to tell Rex what Motorhome Ministry was all about, and we discovered that he was a Christian, as well. Larry sent him off with a brochure and a signature pack of seeds.

Psalm 145:1-8, 21
I will exalt you, my God the King;
I will praise your name for ever and ever.
² Every day I will praise you and extol your name for ever and ever.
³ Great is the LORD and most worthy of praise;
his greatness no one can fathom. ⁴ One generation commends
your works to another; they tell of your mighty acts.
⁵ They speak of the glorious splendor of your majesty—
and I will meditate on your wonderful works.
⁶ They tell of the power of your awesome works—
and I will proclaim your great deeds.
⁷ They celebrate your abundant goodness
and joyfully sing of your righteousness.
⁸ The LORD is gracious and compassionate,
slow to anger and rich in love
²¹ My mouth will speak in praise of the LORD.
Let every creature praise his holy name
for ever and ever.

OCTOBER 6

Happy Birthday to my daddy in Heaven, who would have been the ripe old age of 93 today, had he lived. But he passed a long time ago, at the too-young age of 67. I will always be my Daddy's Girl, and will miss his presence in my earthly life, right to my dying day.

Today was a Thursday. When Diana made her plans to be here in Las Vegas with us, Larry's mom, Lois, said that she wanted to fly out to spend the weekend with us, too. We do have a good time with her, and the four of us have vacationed several times together. She had all her reservations made weeks ago, and was genuinely looking forward to the trip.

Larry's sister, Sherri and her husband, Ron flew to Myrtle Beach for a mini-vacation, to stay at Mom's while she was in Vegas. But no one had planned for a hurricane as part of the equation. Diana had been able to slip out of Myrtle Beach prior to the approach of Hurricane Matthew, hence the weather delays. As the storm moved closer, and Sherri and Ron arrived, mandatory evacuations were posted for Mom's apartment. They all had to evacuate, along with Larry's other sister, Lisa.

I'm so grateful that God had everything figured out ahead of time. Larry and I were always Mom's geographically close support system. After we left, Diana has remained available. But with the three of us heading toward Vegas, it was definitely a God-thing that Sherri and Ron arrived just in time to help Mom with the evacuation. Mom was really bummed that she didn't get to enjoy the weekend with us, but we'll get together another time soon. God is Great!

Diana: *Before getting back on I-40, we stopped at Bedrock Lodge, where I took a picture with Fred Flintstone and the gang.*

Back in the motorhome, we continued on I-40 west to Kingman, Arizona, through the desert, to visit the Route 66 Museum, that was also on Diana's bucket list. It was in a former electrical power building. Parking the motorhome was a bit tight, but Larry managed. He was beat and stayed in the rig to rest, while Diana and I enjoyed the museum. The website teases, "The museum was filled with murals, photos, and life-size dioramas that captured each of the groups that have traveled what came to be known as the Mother Road. Follow the paths of the Native American trade routes and the U. S. Army-led survey expeditions. Travel along with the settlers on their migration west over the nation's first federally funded wagon roads. Feel the hardship and despair of the dust bowl refugees as they journeyed along the Mother Road to a better life. Visit Main Street America as the 50's usher in fun and excitement for Route 66 travelers."[14]

Route 66, "which became one of the most famous roads in America, originally ran from Chicago, Illinois, through Missouri, Kansas, Oklahoma, Texas, New Mexico, and Arizona before ending at Santa Monica, California, covering a total of 2,448 miles."[15]

Just so you know, I-40 through Arizona is one of the bumpiest and deteriorated sections of Interstate that we have traveled so far. The Interstate Highway System was established by President Dwight D. Eisenhower in 1956. I do understand there are nearly 48,000 miles of Interstate highways at present, but what a mess some of those miles are, take my word. These roads are tough on the motorhome, and I cannot imagine being a long-distance truck driver and doing this full-time, every day.

---

[14] kingmancircle.com/gokingman/

[15] en.wikipedia.org/wiki/U.S._Route_66

Diana, on the other hand, is having a ball, checking things off her bucket list. She's taken hundreds of photos through the open window, from her seatbelt on the sofa.

The rest of the day, we traveled northwest on US93 to Hoover Dam. We came over the top of one last ridge, onto the bridge overlooking this massive dam. How could man build such a massive cement structure, back in the early 1930's, with only the equipment, tools, and scientific knowledge that existed at that time? "Hoover Dam is a testimony to a country's ability to construct monolithic projects in the midst of adverse conditions. Built during the depression, thousands of men and their families came to the Black Canyon to tame the Colorado River. It took less than five years, in a harsh and barren land, to build the largest dam of its time. Now years later, Hoover Dam still stands as a world-renowned structure. The Dam is a National Historic Landmark and has been rated by the American Society of Civil Engineers as one of America's Seven Modern Civil Engineering Wonders."[16]

We needed to get this motorhome parked, so we headed to the campground, planning to return to the dam later in the evening, then take the full tour in the morning. We checked into Lake Mead RV Villa, right on Lake Mead, backed up by Hoover Dam. Larry rated it a 10, and I would have rated it a 12.

It was definitely a WOW campground, with manicured, well-landscaped sites, and boasting a view of the bright, blue lake in contrast to the desert browns of the surrounding mountains, red rocks, and sand. Our camp site was planted with beautiful palms, and overlooked the Lake. Setting up, we enjoyed yet another spectacular sunset. The view was awesome, to say the least.

---

[16]usbr.gov/lc/hooverdam/history/storymain.html

Larry plugged in our electric cord, and the electric didn't work again! He was ready to explode! I immediately called Rex and explained that he had to get this fixed, especially after we'd paid that huge bill. We will be at another campground in Las Vegas tomorrow, and he agreed to meet us there, day after tomorrow. We will have his repair, our windshield replaced, and the washer/dryer repaired this week. What a time for all of this to go wrong! Devil be Gone!

---

1 Peter 5:8
Be alert and of sober mind.
Your enemy the devil prowls around like a roaring lion
looking for someone to devour.

We finished set up the best we could and now the sun has set. We decided to go up to Hoover Dam to see it with lights on. It was eerie, passing through a security gate check point with flash lights shined in our faces, and driving over the dam without another soul in sight. We truly enjoyed the stunning aspect of the dam at night. The lights sparkle against the cement and make it glow.

But, it was really creepy in places. Even though the security folks had let us in, we felt like we were trespassing, being someplace where we shouldn't be. I will remember those scenes forever. That's something you don't get to do every day!

OCTOBER 7

We got a good night's sleep and were up early to make the opening of the Hoover Dam's Visitor Center and back before the required campground check out. We watched the National Park Service movie at the Visitor Center, then got my Passport stamped. We didn't take the tour down into the dam because Larry and I had taken the tour years before and Diana didn't like the idea of the underground tunnels.

"Hoover Dam is one of the Bureau of Reclamation's major dams constructed on the Colorado River. These projects control floods; store water for irrigation, municipal, and industrial use; and provide hydroelectric power, year-round recreational opportunities, and fish and wildlife habitat. The dam is in the Black Canyon, spanning the Colorado River between Arizona and Nevada, about 30 miles southeast of Las Vegas, Nevada. It is 726.4 feet from foundation rock to the roadway on the crest of the dam. The towers and ornaments on the parapet rise 40 feet above the crest. The dam weighs more than 6,600,000 tons!

"There are 4,360,000 cubic yards of concrete in the dam, power plant and appurtenant works. This much concrete would build a monument 100 feet square and 2-1/2 miles high; would rise higher than the 1,250-foot-tall Empire State Building if placed on an ordinary city block; or would pave a standard highway 16 feet wide, from San Francisco to New York City.

"The first concrete for the dam was placed on June 6, 1933, and the last on May 29, 1935. Approximately 160,000 cubic yards of concrete were placed in the dam per month. Peak placements were 10,462 cubic yards in one day (including some concrete placed in the intake towers and power plant), and slightly over 275,000 cubic yards in one month."[17]

They had to build a city, Boulder, Nevada to house the workers for this massive construction job. Standing on the dam is an experience of a lifetime. At the middle of the dam you can stand in

---

[17]usbr.gov/lc/hooverdam/faqs/damfaqs.html

two different states, Nevada and Arizona. Seeing the cliffs and the anchoring structure, electric towers and the bridge is a technical marvel of engineering. Remember, this was built in the 1930's!

Diana: *While I gazed out upon the Dam in awe, I suddenly jerked out of the way for what I thought was a wasp. But, on second glance, it was a hummingbird! It hovered and stared at me for what felt like 5 minutes. Then as fast as it had arrived, he was gone.*

I had never been that close to a hummingbird before. For goodness sake, what in the world was it doing at the dam? There weren't any flowers nearby that would have attracted him. I checked Hoover Dam from my bucket list, plus the additional one of standing in two states at once (never did that before, either.)

We finally finished wandering the Dam, returned to the campground to pack up, and off we went for the short drive to Vegas! We took US93 southwest, then I-515. Diana laughed as we drove through Henderson, Nevada. She is an all-time champion CSI fan, and the bad people on the show always seem to live in Henderson. As was passed the airport on I-215, then toward downtown on I-15, we could see everything up close. Wow, the Grandeur of Vegas.

Las Vegas, in Nevada's Mojave Desert, is a resort city famed for its vibrant nightlife, centered around shows and concerts, 24-hour casinos, and other entertainment options. Its main street and focal point is The Strip, just over 4 miles long. This boulevard is home to themed hotels with elaborate displays such as fountains synchronized to music, an Egyptian pyramid, the Venetian Canals, the Circus, New York City, and the Eiffel Tower.

We pulled into the Las Vegas Motorhome Resort, which Larry rated a 12+. The entrance is opulent with the street lined in high palm trees, iron gates at the security check point, and a massive club house. We even had to unload the car from the tow dolly at check in and let them take the dolly to an area where no one could see it. When you make reservations here, they ask how old your rig is; it can't be more than ten years old. The place is like a lush Garden of Eden with exotic plants, flowers, and palm trees everywhere.

> Ezekiel 31:9
> I made it beautiful with abundant branches,
> the envy of all the trees of Eden in the garden of God.

There are privacy hedges between the sites and each is decorated with different types of amazingly beautiful upgrades like Tiki grass-covered patios with a grill, refrigerator, fireplace, large screen TV, even a washer/dryer. Every one of the sites kept a coordinated theme of stainless steel, rock, and Tiki grass, just with different options. Some even had the driveways done in fancy cement coverings.

Larry opened the electric box to see if he could hook up, but we still had no electric. He did find a note stating that this site was for sale, $125,000, and it had no upgrades, just a patio table with a Tiki umbrella! I'd bet some of the other sites could sell for well over a quarter-million—plus fees! There were multiple pools and hot tubs throughout the park, so no one would have to walk or drive far.

They say it's "an RV Resort for Royalty." They weren't kidding. It was even a pleasure doing laundry here. This was sure a whole lot nicer than a National Park or boondoggling at Walmart!

Now that we'd arrived, Diana couldn't wait to see the Vegas Strip. It was evening and the lights were just beginning to glow. The glitz of neon was everywhere. First stop was at the "Vegas

Welcome" sign for a photo op. We parked the car at the MGM and started to walk, and walk, and walk. We walked up and down bridges that went high over the streets, and passed all kinds of landmarks that you see on TV and in the movies. You also see the seedier side of the city, with people passing out all sorts of business cards for any type of vice or sin you could desire. None for us, thanks. Some women were half-dressed or in immodest clothing. There were costumed characters scattered about in costumes, from Mickey Mouse to Darth Vader, trying to coax people to take pictures with them for a fee.

Then there were the homeless. As we have seen in all the larger cities, this city had them everywhere, begging or selling water bottles for $1 out of old, dirty coolers. We prayed quietly for them. We saw all of this in the first hour along the street!

Proverbs 19:17
Whoever is kind to the poor lends to the LORD,
and he will reward them for what they have done.

We had witnessed homelessness before in San Francisco and Los Angeles. But, one thing for sure, the disintegration of the middle class is apparent. In all my sixty-plus years, I have never witnessed the amount of homelessness in America as I have on this adventure. You think to yourself, what has happened to them to wind up like this? Not to judge, but I curiously wonder if it was addiction, or illness, or just giving up on life? Perhaps they have chosen this as their "job", to beg for money?

God says if you believe in Him he will take care of you just like He takes cares of the birds.

Matthew 10:29-31
Are not two sparrows sold for a penny?

> Yet not one of them will fall to the ground
> outside your Father's care.
> [30] And even the very hairs of your head are all numbered.
> [31] So don't be afraid; you are worth more
> than many sparrows.

This city is not our cup of tea, but at least we can say we have been to Vegas. We found a Bubba Gump restaurant on the strip and had a shrimp dinner like Forest Gump would have. I enjoy their restaurants. They're well decorated, and wait staff yell questions about the movie *Forrest Gump* to the diners, and if you know the answers, you can win prizes. We left our brochures for every server that waited on us, in the hopes of spreading the hope of Good News.

We stared in amazement as the Bellagio Casino fountains came to life and danced to music, waving to all who watched. Inside the Bellagio, they had tremendous fall displays that incorporated thousands of live, colorful flowers, lights, bows, ribbons, and fall trees with faces in their trunks. It must have taken a month to get this display ready, so how do they keep all the flowers fresh? We strolled the canals and shops of The Venetian and The Palazzo. We wandered into the Treasure Island hotel as well. We were all beat by 8pm, so we walked back to the car and drove to the motorhome.

Rex had told us on the phone that the warranty company had said that, although we had good coverage, we could only claim part of the component replacement costs because they do not, repeat do not, cover damage done by electric surges. Remember, this electrical cord was tested, repaired, and re-tested only back in Durango, Colorado, so it couldn't be the cord. We've had intermittent electrical problems for months, even a couple of blown plugs and power strips. What in the world is doing all this damage?

OCTOBER 8

Rex came today to once again evaluate our electrical problems. When Larry plugged in the electric cord, it started a fire in the transfer switch and blew the switch again. The smell of burnt electric has always frightened me terribly, and I was beside myself. The smell was all through the motorhome, and the men could see scorch marks on the components. Rex told us he thinks there was a main trunk line in the motorhome that was shorting out whenever we moved the rig. So, he went to work on that and repaired the transfer switch again. Another $3,863.53. This has cost us over $6,000 so far. We prayed that Rex had not assumed that he had a sucker to scam. Larry had to sell some stock investments fast to pay for this. Our retirement was being burnt up for motorhome repairs.

Larry stayed with the repair guys as Diana and I explored the city. There was no sense for all of us to be grounded for the day. We parked downtown close to Binions. They offered to take our picture standing with ONE MILLION DOLLARS for free. It was all encased in a thick layer of acrylic and bolted to a table. It probably weighed a ton and no way it was going anywhere! We posed like silly tourists who had just won that pile of cash. What fun to see so much money. We decided to sign up for Player's Club cards, and when we put some cash in, we automatically received a $5 credit from Binions. We played until we went broke, which didn't take long, but Diana did win $15 to spend in hotel shops, so it wasn't a complete loss! We were invited to spin a large slot machine outdoors for a chance to win One Million Dollars, but all we won was a free pic with the million dollars, which we'd already done.

Before we left downtown, Diana made sure to pick up her souvenirs. There on Fremont Street, were dozens of small shops with everything a tourist could possibly want to take home. Back at Binions, she bought a snazzy hooded sweatshirt. I bought a pretty peach T-shirt for me, and a Las Vegas cap for Larry.

We returned to the campground. I can't imagine what the neighbors thought of all this commotion going on at our campsite. What riffraff had the resort allowed in? That may be another reason they don't let older RV's into the park, we need too much repair! The devil was sure having his way with us. Now, the insurance company was arguing about how much they would pay, since they don't cover electrical fires or surges. It will end up, after everything is said and done, costing us around $3,800 out-of-pocket. But, stay alert: the devil is not done with this yet, though.

Diana: *I remember that Dad voiced his frustrations when we returned. He was upset that he had tried to plan the perfect vacation for me and the devil was ruining it. I tried to explain to him that it wasn't ruined at all. In fact, it was the best vacation ever, because I got to spend time with my parents.*

When the repairmen had departed, Diana and I took Larry down to Fremont Street for the evening. It was a way to bring tourists back down to the older part of Vegas, away from the strip. These businesses and casinos have an amazing light show above the street. The Vegas Experience explains: "The Viva Vision video screen is 1,500 feet long, 90 feet wide and suspended 90 feet above Fremont Street's renowned pedestrian mall, lined by some of the world's most iconic casinos and hotels. Guests can enjoy a variety of light shows with dazzling, high-resolution imagery and state-of-the-art, 550,000-watt, concert-quality sound. The Viva Vision screen is made up of 12.5 million energy-efficient LED lamps."[18] The show was amazing, and we'd never even heard of Fremont

---

[18] vegasexperience.com

Street during our previous visits. Diana had really done her homework.

The street was alive with all sorts of "people". It just shows you the world is made up of all kinds, and they are all here on Fremont street. Enough said.

Well, except for the naked guy with the jock strap walking and dancing down another street singing, "America the Beautiful" while holding an American flag on a pole. Geesh.

OCTOBER 9

Diana had prepared such a detailed Bucket List for this week, and there will still things left undone. One item on it was the Carroll Shelby Museum. The race-car maker displays its most notable models & prototypes of his cars in this showroom. I couldn't afford the match box cars in the gift shop much less the half-million-dollar Shelby Mustangs. They were magnificent pieces of engineering machinery. The museum was full of stories of the man, Carroll Shelby, the cars and their history. Sadly, it was Sunday and there wasn't a soul working in the garage, which took up half of the building.

Diana: *Carroll Shelby made one car. To get people interested in his car, he asked magazines to write articles about it. However, being the smart man that he was, every time that an article was written, he painted the car a different color, creating the illusion that he had an entire line of cars available.*

Somehow, her research had uncovered the fact that there was one, single White Castle restaurant tucked away here in the fancy city of Las Vegas. We just had to go! It was a tiny place, and the lines were long, but the White Castle hamburgers were terrific, as well as the tiny fish sandwiches that I also love. It had been a great way to spend our last afternoon together. It was a favorite from old times.

Diana remembers: *We almost had an argument about where to eat supper. We found an off-Strip Italian restaurant named Sergio's. Dad didn't want to eat there, but girls rule. After we ate, we all agreed they had amazing food.*

Yes, Diana's vacation had rolled to its end and it was time to take her to the airport. Larry and I hated to see her go. If anything, it makes you realize how important family is when you are on the road as long as we have been. You can see and learn amazing things, but family is what you miss the most about home. There were lots of hugs, kisses, and tears as Diana prepared to enter the airport.

Back in the car, Larry had such an emotional moment, he nearly cried. He had really enjoyed this week through Diana's contagious laughter and youthful eyes and already missed her terribly. I took advantage of the moment and suggested that we make plans to fly home to Myrtle Beach for Christmas. Within hours, all reservations had been made.

We had been blessed with a beautiful full moon this entire week. It was especially nice watching it pass overhead, as we enjoyed the hot tub.

Genesis 28:14
Your descendants will be like the dust of the earth,
and you will spread out to the
west and to the east, to the north and to the south.
All peoples on earth will be blessed through you

OCTOBER 10

Diana went home yesterday, and the motorhome seemed desperately quiet today. Since we finally had electric, I took a cool and much-needed nap, and we agreed to eat in tonight. Later that afternoon, I hauled everything up to their laundromat on our street. Larry worked outside and got some maintenance done. We ended the day with an hour-long soak in the hot tub, under another beautiful moon. What a marvelous, glorious whirlwind these past few days have been.

Diana adds one last thing: *When I got home, I returned to a flat tire on my car. And, thanks to Hurricane Matthew, that car was covered in dried paper pulp from some trash can. Yep, the devil had followed me home. Perhaps he will leave my mom and dad alone, at least for a little while.*

OCTOBER 11

Even though we'd been running constantly, Larry wanted to get out and do something, so he got online and found out that the Righteous Brothers were singing at Harrah's.

We drove and parked on the Strip late in the afternoon, then picked up the tickets at Harrah's before they gave them away to somebody else. We walked around a bit, and enjoyed an early supper at The Twisted Kilt. Back at Harrah's, the concert began at 6pm.

Even though Bill Medley is getting up in age, he still performs, as he has since 1963. His voice was straining a bit towards the end of the show, but it was fun taking a nostalgic journey through the legendry music of Bill and Bobby Hatfield. Bobby died a few years ago, and Bill has a new partner, Bucky Heard, who's much younger than Bill. But, if you close your eyes while they sing, you'd swear it was still Bill and Bobby. My favorite has always been *Unchained Melody*. The concert had been a great idea, and we had a wonderful evening.

OCTOBER 12

We were awakened early by the men who arrived to fix the motorhome windshield. They certainly knew what they were doing and completed the job quickly. They reassured us that no one had done this damage on purpose; it was a failure of the bottom section of the gasket that sealed the window. We confirmed that the motorhome was 10 years old, and they agreed that it was not unusual. That did make us feel better about what had caused the damage. Thank the Lord this was 100% covered by our insurance.

We hung around until 1pm, when the washer guys came to replace the main board I'd ordered. It was definitely blown, as it had smoky markings on it. Their bill was another $537.96!

We had stuff to mail, and there was a humongous line at the post office. We both got much-needed haircuts, then went grocery-shopping. We even managed to stop at a small RV show being held at a hotel just down the street. Boy, were there some beauties there…the price tags were beauties, too!

We enjoyed a quiet supper at the motorhome, then a dip in the hot tub, followed by an evening of *Longmire* on Netflix.

Thank you, Lord for another great day.

OCTOBER 13

But today, not such a great day. We had hoped and prayed that our electric problems were behind us, but something wasn't quite right. We discovered them early in the morning, and Rex was called again.

A lesson in Motorhome Power 101. When hooked up to nothing, we can use 12-volt power like you can charge your cell phone in your car, with a special charger. There are also several lights inside that are wired to the 12-volt. They get powered by the bank of batteries in the back of the rig. Also, you can start your on-board generator. It's powered by diesel and can operate a lot of things that electric can, but batteries cannot. But it has some limits: you can't run the air conditioner and use the microwave at the same time. Then, there is plugged-in 30-amp power, which runs everything—to a limit, and finally the king of power: 50-amp power where you can run anything and everything you want.

Also wired into all of this are power converters and inverters. I can't explain all of this, because I'm not that smart, but those components take the electric and generator power and uses it to recharge the batteries. We have a solar panel that recharges them, too. This story is leading to the fact that although our 110v electric was working fine, the batteries were not recharging. He started the generator and found the same problem. These electrical systems were not playing well with the others, and some were not in the game at all.

I had planned to finish my financials and prepare my quarterly sales tax return, but I was fearful of another power surge. I certainly couldn't afford to lose my computer this year, too! Larry had a total meltdown, being sick and tired of this complicated electrical problem. It affected everything that he did daily: his computer, the wifi, his iPhone, software updates that he needed. He was so mad! And it got worse when Rex confirmed that additional parts had now blown and had to be replaced, to the tune of an additional $2,600.

I did the best I could to cheer him up with a special meal. I fixed steak kabobs on the grill and had fresh corn on the cob. It did cheer him up, but just a tiny bit. And, only for a very short while.

OCTOBER 14

We left Las Vegas today for Death Valley. Even after all the desert we'd seen, we were anxious to see what Death Valley, California had in store for us. You wouldn't guess in a million years.

When our Verizon service would allow it, we were trying to call Diana to wish her a very happy birthday. It was a big one—our Bicentennial Baby turned 40 this year—even though we'd already celebrated with her. We finally had a good conversation, which just confirmed how much we were all missing each other. Happy Birthday, Sweetie.

We took NV160 and CA190, where Death Valley is known as the lowest point in North America. The landscape is dry, desolate, and sandy. The whole drive there was arid and barren. The Furnace Creek Campground at Death Valley National Park was located on a small stream, so there were a few trees spotting the area. Larry rated the campground a 6, which is above normal for national parks.

"In this below-sea-level basin, steady drought, and record summer heat make Death Valley a land of extremes. Yet, each extreme has a striking contrast. Towering peaks are frosted with winter snow. Rare rainstorms bring vast fields of wildflowers. Lush oases harbor tiny fish and refuge for wildlife and humans. Despite its morbid name, a great diversity of life survives in Death Valley.[19]

We pulled in after the drive into the valley, found our campsite, hooked up, and Pop! What was that? Another electrical failure! What?! The transfer switch blew again, the converter malfunctioned, and the washer/dryer had blown again as well.

We were all fine one moment, then Larry had picked up the power cord to move it when this happened. Then, we knew, without a doubt, it had been the stupid power cord all along.

We were so upset! How many different men have we paid to test this stupid cord? One after another assured us it was fine. If any one of them had done their job correctly and completely, we would have replaced it months ago and avoided the anger, frustration, and the thousands of dollars we paid out.

Well, we called Rex again and agreed that each of us would drive back to Vegas to meet—him, 3 hours west and us, 3 hours east. We didn't even register for the campsite at Furnace Creek, we just packed everything back up and left. We did stop long enough to get my stamp at the Visitor Center. Larry was furious after paying so much money out for repairs that hadn't fixed anything. I don't like him driving when he's so upset. God please be with him, I prayed. His patience was gone, all used up.

On the way back, when I could get service, I left messages for the washer/dryer guys. Back to Vegas we went and back to the

[19]nps.gov/deva/index.htm

same campground, we even asked for the same site. The pool was close, as was the laundromat, which I'd be needing for sure. We cooled off in the pool, then managed to sleep in the heat. Praise the Lord for the breeze that night!

OCTOBER 15

Rex texted to say he'd be there about 1:30pm. We were not wasting another minute waiting around, so we hid a key for him and went to the movies. He texted again during the movie to say all was finished. When we returned, there was a brand-new power cord and everything worked as it should. And there was no additional bill. It sure was about time—this job was done.

I left 2 more messages for the washer/dryer guys, but they would not return my calls. Cowards…

While we'd been out earlier, I expressed my need for a new bathing suit. Now, please understand that I hate shopping for bathing suits, as most women do. I no longer look for something that makes me look good, 'cause that just ain't happening. I'm just happy to find something that fits that doesn't make me look any worse off than I am. Ha!

Larry drove me to a nearby Target. He stayed in the car with his cell phone for entertainment and I headed inside. I managed to find 5 suits near my size and I headed for the fitting room. The solid black one was perfect. One-stop shopping for a bathing suit, after only trying on five?

It was windy that evening, but we enjoyed another visit to the hot tub. This has been by far the most luxurious campground we have stayed in to date. And, of course, it isn't cheap at about $80 a night for a *standard* site. In these past 6 months, we sure have visited the complete array of campgrounds from unpaved parking lots, to the ritziest of them all, and everything in between.

My journal notes say that today was day # 200 on the road for Motorhome Ministry. Wow. And the journey has really just begun.

OCTOBER 16

We had not been to a church in a while and we felt the need to enjoy some time in the company of like-minded Christians, especially after Vegas. Many of our Sundays are travel days and other times, there's just no appropriate place to worship. Larry searched the internet for a church to attend, and we ended up at Calvary Chapel Las Vegas, a nice contemporary church.

The people were warm and friendly. We sure needed a big dose of friendly, after being on the road and being so unaccepted in some places. The music was modern and upbeat and I even knew a couple of the songs. The message was great and held my attention. We met the Pastor Derek Neider after his sermon and exchanged what we did on the road for Him. He offered to pray for us right there and then, and we most certainly accepted.

We stuffed ourselves at Olive Garden and took a nap in the afternoon to escape the heat. I hauled my undone laundry to the nearby air-conditioned laundry room, colored some in my color pencil book, then called my best buddy, Deb to catch up on stuff. It's always great to visit with her. Miles simply cannot separate good friends.

We finished watching *Longmire* until the end of the season. Now what? When will we learn what happens next? We enjoyed another dip in the hot tub under a full moon for what was hopefully our last night in Vegas. Today had been an enjoyable day, greatly unlike the days of mayhem that have been torturing us lately. Thank you, Lord for a wonderful day.

OCTOBER 17

We set out from Las Vegas this morning to go all the way to the coast. It was a five-hour drive to Hobson Beach County Park, Ventura, California from Vegas. Heading west on I-15 to I-210 to US101 north. Yes, the Route 101 that travels right along the blue pacific.

While on the way, we saw this bright light miles ahead of us. We had no idea what it was—it looked like a blinding star on the ground! Was it a UFO? What? It was so bright! Google quickly explained that the Ivanpah Solar Electric Generating System is "a 377megawatt net solar complex using mirrors to focus the power of the sun on solar receivers atop power towers…and is currently the largest solar thermal power plant in the world."[20] It's located at the California—Nevada border. One regretful hazard of the plant and a grave concern of environmentalists nationwide, is its intense heat and radiation, which has killed birds in flight

I finally got to speak to the washer/dryer guys. They were not sympathetic at all, saying that I had made the diagnosis and he'd only plugged in the part that I'd provided. There was no guarantee that it was fixed—so, no warranty on their work. He offered to order yet another part, but we didn't have time to wait around for that. I

---

[20] brightsourceenergy.com/ivanpah-solar-project#.WRS19-XyuK4

called the manufacturer again. After they heard this whole, messy story, they had pity on the situation. They agreed to send another motherboard and capacitor switch free of charge, and we could probably install it ourselves. Thank you! We gave them the address of the campground we would be visiting in Malibu, California. We will deal with it then.

The last full-time job I had was working in a call center, and the client I served was a California health care provider. Before retiring, I had spent over a year talking to folks all over the state of California, who lived in places I'd never heard of before. Many of those conversations came back to me today, as I read sign after highway sign with names of all those places: Victorville, Fontana, Rancho Cucamonga, Moreno Valley, Riverside, and so many more.

As we passed the signs for San Bernardino, I recalled the terrible killings that had occurred over the holidays last year. What a sad state of affairs that was, so very sad.

And as we continued, we could clearly see the devastation of the wildfire that had roared through here less than a year ago. I personally remembered news footage of the interstate where folks had abandoned their vehicles and run for their lives, trying to beat the path of the fire. I know we traveled over that same, exact spot, as you could see where the road was burned from both sides. I had talked to lots of folks about their health insurance coverages, and they told me their stories of the draught, these wildfires, and how close they resided to these events. I can now personally understand just what and where they were talking about.

Traveling on for hours, we finally made it to the Los Angeles basin on the I-215 and there, we stopped. We have never seen traffic like this in our entire lives, and we've driven through a lot of large cities. All 7 lanes on both sides (that's 14 total) were stopped and filled with glowing lights, going nowhere anytime soon. But, we have since been told that this is normal LA. The roads in California are now the worst we've encountered to date. They need to repair and expand it all. I just couldn't believe the state with the highest gas taxes in the nation had the worst roads. Where is all that gas tax going, I wonder aloud. Man, this is bad! My body was tired, as I'm sure Larry's was. It was enough to make me want to curse out loud. Forgive me, Lord. Are we there yet?

> James 1:26
> Those who consider themselves religious
> and yet do not keep a tight rein on their tongues
> deceive themselves, and their religion is worthless.

The last time we were in California, we met Larry's cousin David and his wife, Sally at a restaurant in Hollywood. Barely knowing each other, Sally and I were trying to find common ground for conversation. At the time, we lived in Indianapolis, and I worked in a high-rise smack in the middle of downtown. David and Sally lived in the "desert", and commuted into the city to work. They explained how their trip was about 90 minutes each way, every day. I was aghast. "How long does it take you to get to work every day?" Sally asked politely. "Uh, about 12 minutes, if the traffic's bad." Her probing eyes didn't know me well enough to decide whether it was true or if I was just being a smart aleck. Not knowing what to say to that, she went back to eating her salad.

Down the mountains, we came into the coastal area. There were miles of farmland and fields of crops everywhere, but, with high rises serving as a backdrop.

We finally arrived in Ventura a little after 5pm. Hobson Beach turned out to be an itty-bitty city park that had about 15 "sites" outlined in a small parking lot, with full utilities and a magnificent walk-up view of the Pacific, which Larry rated a 4. It is a first come, first serve campground, and the price was high for the dirty little, unkempt place that it was. But God went before us and we claimed a site barely big enough for this big rig, right under a couple of high palm trees.

As we pulled in, a woman was standing in front of her car changing into her shorts and underwear—she was buck naked in front of everyone. Welcome to California! Surfer dudes came and went to hit the surf. By sunset, the bright sun had yielded to a gorgeous sunset over the Pacific Ocean.

Our motorhome had been parked in a way that we had a grand view of the setting sun, as we enjoyed the scent of the wood fire some of the surfers were tending nearby. We enjoyed some quick-fix Stouffers and caught up on Fox News. I can't wait for this election to be over!

OCTOBER 18

We rose early to get a head start on this beautiful day. We drove the car to Simi Valley, California to visit the Reagan Library. When we told the clerk that we planned to visit a lot more Libraries this year, he recommended that we purchase a Presidential Pass. From this time on, it would give us free access to most of the other Presidential Libraries. What a money saver! We are now considered patrons.

The library was amazing, displaying lots of photos and explaining in great detail the life of Ronald Reagan, our 40th President of the United States. He and Nancy Reagan's graves are there. His Marine One Helicopter, Air Force One plane, and his Presidential Limousine are all there. The place is huge, all under roof. How in the world they got that Boeing 747 up the mountain and under roof is way beyond my understanding.

One of the most memorable pieces of history was a concrete slab from the Berlin Wall. Reagan said, "We welcome change and openness; for we believe that freedom and security go together, that the advance of human liberty can only strengthen the cause of world peace. There is one sign the Soviets can make that would be unmistakable, that would advance dramatically the cause of freedom and peace.

"General Secretary Gorbachev, if you seek peace, if you seek prosperity for the Soviet Union and Eastern Europe, if you seek liberalization, come here to this gate. Mr. Gorbachev, open this gate. Mr. Gorbachev, tear down this wall!"[21]

And that he did. A piece is outside on the grounds, overlooking the valley on a hillside for all to see. What a memorial to President Reagan, and what he did for freedom. One side is full of graffiti from the free side of the wall and the other is blank from the communist side. The library is massive and elegant with marble throughout and magnificent views of the California mountains and valleys from huge windows. Just imagine the sight of Air Force One, a Boeing 747 in a glass structure under roof. It's all there!

The day was beautiful and we learned a great deal. We stopped at the most pathetic little Walmart on the way back, but they didn't have a single thing we wanted or needed. Fox News served as our evening's entertainment again, and I must say I'm so sick of the political mud-slinging. Yuck.

---

[21]reaganlibrary.gov/major-speeches-index/35-archives/speeches/1987/6925-061287d

The view here is fantastic and the sounds of the ocean just a few yards away is so nice. We will be in Los Angeles for weeks to come—I wonder what great adventures will be revealed?

OCTOBER 19

Today we rose early because we had someplace important to go—we had audience tickets to *The Price is Right!* Fighting traffic, we arrived early at the CBS Television Center on Beverly Boulevard in Hollywood. Our tickets were first come, first served. We stood in a long line outside the secure fenced area and waited. Since we were so early, I jaywalked to the vitamin store across the street to purchase some sustenance. It was a good thing that I did. We had no idea that this line would turn into a 4-hour audition and taping.

They finally took us through security and into a shaded holding area. We were given a tag with a large number on it, then another tag with our first name. It didn't take us long to figure out that we were all being watched. At one point in the line, they told Larry and I to get in front of this fancy backdrop. They explained that they would cue us, and they wanted to see how we'd react to learning that, "You won a new car!" So, we jumped in the air and threw our hands up and had this great look of surprise on our faces. We bought the pic. It's silly, but what a pic it is!

We were told to stay in numeric order, but the woman behind me kept wandering off. She was a tall, skinny black woman. And she was odd. She was wearing a one-piece fleece contraption that looked like a sleeper you put a baby in. With a hoodie. It was hot today, and she never even removed the hood. She just couldn't sit still and would disappear for half-hours at a time. Weird.

There were over 200 of us in line. When we were moved to another waiting area, they called small groups of us up to stand in front of some cool, relaxed guy who would ask each of us a question. He only asked me where I was from. How great can you say, "Myrtle Beach, South Carolina?" The guy recognized Hoodie Girl, saying, "You've been here before, haven't you?" Who could forget her?

Then we were moved again, where we could watch past show clips on the TV's above, being sure that we all took potty breaks before entering the studio. Miss Weird Person finally spoke to me for the first time. "You need to sit forward on this bench; I'm tired of looking at your back." I was stunned. I stumbled for a polite response. "I'm turned to speak to my husband, so I'm sorry you have to look at my back." She never said another word. Larry speculated later that the scars on my neck made her uncomfortable.

Finally, it was time for the show! They turned up the lights, queued the music, and announced, "So and so, come on down!" We were sitting near the left end of the audience, just a few feet from Drew Carey's exit between takes. He was nice, making eye contact and asking how we were as he passed by. It was fun to watch all the behind-the-scenes stuff going on. We had a great time.

But, by the time we arrived back at the motorhome, we were bushed. We had left around 9am and didn't make it back until after 8pm. And, oh darn, we missed the final presidential debate. We hit the shower and we were off to bed. What a day of memories!

OCTOBER 20

As I awoke this morning, the first thing I noted was today's date, 10/20. This day, exactly 1 year ago, my life changed. It was on this day last year that I broke my neck. That whole incident was such a God thing, and my life will never be the same. Every single day I am so aware that God has a continued plan for me, or He would have left me for dead that very day, that very moment. I pray daily that He will use me as He wills, and always for His glory. I am His. I am only here today because of Him. I owe Him my everything.

> Jeremiah 29:11
> "For I know the plans I have for you," declares the LORD,
> "plans to prosper you and not to harm you,
> plans to give you hope and a future."

We packed up the motorhome and took US101 south to the Malibu Beach RV Park this morning, which Larry rated a 6. You know, the stars live in Malibu. Just for fun, we picked up one of those Homes magazines at Walmart and it only showed a few "shacks" for $750,000—everything else was in the multi-millions.

On our way into Malibu, we were shocked to see a string of older motorhomes parked along the left side of the highway, up against the mountain cliffs. Some looked like they hadn't run in years, some were even jacked up. They were parked on the right-of-way and I'm amazed the upscale area allowed it. I guess they've found some loophole that allows them to stay there—for free—with no hook-ups and no one to bother them. And the view is fantastic, of course. To each his own, I guess.

We found Malibu RV Park set on the side of a tall cliff. The drive up into the Park was very steep and there were 3 levels of campsites. We were assigned to a second-row site, located in the lowest section. Lowest being relative, as we were a good 500 feet above US101. The views of the Pacific, Catalina Island, and downtown LA were unbelievable. This is basecamp for a week.

We got settled in, hooked up, and Larry put out the banner and the Kid's Packets. As soon as it was up, 2 girls about 10 years old were riding their bikes past, and took notice. After riding back and forth several times, I went outside to ask if they would like some packets. They said, "Sure. Yes, ma'am." I had been watching them from inside the motorhome. They looked like they wanted them but were afraid to stop and take them, so that's why I offered. They were excited that the goodies were about Jesus, and my heart swelled that these young ladies were being brought up in faith.

Larry spent a lot of time today on the computer, getting us more tickets for whatever shows he could find. He managed to get us on *Conan O'Brien, Jimmy Kimmel Live,* and *Wheel of Fortune.* He even managed a fair price for concert tickets to hear Norah Jones live in Griffith Park. Larry really enjoys her soulful jazz.

We didn't want to venture far, but really wanted some fresh seafood. There was such a place so close that I could have hurled a rock over the cliff and it would have landed there. But to drive there was a whole different 15-minute matter. We drove the car down the steep hill and was forced to turn right because of the concrete median on US101. We drove a mile north to the median break, made a U-turn when the light turned green, drove past the RV park, past the seafood place (on the same side of the road as the RV park), then up the road another mile in the wrong direction, to another median break. Made another U-turn at the light and finally, turned into Malibu Seafood.

Inside, I walked up to their small counter to order, while Larry claimed a picnic table outside. There is no indoor seating here, just carry out and picnic tables with fantastic views of the Pacific Ocean. They offered fresh fish, shrimp, crabs, and more. I walked back outside to wait at the pickup window. Lots of folks came and went while I was waiting, picking up orders they had called ahead. This place was hoppin'. Our order was finally ready and we enjoyed every bite. No wonder this place is so busy.

As I said my prayers at bedtime that night, there was much to pray about, camping on the side of this gigantic cliff on the coast of California. I always thank the Lord for the hedge of protection He's had around me all day and I pray that He will bless us with another hedge again tomorrow.

There have been well-televised wildfires in this area, and I prayed that no such fires would overcome us here. Earthquakes are certainly not new here, so close to the San Andreas Fault, and I prayed that no such earthquakes would come during our stay. Despite the drought, if heavy rains were to come, Malibu is infamous for terrible landslides, and I prayed that no such landslides would happen during our stay. I think we're safe up here from tsunamis, so I didn't bother to pray about them. Those were some pretty long prayers, and God answered every single one.

> Psalm 91:9-12
> [9] If you say, "The LORD is my refuge,"
> and you make the Most High your dwelling,
> [10] no harm will overtake you, no disaster will come near your tent.
> [11] For he will command his angels concerning you
> to guard you in all your ways;
> [12] they will lift you up in their hands,
> so that you will not strike your foot against a stone.

OCTOBER 21

Anticipating a busy week, I caught up on housework and laundry, then we went adventuring, just to get our bearings.

We headed to the famous Santa Monica Pier. We paid and parked, then walked quite a way and up lots of steps to get up on the pier, where you could see the beach and ocean for miles. There were plenty of sun worshipers laying on the sand. It was a Friday afternoon and kids were in school, but the area was still pretty busy.

There were plenty of so-called "musicians" playing for tips, and one looked and sounded just like Ray Charles. There were lots of little shops tucked about the pier and lots of little places to buy food and drink. The rides were running, the place was generally clean and tidy. One night when we were watching cable, Larry pointed out that a commercial for irritable bowel syndrome medicine was filmed in that very same place! And I concur. I've been there!

We got back in the car and drove to Venice Beach. We went to park in a city lot, but the first parking space was occupied by an unkempt fellow, stretched out in the hot sun, oblivious to everything around him. We parked in the next space, then got out and walked up the street. I was uncomfortable with this whole situation—the whole place seemed dirty. Of course, we had TOURISTS written all over us, and there are bad people in the world who interpret that as VICTIMS.

There were plenty of roller bladers, dog walkers, and bicyclists on the famous concrete path by the beach. There were a few street vendors lined up against the sidewalk, who were offering questionable items for sale. I did enter a cluster of permanent shops on the other side of the street, and I felt sorry that these quality vendors had to share the streets with the likes of those outside. I prompted Larry to get back into the car and leave. He agreed.

But it was fun, walking the streets that we've seen so often in the movies. Just to name a few: *China Syndrome, American Gigolo, Down and Out in Beverly Hills, Dragnet, Speed.* Just about anywhere you went, you would see streets blocked off and signs telling you that filming was in progress, whether TV shows, movies, or commercials.

Then we had this idea that we'd go to Costco to pick up some things, since we'd be in the area for a while. It was only a mile away, simple, right? What a hair-brained idea that turned out to be! With the one-way streets, the blocked off streets, and construction at the store, it took over an hour to go that one mile. We had to drive around the block twice to even get into the parking lot. The store was even worse! People were packed in there wall-to-wall, with no room to move. The checkouts all had long lines. The traffic just getting in and out of their parking lot was terrible and the 14 miles to get back to the park took us well over an hour. Get me outta here!

We would have to be sure to leave in plenty of time to get to the events we have tickets for. Traffic moves at a snail's pace here, and the city is spread out in all directions. We'll be sure to pack water and food for each trip.

If you think I'm kidding, you will soon find out that I'm not.

OCTOBER 22

Today was a lazy day. I slept late, then laid in bed enjoying Facebook. In the afternoon, we decided to go into Malibu to see a movie and were shocked at their west coast prices. Yikes! But, it was also the first time we had ever watched a show in recliners—they were great. I think we went to see *The Accountant*, but I'm not totally sure. Whatever it was, we enjoyed it, because at least we were comfortable.

But the real entertainment had been on the way to the movies. Larry noticed a guy walking erratically on the sidewalk, while we were waiting at a traffic light. The guy stopped, turned himself to face the street, unzipped his pants, and peed right there in front of God and everyone. What is the matter with folks nowadays? He could have easily stepped behind the tree at arm's length and did his business in private. Was he under the influence or making a social statement?

When we went back to the motorhome, we decided to watch another movie on DVD, then went to bed.

The sunset from our vantage point was absolutely beautiful.

But the best part of the day? Diana texted to say she had found a prescription bottle of Ambien with Larry's name on it. Now, if you haven't read my first book, you wouldn't understand the big deal, but it had been a very big deal indeed, last July.

Larry uses the prescription to sleep, and when he ran out, it was a terrible thing. He had been angry at me for weeks, saying I'd lost the bottle or had thrown it away. I vehemently insisted that I wouldn't have done such a careless thing. It had been like pulling teeth to get his doctor to write another one, then to get the insurance company to fill it. What's the date on it, I asked her. July 18. I am innocent! Redeemed! Vindicated!

> Psalm 7:8
> Let the LORD judge the peoples.
> Vindicate me, LORD, according to my righteousness,
> according to my integrity, O Most High.

OCTOBER 23

Today was busy! After I'd looked at a lot of reviews for church this weekend, we drove all the way downtown LA to attend Hillsong Church. We found their signs outside a historic theatre, an older Arts Building called the Mayan. There were Mayan designs covering the outside, with a long line waiting to go in.

It's the only time we've ever seen a line to get into church! We learned later that there are Hillsong churches around the world. They started out in Australia with just 45 people. Now, they are in just about every major city in the world. Their aim is to serve their city by being the hands, the feet, and the voice of Jesus. They want to bring hope and the gift of grace wherever they go.

We were not disappointed. We were by far the oldest folks there and the message was spot on. A traditional service as this was, the pulsating lights and loud music were just icing on the cake. We thoroughly enjoyed it all.

Then, as we're leaving, the homeless are lined up on the sidewalk, begging for money. I don't know whether they bothered to come in to hear the Word, but they were sure ready for us. LA's homeless problem seems to be even worse than what we witnessed in San Francisco. In the numerous bone-dry viaducts, we often saw entire "tent cities."

After wandering all kinds of freeways and side streets, we enjoyed lunch at the Roosevelt Restaurant, a small café in Griffith Park. We spent the entire afternoon at the Griffith Park Observatory and the Planetarium. It was a bit crowded, but we enjoyed every minute of it. Leonard Nimoy had narrated the film shown in the theatre named for him.

Again, there was a long list of movies and TV series that have been filmed here: *Beverly Hills 90210, Terminator, MacGyver, Charlie's Angels: Full Throttle, Jurassic Park, NCIS: Los Angeles, La La Land, Lois & Clark: The New Adventures of Superman, Adventures of Superman, Star Trek: Voyager, 24, Melrose Place*...and that's just the short list.

The view of LA from up there was amazing, and we continue to see views from that vantage point in lots of movies and on commercials. You can see the LA City basin and the Hollywood sign on top of the mountain. The smog lining the LA Basin is real, too.

Driving all over the area, we were on lots of roads made popular over the years. Laurel Canyon Road was famous for the Manson Murders. You've heard of Mulholland Drive, Wilshire Blvd., Beverly Hills Blvd., Rodeo Drive, Sunset Blvd., Hollywood Blvd., and we drove them all.

Just above Warner Brothers Studio in Studio City, we drove off Franklin Canyon Drive to get to the Upper Franklin Canyon Reservoir. They have a park there where the opening shots of the *Andy Griffith Show* were filmed a very long time ago. Larry just had to take a picture of the place where Andy and Opie had walked so long ago, with fishing poles in hand. It's just a regular road with regular houses leading to a small park and waterhole. It was fun to see it and it was so peaceful there. There was a professional photographer shooting some lady's pictures there. Only in LA. Larry was whistling that tune all afternoon. After you read this, you'll whistle it, too.

Heading back to the rig, we stopped at D'Amore's, a little-bitty pizza place in Malibu. There were pictures of stars all over the walls, and we had no idea how great this little place was to the community. Their website gives their entire history, starting with Grandma **Mommanonna**'s pizza recipe. There are pictures and stories of Pierce Brosnan, Ray Romano, Gerard Butler, the Jenners and the Kardashians. And we were there! Tiny little place—mostly for pickup, carryout, and delivery--but they have quite a few full-service restaurants throughout the city. They import the flour, olive oil, and the water they use to make pizza crust, directly from Italy. It was west-coast pricey, but it was great pizza.

Its slogan is "Pizza of the Stars." Even Joe D'Amore's wife, Christiana is in the industry. She was born Christiana Deborah Capetillo in 1965. She is an actress and director known for *Malibeauties, Christiana D'Amore: The Future Soon Becomes the Past* (2014), and *Only Now Existing's Escape Artist* (2017). She is an actress, director, and producer, as well as a model, singer, and songwriter. Oh, and pizza maker.

When we arrived back at the motorhome, Larry surfed the satellite and found a rerun of *A Few Good Men*. It had been a long time since we'd seen it and it was all new to us again. Great movie. "You can't handle the truth!"

It had been another wonderfully blessed day, which ended again with wonderfully-long prayers.

OCTOBER 24

This was a day of chores. We're still waiting for the washer/dryer parts to arrive, so I dragged everything up to the little laundromat at the RV Park. It was a short walk, so I kept walking back and forth instead of hanging out in the heat. The sound of the surf even way up here is so nice.

The sky is so blue and the sun so brilliant today; it glistens like diamonds on the endless Pacific. It was stunningly beautiful.

I made a note in my journal that I made a new recipe from scratch and Larry really liked it. I cut down the original recipe "Big Mexican Crock Pot Chicken" so we wouldn't have to eat it for days. The original proportions are in the back of the book.

This evening's entertainment was *The Pacifier* on satellite. Again, we'd seen it before but I enjoyed it more this time around. It's such a cute movie.

Chores were all caught up and it had been a great day. Those lengthy nightly prayer concerns have been just that—nightly. Amen.

---

2 Timothy 1:3
I thank God, whom I serve, as my ancestors did,
with a clear conscience, as night and day
I constantly remember you in my prayers.

OCTOBER 25

Today was a full day!

We drove downtown to Warner Brothers Studios to be on the *Conan O'Brien* show—free entertainment. After fighting the usual LA traffic, we parked and found a nice herding area on the first floor of the parking garage. When everyone with tickets had finally arrived, they took us as a group across the street to Studio 8, as Larry recalls. You have seen pictures of this place many times, at the beginning of every Warner Brothers movie. As we were guided through dozens of huge sound stages, we noticed plaques by the doors of each one, showing the many TV shows and movies that had been filmed there. I saw where *The Waltons* had filmed for nine seasons. *Two and a Half Men* filmed there for more than a decade.

Other TV series included *Dragnet* and *Twilight Zone*, and just a few of the infamous movies were *Gremlins, A Star is Born, My Fair Lady,* and more recently, *Sully, the Legend of Tarzan, San Andreas, American Sniper,* and *Jersey Boys.* Some of the buildings had the doors propped open and we could see folks hard at work on the sets inside.

We finally arrived at our destination. We entered the building and hiked up some old wooden stairs, from here, it was all scaffolding and backstage stuff. There about 250 tight but comfortable seats, under rafters, wires, cables, and lights. We watched in awe as last-minute tasks were being completed: camera placement, sound checks, sweeping and buffing the floor to make it shine.

As we were preparing for the taping to begin, the announcer came walking through the audience, walked straight up to me first and told me to head down to the stage floor. What? I was dressed nicely, but I guess I looked like a wild and crazy grandma. When he'd finally selected a half-dozen others, they played music and told us all to do our best butt dance!

I can't dance one speck—especially with my butt, —all my music is in my fingers and my voice. But everyone was laughing hysterically, as we did as we'd been told. One lady approached me, said she couldn't dance either, and gently took my hand to dance together. Each of us were given a Conan T-shirt for our ridiculous efforts. It was too small for me, but Larry gets good use out of it. We sure got the audience warmed up!

They announced that Ron Howard would be interviewed on today's show. Wow, Ron Howard! He was here to promote his third movie *Inferno* based on Dan Brown's series, and starring Tom Hanks. He also talked about his new series *Mars*. His interview was great. Ron is our age, and I have always admired his accomplishments. He seems to be a grounded soul in Hollywood. In contrast, I did not see Conan speak to even one member of the audience, and didn't mix with the production staff, either. Was he "staying in character" during taping or just way above it all?

Larry and I are both in bed long before the late-night shows come on. But what we learned by Conan and eventually Jimmy Kimmel, these "live", late-night shows are all filmed in the afternoon! I always assumed they were live. Silly me. It was fun watching the lights, camera, action of everyone doing their jobs. Nobody messed up. Everyone had a certain job and did it with perfection.

Part of today's show was a guest band, which had been pre-recorded, so our taping went quickly.

From there, we drove straight to Griffith Park. Tonight, would be special—an evening with Norah Jones. The concert was at the outdoor Greek Theater, and we enjoyed a sandwich and a soda there, once we were parked. It started a little late, but there wasn't a bad seat in the house. It was outdoors under the stars. It was getting chilly, so we were so glad we'd brought our brown matching Alaskan-worthy sweats. She sang her heart out, performing hits like *Come Away with Me, Don't Know Why, Sunrise, Turn Me On, Thinking About You, and Happy Pills.* Sitting outside in the chilly air under the stars was great. Norah Jones is an excellent music artist and she did a wonderful job.

Psalm 150:1-5

Praise God in his sanctuary;
praise him in his mighty heavens.
2 Praise him for his acts of power;
praise him for his surpassing greatness.
3 Praise him with the sounding of the trumpet,
praise him with the harp and lyre,
4 praise him with timbrel and dancing,
praise him with the strings and pipe,
5 praise him with the clash of cymbals,
praise him with resounding cymbals.

On a personal note, I think she should have run a brush through her hair beforehand, but I guess she didn't feel like it. As my mom would have said, "Her hair was a rat's nest."

Another personal observation: her warmup singer was terrible! Her name was Valerie June and that night she was awful. How many ways can I say dreadful, rotten, appalling, atrocious, terrible, unpleasant, horrible, frightful, foul, horrendous…well, you get the picture. Although Larry likes music, he admits to having a tin ear. My immediate reaction when she began to sing was I wondered if she was a comedy act.

When she continued on and on that way, it wasn't funny anymore. Then she started another song. Larry finally leaned over and asked, "Is it just me or is she really bad?" I wondered if it was the acoustics or something. It was like listening to a cat with his tail in a door. Can you say caterwauling? Anyway, we were so relieved when Norah finally came on stage and began to sing. She is a great pianist, a great singer, and a pretty darn good guitar player. She said she was just learning, but who knew she played guitar? And the acoustics were perfect.

Trying to get out of the parking lot with everyone leaving at once was disastrous. Traffic was again a disaster, but the day was great. It's amazing in LA that EVERY road you go on whether it be expressway, highway, street, or alley is ALWAYS backed up bumper to bumper. Where is the mass transit system? If there is one, why doesn't anybody use it? And the roads are in such bad need of repair.

OCTOBER 26

From all the running around and fresh air, I slept in 'til noon, without an ounce of guilt. The parts for the washer/dryer finally arrived, so Larry and I worked together, replacing the mother board and a capacitor. Not too bad for two old farts. It even worked when we were finished. Gee, we could have saved ourselves over $500 if we'd known that the first time.

I wasted an hour on the phone with Social Security, addressing a problem with my benefit check, then had to call the US Department of Treasury regarding the same problem.

> John 4:24
> God is spirit,
> and his worshipers must worship in the Spirit
> and in truth."

I was having problems again with QuickBooks, so I wasted yet another hour of this beautiful afternoon, trying to take care of little, stupid, annoying but absolutely necessary stuff.

OCTOBER 27

We really put on the miles today, all of it in horrible traffic. The water and snacks sure came in handy today! Our first stop was to see the Space Shuttle Endeavor. It's a "retired orbiter from NASA's Space Shuttle program and the fifth and final operational shuttle built. It embarked on its first mission, STS-49, in May 1992 and its 25th and final mission, STS-134, in May 2011."[22] Seeing it right in front of you and knowing this was in space was amazing.

We watched actual footage of it being maneuvered in by inch through downtown LA to its final home, and that was an engineering feat in itself. As this massive machine was being towed through the city streets, into place at the Center, traffic lights, electrical wires, street lights, and even trees had to be moved and replaced. We were looking at a machine that cost 196 billion, that is BILLION, $196,000,000,000. We visited the entire museum and learned all kinds of things from the environment, the sea, and Mother Earth.

Larry's myositis makes it difficult for him to drive in stop-and-go traffic—his leg muscles tire so easily, so I was driving today. We left the Center and drove through Beverly Hills. We passed the

[22] en.wikipedia.org/wiki/Space_Shuttle_Endeavour

Beverly Hills Hotel and all those beautiful, slender, and so-tall palm trees that line the streets. Myrtle Beach palm trees look like pygmies compared to these.

I drove down Rodeo Drive, past all the stores for rich people. Larry says aloud he probably couldn't afford a pair of shoestrings in any of those shoe stores. Yes, there were beggars on the corners of Rodeo Drive, as well. It's so fancy here, they don't even pronounce it like the rest of us do. "Rodeo: [**roh**-dee-oh] a public exhibition of cowboy skills, as bronco riding and calf roping."[23] Rodeo Drive: "[roh-**dey**-oh]"[24] well, you get the idea.

A surprisingly short distance from the Rodeo Drive shops are the La Brea Tar Pits on Wilshire Blvd. Natural asphalt has seeped up from the ground in this area for tens of thousands of years. The tar is often covered with dust, leaves, or water.[25] Some of the pits bubble up debris from below. Lots of animals, like Mammoths, Saber Tooth Tigers, and more have lost their lives in these pits and fossils have and currently are being dug up. We saw their educational movie and toured the grounds and museum. I tell you, kids should do a year on the road like this, they would learn more in a year than they would ever in school. Plus, they would have a ball doing it.

Needless to say, there was plenty of rush-hour traffic to keep us on our toes. I am so glad I was driving; Larry was a wreck! We enjoyed pan-fried shrimp and coleslaw for dinner at the motorhome. Yum!

---

[23] dictionary.com/browse/rodeo?s=t

[24] dictionary.com/browse/rodeo?s=t

[25] tarpits.org/

Lots of prayers, then early to bed tonight. It had been another amazing day.

OCTOBER 28

Today was a day for running errands. We drove to Walmart for stuff, picked up prescriptions at CVS, and went grocery shopping at Ralph's. We didn't pick up many groceries, because we're trying to get the freezer inventory down before the cruise. Did I say that? We have another cruise soon! I can't wait.

OCTOBER 29

Today was my kinda day. I did laundry and a bit of cleaning. I enjoyed coloring with my pencils and beautiful coloring book today. My plans are to have a few framed for special people in my life as Christmas presents. Coloring is so relaxing for me. It's my little creative world. I can use whatever colors I want and even color outside the lines, if I choose to. And it's beautiful when I'm done.

Did you know that the first person to be filled with the Holy Spirit was Batzalel and he was an artist in charge of building the Tabernacle and the Ark of the Covenant to God's specifications? His creative talent was given to him by God. We are all given talents with which to serve Him. This book is a testament of one of my talents.

Do you know what your talent is? Ask Him to show you, then use it in service of others.

| Exodus 31:3 |
| and I have filled him with the Spirit of God, |

> with wisdom, with understanding,
> with knowledge and with all kinds of skills—

Larry had DVR'd the remake of the mini-series *Roots* recently, so we watched some of that. I fixed pork fried rice for dinner.

It had been a calm and peaceful day. Nowhere to run, nowhere to go, we chose to stay off those crazy traffic-jammed streets for the day. My heart is at peace. I am blessed. Thank you, Lord.

OCTOBER 30

I wrote only 3 words in my journal today: rainy, cloudy day.

And, as *Forrest* Gump would say, "That's all I have to say about that."

OCTOBER 31

Late last evening, I was sitting in my recliner as I usually do and heard something snap. Further examination revealed it was a weld on the chair frame that had broken. We set out today, with the chair in the car, trying to find a welder who would be willing to do this small repair. We Googled welders, called up some, tried to drive to others, spoke to quite a few. We finally gave up when one of them told us that it would be very dangerous to attempt to make that specific repair.

The upholstery part of the chair was not designed in a way to remove it from the frame without ruining it. And if he attempted repairs the way it is, there's a good chance that the heat from the weld would catch the upholstery on fire. Nope, he wouldn't do it.

Alright, then.   After several frustrating hours of LA traffic, point taken.

We Googled again, this time for the nearest Camping World. We found a nice-looking chair there and we agreed to purchase it with the understanding that they would dispose of this broken chair. Deal. Nearly $400 later, we were back in the motorhome.

We were sure to be back in time for the Trick-or-Treaters. We figured there would be some, up there on the hill, but there were only 2 who stopped by for treats. What a shame. This year, I'd bought the good stuff. I guess we'll have to force ourselves to eat it all. Dang.

NOVEMBER 1

This day was barely off and running when crises arose. Larry usually checks our bank balances first thing in the morning. When he checked our business account, he found it to be hundreds of dollars overdrawn. What! He frantically made lots of calls to get someone working on this. It would take a couple of days to get it all straightened out. Yikes. We will have to sort things out later.

We needed to get to Hollywood. We had tickets for the *Jimmy Kimmel Live!* Since we never know how long it will take to drive anywhere, we left hours early and then had plenty of time before the show. We wandered the streets nearby, waiting for the curtain call. We checked out all the imprints at Grauman's Chinese Theater. We walked only a small portion of the famous Hollywood Walk of Fame—the entire Walk goes on for 18 blocks of Hollywood Blvd. and Vine Street. There are more than 2,600 terrazzo and brass stars embedded in the sidewalks.

The one star that really stood out could not be viewed. Donald J. Trump's star had recently been vandalized and hadn't yet been repaired. It was covered in plywood and had street barriers around it. There were derogatory remarks on the plywood, but that wasn't all. There was a woman standing next to the barrier. She was yelling and screaming and pointing various fingers at the plywood. She was really giving our POTUS an earful. It was creepy, and we gave her a wide berth. Check out www.walkoffame.com to learn lots more about it.

Of course, there were plenty of odd folks selling souvenirs, street entertainers, and lots of folks trying to sell tours. There were plenty of beggars, as well. A lot of the stores sold a Map to the Homes of the Stars for $19.99. No, thanks.

Jimmy Kimmel Live is not live at all. Taping was at 4:30 in the afternoon. The show was taped at the former Masonic Hall, just a few steps and across the street from Grauman's Chinese Theater and the Kodak Theatre, where the Oscars are presented.

Larry asked one of the show's greeters how the street was set up for the Oscars. Using a lot of hand gestures, he explained how they close part of Hollywood Blvd. to set up barriers and stages, as well as roll out the red carpets.

We killed a couple of hours, then got something to eat. We were finally ushered into a small studio that sat perhaps 200 people. They seated us in the front row, I suppose since Larry was using his cane today. We were less than 20 feet from the set. Wow.

They got right down to business. Kimmel opened with a skit, "Jimmy Kimmel for Vice President" and went rambling on for a few minutes. Things settled down and Jake Gyllenhaal came out from backstage. He was there to promote his new movie, *Nocturnal Animals*, also starring Amy Adams.

I was surprised that Gyllenhaal, Kimmel, Sajak, and Conan are all very small and slender men in person. Kimmel didn't interact with the audience, either. It's like the audience wasn't even there.

The second guest was a young newcomer to Hollywood, Hailee Steinfeld. She's an American actress, model, and singer. She achieved instant stardom in her role of young Mattie Ross in *True Grit,* and nominated for an Academy Award for Best Supporting Actress.

Traffic was just as wretched that evening, as we tried to get back to the campground. We decided to stop for dinner at Vittorio Ristorante & Pizzeria, Pacific Palisades, off Sunset Blvd. We hoped that, by the time we were done eating, traffic would be lighter. It was a family-friendly restaurant known for their garlic rolls & pizzas served in a bustling setting. The food was authentic and terrific. We had a nice, quiet dinner off the beaten path.

This was quite a day. Thank you, Lord for safety.

NOVEMBER 2

This is our last day in Malibu. After hours of phone calls with the bank over the past few days, it turned out that one of our web customers decided to check a little box to upgrade their software to something bigger. When she did, it charged a $900 annual fee to **our** business PayPal account. When the cash wasn't there, it charged our secondary business checking account, and it wasn't there either. Oh, my goodness! She won't be doing that ever again.

And the new recliner is just not right. It's not adjustable like the other was, and this lays you back so far that you can't work on the computer! We'll be taking it back, for sure.

In the afternoon, I went to the local grocery store, Ralph's by myself. It's part a chain owned by the Kroger company in Cincinnati, our old stomping ground. Before heading back to the motorhome, I confess to exploring on my own. I drove the street behind Ralph's, which would have homes on the Malibu waterfront. Toward the end of the road, I recognized someone I had seen many times on TV—Richard Schiff. There was no doubt in my mind that it was him. He was standing at the bottom of his driveway, talking to a neighbor across the street. You've seen him, too on *West Wing, Jurassic Park, NCIS, Once Upon a Time, White Collar, Monk, ER*, and many more. Just a regular guy, doing what anyone else does on a day off.

And you know you're in Malibu by the cars that drive by: Bentley, Maserati, Jaguar, Tesla, Porsche, Land Rover, Range Rover, although Mercedes-Benz and BMW's have become mainstay nearly everywhere. They're all beautifully detailed. Our poor Ford Escape was dirty from being on the road and badly needed a bath. We were reminded again that we were not among our own kind here.

Diana texted later that afternoon to say she'd had a fall. Her knee and leg are swollen and hurt terribly. My best buddy Deb is an expert by experience of knee and leg injuries, so I called her for advice: apply heat or cold, wrap or not wrap, what to do? Deb had all the answers, so I called Diana back with instructions. It's always something with that girl.

It'll be good to move the motorhome to a new place tomorrow. It's been great here, but I'm ready for a change. One last time, I prayed that all earthquakes, landslides, and wildfires stay away for at least one more day, until I get off this cliff. Amen.

NOVEMBER 3

We headed south on US101—also known as the Pacific Coast Highway—again, via I-405, aka The Dreaded Four Oh Five. How do people live like this with this traffic every day? The lanes are all so full, and each time we need to change lanes with this big rig is like parting the Red Sea. My nerves are shot and I'm not even driving!

It took a while, but we finally traveled the 67 miles to arrive at Orangeland RV Park, located in South Los Angeles. Larry rated this one a well-deserved 9. It was conveniently located within 5 miles of Disneyland and other large attractions. After checking in, we were escorted to our well-manicured site, and they expertly assisted us in backing up among the fruit trees, heavy with citrus. The fruit trees were throughout the park, with fruit all colors and shades of orange, green, and yellow.

I noticed while checking in there were signs encouraging everyone to pick whatever fruit they could use. They offered you the use of extension pickers at no charge. There was even a large map to show what fruit trees were planted where: oranges, limes, lemons, and even grapefruit. After setting up, I came back to check out the picker and Larry and I had such fun gathering some fruit. I made a mess eating 2 fresh-picked oranges right away, and I always enjoy lime in Diet Coke.

We had a bit of trouble setting up the cable service, but we finally got it right. The office had forgotten to offer us a special cable box needed to get cable channels. Once connected, everything worked fine. Larry grilled the rest of the cod from the freezer tonight. It was delicious.

The hot tub provided us a great deal of relaxation. There was also a nice pool, but it was a bit cool for my taste. We didn't realize that spending a few nights in the hot tub this week would bring some heated political discussions, which involved a very liberal democrat who didn't want to hear anything from a conservative point of view. He especially didn't want to hear anything about Jesus. We tried, but he just wouldn't have it.

God is very clear in His Word that He wants us to go forth and spread the Word. As Christians, part of our duty is to try to reach out to as many people as possible. It is important for us to revisit the Bible regularly to reflect on key passages and rediscover our purpose. This guy just wanted to tell us what was wrong with Trump and how great Hillary was. Not even a discussion or nothing up for debate. His way or the highway. How could we be so stupid?

Little does he know he will be on his knees one day being judged and giving an account of his life, along with the rest of us. Pride is a deadly sin.

Mark 16:15
He said to them, "Go into all the world and
preach the gospel to all creation."

I called to check up on Diana's knee. It's still really swollen but at least she's able to get around and earn her paycheck.

Sleep came easily under the orange tree. And now that we were back on flat ground, my prayers were much shorter tonight.

NOVEMBER 4

Our goal this morning was to find a place to park the rig while we were on the cruise. We set out in the car and drove to a few places close to the port. One was out of business, the other pricey, and filled to capacity. Phone call after phone call was made. Near and far from the port, we called. We even tried whining, but it didn't work at all.

We decided to take a break from this challenge today and go to the movies. We went to see *Hacksaw Ridge*. It starred an actor I'd never heard of, Andrew Garfield, playing a soldier whose story I'd never heard. "WWII American Army Medic Desmond T. Doss, who served during the Battle of Okinawa, refuses to kill people, and becomes the first man in American history to receive the Medal of Honor without firing a shot."[26]

Medic Doss was a Seventh Day Adventist and, although he desperately wanted to serve his country, he refused to carry a gun. They all laughed at him and told him that if he really wanted to go charging into war without one, it was sure okay with them. He wanted to use his God-given talents to save the victims of war, not to create more.

The movie was amazing. Directed by Mel Gibson, it showed Doss achieving acts that only God Himself could have enabled him to perform. It was breathtaking. Yes, it was ugly with the horrible acts of war, but the movie was such a tribute to someone of faith. Go see it. You won't regret it.

---

[26] imdb.com

We both filled up on popcorn, so when we returned to the motorhome, there was no point on fixing supper, we just snacked a bit until bedtime.

Thinking again of that movie, I thanked God that the men (like my husband) born in 1954 were the first ones not to be called up in mandatory draft service to the military. My daddy was in the Army Air Corp. long before I was born, and spent his war years as a radioman in Reykjavik, Iceland. I thanked God that I have not personally been touched by the loss of a loved one in times of war, although I know many who have been. I prayed for them. My heart was solemn as I laid in bed to pray tonight. The movie was a hard reminder of the real world outside my small circle of life.

Thank you, Lord for this time and place you chose for me. I am so very blessed.

NOVEMBER 5

Today was set aside to visit the Richard Milhous Nixon Presidential Library, in Yorba Linda, California. He was the 37th President of our United States. Larry and I were in high school during his presidency, and I was engulfed in more pressing matters than the nation's state of affairs.

Of course, back then, the headlines were just the first 6 to 8 minutes of the 6pm news and the 11pm news (when I was in bed). If you didn't catch it then, you missed it. It was certainly quite different than things are today, in our world of instant news 24/7, and right in the palms of our hands.

Back then, I never read the newspaper and my view on world events and current news was limited, as was much of the rest of the country. No internet, no CNN, no Fox, no MSNBC. You remember those times, don't you?

Before our visit today, all I knew about Nixon was Watergate and that in 1974, he became the only US President to resign from office. Today I learned countless new things about Nixon, his wife, Pat and their 2 daughters. We have really enjoyed these presidential libraries and the opportunity to see what the political lives, as well as the personal lives of these great men were like.

We were privy to see his boyhood, his rise to power, his run against Kennedy, and the first debate that had been televised live. We learned details about his dealings with China, which at the time, was a remarkable feat. He was also a family man, who cherished his wife and daughters—as heard from tapes of his affectionate phone conversations with them.

And then there was Watergate. Those 18 ½ missing minutes of evidence in Watergate. "The President had been using a voice-activated tape recording system. Nixon's Secretary Rose Mary Woods took the blame for the first five minutes of the erasure. She said that she had been transcribing the tape, and when she reached to take a phone call, her foot hit a pedal on the recording machine, inadvertently causing the tape player to record over the original tape's contents.[27] But the other missing minutes remain a mystery. The tapes are there for you to listen to, and they are indeed missing.

The Library was built on the grounds surrounding his boyhood home, which stands there still today. We learned that the cottage was built from a "kit"—a mail order home. His Marine One helicopter is there to walk through, as well. He and Pat are both

[27]washingtonpost.com/news/volokh-conspiracy/wp/2014/06/16/the-missing-18-12-minutes-presidential-destruction-of-incriminating-evidence/?utm_term=.0299c79d68fd

buried there, in the gardens with award-winning roses. It's a beautiful place and lots of folks were scurrying around, preparing for a wedding that would take place later that day. The bride and her ladies were getting their pictures taken in Pat Nixon's rose garden. There were wedding flowers galore and nicely-dressed guests milling about in the afternoon sunshine.

We weren't in any hurry to leave this beautiful place, but there were other places we wanted to see. We learned that there is so much more to President Nixon than Watergate and he still deserves great respect for his accomplishments in American and world History.

> Proverbs 16:12
> It is an abomination to kings to do evil,
> for the throne is established by righteousness.

We drove on to Garden Grove, California to see the Crystal Cathedral, the church that Rev. Robert Schuller built through the Hour of Power television program. We had been in the cathedral once before, for their Passion Play in 1987. It was an amazing production. And when Jesus ascended, he indeed ASCENDED. My only regret was that we were there at night. Those 12,000 panes of glass must be something to see in the bright sunlight.

Now we were back in Garden Grove in bright sunlight, but we were not able to go inside. I hadn't done my homework and had no idea that the Rev. Robert Schuller's dynasty had ended in bankruptcy a few years ago. The Catholic Diocese of Orange had purchased the church for a song in 2012. There were no tours allowed. I was so disappointed.

Already in the car, we made a quick trip to Walmart and then grilled fresh hamburgers for supper. With full tummies, we cooked in the jacuzzi for a while, listened to the local democrat there, and sleep came quickly in the cool air conditioning.

It had been yet another amazingly beautiful, educational, and enjoyable day.

NOVEMBER 6

From information online, I chose Sovereign Grace Church to worship today. It was a small church in Old Orange. Once again, we were the oldest ones there. They were a friendly little group who greeted us openly. Eric Turbedsky, the senior pastor did a great job as he spoke from the first 12 verses of Ecclesiastes. The praise music was upbeat and I even knew 3 of the 4 songs! I would certainly go back there again, if I ever had the opportunity.

> Hebrews 10:24-25
> And let us consider how we may spur one another
> on toward love and good deeds,
> [25] not giving up meeting together,
> as some are in the habit of doing,
> but encouraging one another—
> and all the more as you see the Day approaching.

The day was sunny and warm, so we chose to walk around this little historic town. We discovered Watson's and decided to do lunch there. It turned out to be California's first soda shop, built back in 1915. They were packed, so service was understandably slow, but the food was worth waiting for.

Everything else we did today was in order of importance. Nap. Laundry. Supper. Hot tub. Fox News. Bedtime. It had been another great day for the books.

NOVEMBER 7

Today was a stay home for a while, taking care of business day.

We have been leasing Ford automobiles for several decades now. Little goes wrong within your lease term and if something does, they have to fix it. We just keep up the regular maintenance and all goes well. The lease for my beautiful blue Ford Escape is coming up at the end of the month. We had already gone to a dealer here in California to explain our situation, but we had to have a permanent address here for them to lease me a car. What? So, I called Ford Credit to explain that we wouldn't be home with my car until March. What options do we have? I asked for an extension due to circumstances, but they said no.

Well! What were we supposed to do now? Not 30 minutes later, a young lady from Ford by the name of Jessica called to confess that, after the phone call, she'd taken the liberty to take our situation to her supervisor's supervisor. As a good customer service person, she knew that we weren't being a problem, just that we had a unique problem that required a unique solution. After some discussion, they granted us an extension all the way to April 19— plenty of time to get us home! God bless Jessica for going beyond her call of duty on behalf of a customer in need. You really blessed my life today!

This same day, we learned that National General declined most of our claim for our electrical problems. They concluded that it was due to a "power surge" and our coverage does not pay for surge damage. We kept asking, "But who determined that it was a power surge? How do you know this?" They really couldn't answer that, but emphasized that nearly $4,000 of the claim would not be paid.

Well, Lord, we know that you will supply our every need. We need to believe and have faith.

And we do.

> Philippians 4:19
> And my God will meet all your needs
> according to the riches of his glory in Christ Jesus.

We had determined that this new recliner was just too reclined for practical use. Larry couldn't read his computer screen while sitting in it, and it was so reclined that I couldn't even watch TV in it. We drove it back to the Camping World and insisted the Manager on Duty sit in it. Yeah, he agreed that it would be difficult to do anything other than recline in it. They kindly agreed to give us full credit on the chair, and we chose a simple wooden folding chair instead.

While we were out and about, we decided to get the Monday Night Fajita Special at Chili's. That's always a yum.

Back at the campground, we took another soak in the hot tub, lulled by Fox News, then went on to bed.

NOVEMBER 8

Today, in the United States of America, the country would come together and vote for the 45th President of the United States. Larry and I had voted weeks before by mail, as we knew we would be on the other side of the country on election day.

While the rest of the country was voting, I decided it was the perfect time to buy me a new pair of shoes. It was way past due and my feet hurt so bad from worn down shoes. Earlier in this decade, I worked part-time for Marshalls, so I Googled them first. Traffic was terrible in every direction! And once we arrived, we had no luck at all. We walked in a nearby mall and Larry received his very first lesson on just exactly how expensive "gym" shoes have become. $160! I had to lead him out of the store before he got us both kicked out. We drove to an even bigger mall with a bigger Marshalls, and after much searching, we finally both got lucky with new, affordable, name-brand athletic shoes.

We figured out some backroads to get us back to the campground. The rest of the evening was spent watching election results. Larry conked out about 11pm, which was already way past his bedtime. But there were so many states that refused to declare a winner, results didn't come until well after 1am on the west coast. I stayed up because I just had to know. And then word came: Donald J. Trump had won the election. I almost couldn't believe it. Wow.

"What happened?" the other party cried. They literally wept. It was sad and pitiful to watch. "This can't be right." "That's impossible." "What happened?" they asked again. They had absolutely no doubt that they would win. What a surprise—to them.

You know what I think happened? GOD happened.

I believe that we "Evangelicals" is what happened. Franklin Graham had lit the fire in evangelicals. We had all been watching our country slipping away for quite some time now, but what could we do? How could we possibly make a difference?

The answer was quite simple: we could pray. And we could vote. He visited all 50 states in 2016 to encourage us to pray hard for our country. To pray for forgiveness as Americans. Millions of us prayed and prayed for this country, to stop the downward spiral of political correctness that was driving us further away from Him. And pray we did. The Bible says:

> 2 Chronicles 7:14
> If my people, who are called by my name,
> will humble themselves and pray and seek my face
> and turn from their wicked ways,
> then I will hear from heaven,
> and I will forgive their sin and will heal their land.

I have seen that God forgives sin and I truly believe that He answered our prayers. Having said that, I believe that He will allow healing of our land, if we continue to work hard enough. We needed something different, as the old way just isn't working. We needed hope. At least now, we have some sort of hope.

NOVEMBER 9

Considering I didn't get to sleep until well after 2am, I slept in while Larry was caught up on all the details from Fox News. When I finally got up, I knew I needed some prescriptions refilled, so I got in the car and Googled the closest CVS. It really wasn't that far and I really didn't need all that much. But, between traffic and confusion in the pharmacy, I didn't get back until an hour and a half later.

The 90-degree temperature and bright sunshine were perfect today, so we spent some time in the pool. What a lovely way to spend an afternoon. I prepared something simple for supper, then listened to lots of folks discuss yesterday's election results. Everyone asked the same thing: what indeed had happened?

NOVEMBER 10

Today was a big day: we had tickets for *Wheel of Fortune*! We had known it should take about an hour to drive to Culver City and park at Sony Entertainment Studios. Anxious about missing this great opportunity, we left two and a half hours early, just in case. Gratefully, we arrived in plenty of time. Unlike *Price is Right*, the contestants had been chosen many months in advance. We were just there to enjoy the show.

While waiting, we saw lots of posters for recent movies filmed here: *Passengers, War Room, Inferno, Magnificent Seven,* and *Money Monster*, just to name a few.

Once cleared through security, we were escorted through the Sony lot. Again, there were lots of sound stages and workers were busy all around us. A lot of them were riding bicycles going from one building to another. We saw a high-end luxury car being off-loaded. It was probably a prize for an upcoming show, as *Jeopardy* is also taped here. When we arrived at the building for *Wheel of Fortune,* there were about 10 private parking spaces there, and Larry and I were sure that Vanna White and Pat Sajak's cars were among them.

We entered the building to find a long hallway with all sorts of pictures, awards, and memorabilia from times gone by. We learned that this stage was formerly home to the historic M-G-M Studios, where some of Hollywood's favorite movie classics were filmed, including *The Wizard of Oz* and *Gone with the Wind.*

It's currently the home of Columbia/TriStar Pictures. We learned that *Wheel of Fortune* is one of the longest running game shows in US history. We also learned (and this is very important) that Vanna has never worn the same dress twice and she returns every one of them when she's done. They have aired over 6,500 episodes. Now this was the most amazing part: they tape 6 shows a day for only 38 days to produce an entire year of shows. Do the math: 6 shows a day for 38 days = 228 episodes. They air 5 shows a week, so that makes 45+ weeks of shows. Consider holidays and pre-empted slots, they have plenty to last them the year.

As we entered the studio, although it was only mid-November, a beautiful Christmas set greeted us. There were millions of little twinkling lights all over a Christmas snow village. It was all shining on a newly buffed and waxed floor. There was the Wheel, there was the huge Puzzle, and there was the new car! There were people chatting away at the contestants, coaching them on how to speak loudly. Other crews were checking lights and sound. What surprised us the most is how small the whole shebang was.

The hardest part for me to play at home is that I can't remember what letters have been guessed. Well, not so on the show. Just like playing BINGO, there's a large out-of-sight monitor where all the called letters are lit up, so there's no excuse when a contestant flubs up and asks for it twice. That must just be the nerves talking.

The guy in charge of warmup comes out and give us a quick lesson on how to yell "Wheel...of...Fortune" at the beginning (as though any one of us wouldn't know how to do that!) He also made sure we understood when to clap and when not to clap.

The first taping began promptly at 1:30, and there were Pat and Vanna. Pat is another small guy, and Vanna is every bit as skinny as she appears on TV. Pat wore the same suit for all three shows we were in, but Vanna would never be so vulgar, so she changed into different dresses for each one.

Pat didn't engage with anyone except the contestants, and he did a good job of that. Vanna promised to come out and talk to us between the second and third shows, as soon as she had changed her gown for the third set. When that time came, I stuck my hand up, stood up quickly and yelled, "Greetings from North Myrtle Beach!" I knew that she had grown up there and knew it would catch her attention, which it did. She smiled hugely and thanked us for coming. Larry won a small light-up Wheel pin by answering the correct year that Vanna started on Wheel, in 1982. He had been paying attention while viewing the memorabilia out in the hallway.

We watched and enjoyed the taping of three full shows. Nobody won the car, but they won vacations and lots of cash. I'm usually pretty good at solving puzzles and, with the used letter board, today was no exception. But I must say that Larry's better than I am with the little 10-second mini puzzles they do. By the time all 3 shows were done taping, our hands stung from clapping so much. It had all been so much fun, seeing it all in person.

It took us nearly 2 hours of stop and go traffic to get back to Anaheim. My neck was killing me by the time we arrived at the campground. I changed, grabbed the big ice pack, and with the help of a pain pill, took the next hour to feel better.

Later, Larry got a phone call from his cousin, David. He and Sally live in Texas and I recall only meeting them twice in all our years of marriage. It just so happened that they were in town visiting David's mom and dad, just down the road in Escondido. We had been planning to spend a day driving to visit with Uncle Tom and Aunt Marilyn, but this would be a double bonus! They quickly made plans for us meet them all tomorrow. We can't wait.

NOVEMBER 11

It was a nerve-wracking 2-hour trip down the I-5 today, but it was worth every minute. David and Sally are our age and Tom and Marilyn are both well into their eighties, maybe even their nineties. We hadn't seen any of them in years, and conversation came easily. There was lots to catch up on!

It's getting to the point in our lives that each time we see someone, it just might be our last, or theirs. We chatted for a couple of hours, and Tom delighted us with old photo albums. He took us outside to see his citrus trees and his jigsaw puzzle room, both of which he was so proud of. We set out in separate cars to meet for dinner, as we would head directly back to Anaheim after we ate. After a great meal at the local Marie Callender's, we collected hugs all around and made promises to see David and Sally when we traveled through Texas in a few months. It had been so good to see them all. It was a wonderful visit. On the road, I do so miss spending more time with friends and relatives. Oh, so very much.

Now evening, the traffic was so much better—it only took us an hour to get back to the campground. What a priceless day with family.

And I'm so grateful that I did some packing ahead. Tomorrow is cruise day!

Proverbs 3:23-26
Then you will go on your way in safety,
and your foot will not stumble.
24 When you lie down, you will not be afraid;

> when you lie down, your sleep will be sweet.
> ²⁵ Have no fear of sudden disaster
> or of the ruin that overtakes the wicked,
> ²⁶ for the LORD will be at your side
> and will keep your foot from being snared.

NOVEMBER 12

We were up early with bells on to finishing packing for the cruise. We've loved cruises for a long time now. Long before cell phones, and back when we owned businesses, Larry concluded that nothing was so important to spend the $14.95 a minute to phone ship-to-shore. Even if the place burned to the ground, he made sure the crew knew to call the insurance agent, not him. Cruises seemed to be the only times that we could fully escape work.

It would be our first time on the west coast of Mexico. We had priced cruises to the Riviera for years, but airfare was costly from the east to the west coast, where all the Mexican cruises departed. But now we were already here, so why not? We reasoned that we would save money in the long run.

We were excited. And then the devil reared his ugly head.

We had found a place to park the entire rig intact, so although the trip this morning was short, we were going to tow the car. I was busy inside, finishing up details. It had rained the night before, and Larry had noticed that the tow dolly ramps were wet. As he attempted to drive the car up the ramps himself, the tires slid, then grabbed, then completely overshot the dolly—the dolly was now completely underneath the frame of the car.

Apparently, he spent some time sitting there in the car, before he came inside to tell me. He wondered what in the world could he do. This is a big problem! How could we lift the car up off the dolly without a crane? And the cruise boards in just a few hours. Lord, we prayed, what can we do?

As he led me outside to show me the problem, a nice black man who worked at the campground came to see what was going on. "Mm, mm," he said, "I'd say you have a problem." He was so nice. He told us that he was a pastor in a nearby church and worked here part time. He wanted to know what we did on the road, as he had seen our banner, then encouraged us and thanked us for our service. His lovely wife also works there part-time and she came over to encourage me. A Mexican worker joined as well, everyone agreed that the car needed to be jacked up above the dolly. But how?

They scurried to find some blocks and got to work. The first attempt failed, and they quickly regrouped. Larry had disconnected the dolly from the rig, so when their plan "worked" the second time, the dolly slid out from underneath. But, then they knew they were on the right track. Larry backed up the motorhome and they all struggled to re-hitch the dolly. The third time was charm.

Praise the Lord that there was no damage to the undercarriage of the car, just some cosmetic damage to one of the doors. We praised and thanked all of those who came and helped so energetically, when they had no obligation to help at all. We promised to pay their kindness forward and thanked them again.

We were finally on our way to the Long Beach City Port Parking.

Thankfully, traffic wasn't bad at all, considering it was early Sunday morning, and we arrived quickly. We found the only lot we could park in, the very last open lot that was already half-filled with old storage trailers. We looped around in the space that was left, so that we parked face out, ready to go, but nearly jack-knifed the dolly when making the tight turn. We'd been told the 7 days would cost us $225, and we feared for the rig's safety, since this was our home. The only redeeming factor was that the toll workers had a booth within a few feet of the end of the lot. We prayed and left our home in God's hands. God is always in control.

We crossed the parking lot and waited in line to board the Carnival *Miracle*. We were on our way.

> Ecclesiastes 3:1
> There is a time for everything,
> and a season for every activity under the heavens:

We pulled away from the docks at 5pm. The ship was lovely, as they always are. Our itinerary would include the ports of call of Cabo San Lucas and Puerto Vallarta, Mexico. We had been assigned a dinner table with only 4 other people, and that should make for easier conversation than our last cruise.

One couple was probably close to our age, originally from Ukraine. They had been in the Los Angeles 20 years, but both of their accents were still very heavy. Factor in all the background chatter and noise, sometimes it was difficult to understand them. Over the week of conversations, we would learn that she was an attorney, and he was a high-stakes poker player—who cruised to play—and who claimed to do very well on this cruise.

The other couple was from Oregon, nearly newlyweds named Kimberlynn and Kris. Now, they were a hoot. They were a devoted Christian couple and so much fun to talk to over dinner. Oh, the stories we all told each other. And laugh. I love to laugh, but life seems to be so serious at times. We had both missed socializing with others. We need to do more of this.

It had been a chilly 60 degrees when we'd left Los Angeles, but there were promises of warmer temps as we sailed south of Baja, California. From the port side of the ship, the cities' lights twinkled from the coast, under a half moon. The bright lights of San Diego really stood out, as we passed that city several hours later. We saw another ship heading south with us, off the starboard side. The sea was calm, great for a good night's rest after such a stressful morning.

Sleep came quickly. God is good.

NOVEMBER 13

This cruise had been cheap for us. I don't like inside cabins because it messes with my inner body clock—you can never tell whether it's day or night. And I hate to pay for outside cabins because they're so much more expensive. For this trip, we took advantage of a special on a cabin with an obstructed view. It lets daylight in through the window, but it was up behind a lifeboat, so it was up above where anybody could peek in. It was the best of both worlds.

We had indeed slept well, and with no port of call, today will be a relaxing day on the ship. After a hearty breakfast, we hit the outside morning sun. The warmth was delightful, so you could tell we had quickly cruised away from the cool weather of the US.

We found places in the hot tubs and were quickly drawn into conversations, at least those in English. So soon after the election, politics was a hot and potentially dangerous topic. I was firm in my choice of Trump, but until one can test the waters (pun intended), I chose to keep my mouth shut.

We would always take the opportunity to tell folks about our Motorhome Ministry. Some would chime right in and make conversation, where others seemed to ignore your comments or simply roll their eyes. That's just fine with us. We don't judge. We plant seeds. We even water them a little. Perhaps that eye-rolling memory will come back to them another time, when we're nowhere around.

We'd have to be in the "third date" stage with someone new to share how God spoke to us personally at the time of Bobby's death. Even beyond that for Larry to share his visit in heaven. Any time before that, they would simply assume we're really weird. But folks who have listened to us really appreciate stories of a personal God. Although I'll never meet most of you reading these words, my prayer is that you will appreciate those stories, too.

I truly believe that God provides situations for us to share our beliefs in Him all the time. That we chose a certain restaurant because a server there needed a calm touch from God. That we camp next to someone that needed a nudge from the Lord. The cashier in the line you chose at the store. That when I wish a call center representative a "Blessed Day," they respond in a way that you knew they needed to hear that right now. Every encounter in our lives is for purpose. Do you fulfill what is expected of you? Do you walk away from those encounters, or do you take the opportunity to bless someone in even a small way?

Suppertime came and we were back with our 4 new friends. Our wait staff was attentive and friendly, bringing us delightful new entrees to enjoy.

NOVEMBER 14

Ditto November 13. Another sunny, peaceful, enjoyable, food-filled, fun day at sea.

NOVEMBER 15

Today we anchored at the pier in Cabo San Lucas, Mexico, for the first of two days. It was a beautiful, hot, sun-filled day. There were all sorts of boats docked there, all styles, sizes, and colors. Some of the boats had small platforms in the aft, by the outboards. It was comical to watch as practiced seals jumped from the water onto the platforms, hitching a free ride into port and expecting to be fed. Pelicans and other sea birds were flying and diving around us, trying to catch lunch, and many more were settled on the rocky shore.

We walked around the large harbor and stepped into many of the small shops. We stopped to enjoy a cold drink and Larry left some Ministry brochures, hoping someone would pick them up later. More seeds planted.

The heat quickly took its toll on both of us, so we took the long walk back to the ship for a cool nap. Soon it was time to get dressed for another great meal with great conversations. K&K were there and we learned that the gentleman from Ukraine had won big in the casino the evening before, and was very chatty tonight. Forgive me for not knowing their names. At the time, I hadn't been planning to write a book, or I would have written them all down. No disrespect to them at all, I couldn't understand their names, couldn't have repeated them, and much less spelled them. Forgive me.

NOVEMBER 16

We filled up on breakfast and headed into Cabo for our shore excursion. Weeks ago, we had arranged a tour of boating and snorkeling on the *Odyssey*. It was another hot, sunny day and the water would feel terrific. As we tendered in however, we noticed the seas were rough this morning. The crew even mentioned this was the roughest they'd seen it in a while. We arrived safe and sound.

We saw lots of interesting things while walking the docks. Of course, there were street vendors selling wares, Cuban cigars, and lots of tequila—both by the bottle and by the shot. The strangest thing we witnessed were chairs with a tank in front, which reminded me of a place giving pedicures. But the tanks were filled with minnows! You paid to sit in the chair with your lower legs in the tank, for a Minnow Massage. Curious, indeed.

We checked our tickets and had a very difficult time finding that specific slip at the docks. When we finally found the slip, there was no boat. After asking several people (and finally found folks that spoke English), we asked about the *Odyssey,* we finally learned that the boat had been taken to another port just yesterday. This guy calls another guy who called another guy who instructed us to take our tickets to another boat, the *Caborey*. A God-thing for sure! It was a modern boat, a large, sleek white vessel designed for parties and dinner cruises. We were informed that the harbor master had shut down all excursions because of the rough seas and currents, so there would be no snorkeling today. I have complete respect for people who make safety decisions on our behalf. We were disappointed, but God had a reason, I'm sure.

They took us all for a nice boat ride around the harbor, to the rocky shores of Land's End to see the famous arch at the end of Baja, California. The sea had that beautiful tropical color to it—that blue-turquoise—and white caps were spilling over the waves. We could see the beautiful hotels, cabanas, cliff houses, and condominiums on land. There was even a large, white cross set on top of one of the nearby mountains. It was a little rough in the water, to say the last. If you dared get up, you walked like a drunken sailor. They had bar service come to us, so we stayed put and enjoyed a sweet tropical drink the bartender recommended. It was just one, and we shared.

They served a great Mexican lunch at the tables inside, then it was time for tips and goodbyes. As always, Larry left a brochure and a seed packet. The crew of the *Caborey* did a fine job of entertaining us for the afternoon, despite our disappointments. We were tendered back to the *Miracle* in time for a nap before supper.

Kim and Kris were late to supper tonight, but the Ukrainians didn't show at all. We were worried that we'd offended them somehow, despite doing our best to include them in difficult conversation. Perhaps tomorrow night.

Adios, Cabo.

NOVEMBER 17

We were already docked in Puerto Vallarta, Mexico when we crawled out of bed. It would be another hot and picture-perfect weather day. We ate quickly and headed out onto the pier. We had tickets for another shore excursion, one that would take us on a tour of the city, to a Tequila factory, then lunch in the jungle. There was only one problem: what time are the tickets for? The ship had made it clear that they would keep "ship's time" for all arrivals and departures from port. But our excursion tickets were not from Carnival, so were they for ship's time or local time? After asking several crew and officers, no one could answer our simple question. We finally decided to leave the ship, and walked past the check-in point at the end of the dock. It was a long walk and we had no idea what or who we were looking for.

God was with us for sure, because at the end of the walk was our tour operator! We were directed to wait for the others outside a nearby convenience store. Those of us gathered were all soon rolling in laughter. None of us read Spanish, but there were signs posted that we loosely and collectively interpreted as "if you want to use the restrooms here, they are free. But, if you need toilet paper, it will cost you $1 in pesos." It was just really funny.

Once everyone arrived, we were guided down the uneven and cracked sidewalks for a few blocks, past old store fronts, to a waiting air-conditioned bus. Thank you, Lord for air conditioning! Our first stop would be a leather store in the old city.

We drove awhile, past large estates overlooking the ocean. There were old, abandoned stores as well as the hopes and dreams of new ones. We reached a crowded section of the old city. Here, the poor lived right next door to the wealthy. Electrical lines draped dangerously across the roads and between houses were mixed with clotheslines full of laundry. The roads were crumbling in parts and some of the potholes were man-eating size. Tropical flowers grow wild here and there were everywhere. Larry voiced that some of the poorest areas reminded him of places he'd seen in Guatemala.

One thing that greatly influenced this city's growth was due to the fact that *Night of the Iguana*, with Elizabeth Taylor and Richard Burton had been filmed here. Taylor had even owned a home here. After fans viewed the film, they wanted to come here, to see it for themselves. The sleepy town instantly became a world tourist destination. The tour bus passed a statue of the 2 stars together, near the home she once owned.

The bus pulled into a large blocked-off space directly in front of the leather shop. Larry supposed that the owner of the shop paid a hefty fee for the tour buses to stop here. We politely looked around the shop, then headed back out to the sidewalk. We were more interested in the kitchen shop next door. It offered all kinds of kitchens that had been decorated in colorful tiles. There were full kitchens, complete with sinks and cabinets. They were certainly different than kitchens found in America!

We reentered the bus and were taken only a few blocks before we got out again. We walked several blocks to an old church in the old city named *Our Lady of Guadalupe*, known to the locals as *La Iglesia de Nuestra Senora de Guadalupe*. There are Catholic influences throughout Mexico. It was a beautiful church.

Being Christian—not Catholic—and living with a personal relationship with God, I can't help but wonder why they believe the way they do.

I saw one example of this recently, during President Trump's inauguration weekend, as the media showed him and his family attending Mass that Sunday morning. The Priest was droning on and on in Latin. In today's world, what did that accomplish for God's Church? I would safely venture to say that absolutely no one who listened to that broadcast understood a single word of what he said. With millions tuning in, wouldn't that have been a wonderful time to skip ritual and read the Gospel aloud in English?

Purgatory is another area that confuses me personally. Nowhere in the Bible can I find instructions to pray a deceased loved one—whose salvation was questionable—out of this "holding area" into Heaven. It's not my right to condemn, I just don't understand. There is so much pomp and circumstance—do such traditions add to or take away from the whole point? Accepting Jesus' free gift of grace is so simple. A personal relationship with God is so simple. Following Him is so simple. Larry encountered folks in Guatemala to whom he would offer this gift of grace who responded, "I will

have to ask permission from my Priest to accept Jesus in my life."
Huh? I truly do not understand this at all.

After a brief walk around the sea wall, we got back on the bus. We drove out of the city, over a scary mountain road and into the jungle. It was a winding, unpaved road full of ruts. Larry and I both felt that no bus this size should be here! We were so relieved when we arrived at a dirt parking lot. We were led up a path to a clearing with wooden benches and an outside fire pit.

The tour operator gave us the history of Tequila and how it's made from the blue agave plant. The juice of the plant is cooked and fermented. When he was finished speaking, he offered us samples of different grades of tequila, from the poorest quality to the best. Then, of course, came the "great deal" offers. Naw, none for us, thank you very much. Do they even have health inspectors in Puerto Vallarta? There's probably enough alcohol content to kill anything, including the worm, but you just can't be too careful sometimes.

We were led up another path to a large, beautiful open-air dining area, built up in the close jungle like a huge treehouse. All kinds of trees and flowers surrounded us. Bananas were hanging from the trees; there was a parrot squawking from atop a large cage. We could hear the tourists screaming from nearby zip lines. Our waiter was young, very new at his job, and brought our fajitas quickly. Although clumsy, he did his best to serve us well, so we tipped him well. We hoped someone would translate the brochure and seed packet we left him, too. That could turn out to be his greatest tip ever.

Back out the dirt road, we made it safely to the ship. The night seemed to come early. We walked the upper decks before dinner to view the city lights. The moon was already high in the sky.

It was as though God Himself was smiling down upon us, shining His light on us. It was wonderful.

The Ukrainians had not attended supper now for 2 evenings, and we worried about them. We had done everything we could to include them. Perhaps they were eating in a premium dining room tonight. We hoped they hadn't taken ill on the cruise.

Our meal was full of laughter tonight. The youngest at the table, Kim and Kris told us they had walked several miles from the old city to the ship in port. Just listening to their story made me ache all over, but especially made the soles of my feet hurt. Escargot was on the menu, and none of the 4 of us had ever tried them. We sounded like little kids, "I'm not gonna try 'em, you try 'em." "I will if you will." I added that, "I'll try anything once, as long as it's dead."

Kim said there was no way, count her out. She tried to defend her stance on not eating critters, then we all laughed because she was eating fish! We called her "chicken" and laughed some more. I ate one first, and liked it. Larry bravely tried one and admitted it was salty, but not too bad. It kinda tasted like sausage. Kris agreed with Larry. Not wanting them to go to waste, I ate the few that were left.

The rest of dinner was so nice. We talked quietly about our life experiences, our jobs, our families. We shared our faith and our Motorhome Ministry. Life is good.

NOVEMBER 18

Today was another day at sea. By now, rules had been relaxed and there were kids everywhere in the hot tubs. And they're relatively small hot tubs. I was content to read in the warm sunshine, and Larry wandered off on his own. He told me later that he'd gone to the Serenity Spa up on the Lido Deck. There was a large hot tub there, and he was the only one in it. It sits deep within the spa, and I guess folks assumed you had to buy spa services to be in there. He said it had been heaven, in the quiet.

It was another laughter-filled supper, and tonight the Ukrainians were back to join us. They had indeed been at the premium dining rooms, and we were all privately relieved that we'd not offended them in any way. He was still winning at the tables and we celebrated with them.

At one point, Larry felt brave enough to propose a hotbed question to them: "as immigrants, how do you feel about Trump's stance on illegals?" Hers was a quick and heartfelt response. "There's a right way and a wrong way to come into this country. Twenty years ago, we did it the right way. There was lots of paperwork to complete, a long time to wait, and in the end, it cost us about $20,000 to come here legally."

Being an attorney in LA, she was very upset about what the illegals were doing to the economy, and didn't hesitate to say so. She had said more in those ten minutes than she had the entire cruise. And I agreed with her every step of the way. And then she added that Putin was a murderer and a mobster. Wow, did she have an uncandid point of view!

NOVEMBER 19

It was our last day at sea. We had been blessed with great weather, while folks back home were already getting snow. We spent another day in and out of the hot tubs, a pleasure we would probably rarely enjoy, once we arrived home.

We ordered our last supper together. Our waiter brought us some "extra" escargot, because he knew at least some of us liked them. That was certainly all we needed to get into another game of teasing Kim into trying one. Uh-huh, no way. Kris and I had to admit they actually pretty good, covered in cheese, so we wound up eating them all. Larry and Kim were just fine with that.

Mr. Ukrainian must have bet plenty on the tables, as Carnival presented him with a bottle of champagne. He insisted the waiter bring champagne glasses all around, so that we could all celebrate with him. As I'd been sitting next to him all week, he chose tonight to get chatty with me. I think he was telling me all about how much he'd won this week, but I really couldn't be sure. I smiled and nodded and laughed when he did. It was nice.

We gave everyone a business card and brochure, so they could keep track of us. Kim would contact us on Facebook, so I could keep track of them. We had made new friends this trip, no doubt. We still couldn't pronounce the names of the Ukrainians, but they now have a place in our hearts, too. We prayed that our ministry would encourage all of them to enjoy the peace that we have in Jesus.

One of our greatest joys while on this Odyssey is meeting the people from different backgrounds, cultures, and countries and knowing we all have the same joys, sorrows, and problems in life.

We are all humans in God's kingdom.

| Acts 17:26 |
| From one man, he made all the nations, |

> that they should inhabit the whole earth;
> and he marked out their appointed times in history
> and the boundaries of their lands.

NOVEMBER 20

We were up early to depart from the ship, through customs and security. After such a fun week and being treated special, this is always my least favorite part. But it was so much simpler this time. We had no plane to catch, no transfer transportation to find. Our home was right over there in the parking lot, and we could see it from the ship. There was no rush at all.

God had indeed kept a hedge of protection around the rig. Everything was still there and just fine. The propane refrigerator was still cold, and the solar panels had done their job by keeping the batteries charged for ignition. Let the adventure continue!

We headed south again, down I-405 to I-5 and almost to the Mexican border in Chula Vista, south of San Diego. The reservations we had in place weren't until tomorrow, so we decided to spend tonight at San Mateo State Park in San Clemente, California, which Larry rated a 6. It was at Camp Pendleton, a Marine base with special helicopters called Osprey. They're capable of both vertical takeoff and short takeoff, combining the functions of a helicopter and a fixed-wing aircraft. We saw dozens of them in various stages of flight.

There were short, fat, wooden posts lining the roads and sites, to keep you from driving over the grass. I was behind the rig, barking instructions on the radio, to back into the site. From back there, I failed to see the single short post at the opening, and Larry was upset when he brushed up against one. No damage, just a smudge. No harm, no foul. Is it a guy thing? Always jumping right to the worst-case scenario. What could have been, but didn't.

Everything was a-okay.

NOVEMBER 21

The next morning, we drove to Chula Vista RV Resort, Chula Vista, California. Larry rated this one a 10! It was only a few miles from the Mexican border and most importantly, had a pool and a hot tub for us to enjoy. It was beautifully landscaped, with a marina located on the San Diego Bay. The only drawback was that we seemed to be on the flight path for some fighter jets from the Naval Base. We only heard a few of them, but you sure heard them when they arrived!

NOVEMBER 22

We spent hours today in the car. We drove first to La Jolla, California, a hilly seaside community within the northern City of San Diego, occupying 7 miles of curving coastline along the Pacific Ocean. The Pacific coast was stunning, on this sunny and warm November day. As we were walking on one of the trails, taking pictures of the sea birds flying above us, a bi-plane photo-bombed the serenity of the moment.

The perfect blue sky and the waves crashing onto the rocky shore made for some mighty fine pictures. A short drive up the coast brought us to La Jolla Cove and beach. Larry told me that he had been here once before, a long time ago, in 1969. His grandma and grandpa, Uncle Tom and Aunt Marilyn and their kids, Dale and David had all come to this beach. It was indeed beautiful; no wonder he remembered it so well. The sand, the sun worshippers, and the surfer dudes in the water--these were scenes that the *Beach Boys* sang of.

Larry and I had lunch at Rigoberto's Taco Shop, located on the main road in La Jolla. We enjoyed the delicious and cheap Fish Tacos. It was a whole lot of food for the prices, and as usual, we couldn't eat it all.

While we were eating, we couldn't help but notice a flamboyant black man dressed as a woman come to pick up a carryout order. We were not in Kansas anymore, that's for sure. I don't understand this whole gender thing, but I will not be one to throw stones. We are all sinners and in God's eyes all sins are the same. By grace, we can all be forgiven, if we just ask. I can only speak to them from the Bible:

Leviticus 18:22
Do not have sexual relations with a man
as one does with a woman; that is detestable.

1 Timothy 1:10
for the sexually immoral, for those practicing homosexuality,
for slave traders and liars and perjurers—
and for whatever else is contrary to the sound doctrine

NOVEMBER 23

Today we drove to Cabrillo National Monument, an old lighthouse that stands even today above San Diego's skyline to guard the bay. We drove all the way to Point Loma, at the end. It was yet another beautiful, sunny, warm day, although a bit windy. The view was postcard perfect as was the rocky coast on the other side of the point.

As you drive along through the Naval base, there is a National Cemetery that looks just like Arlington National Cemetery in Virginia. It's smaller, but everything here was kept in the same geometric and pristine condition as other national cemeteries. Especially on green rolling hills, it's a mystery to me how they place the stone markers so perfectly.

From a distance, you could see that the high walls surrounding the cemetery were actually outdoor crypts. Standing here among the dead really touches your heart. It makes you stop and remember the brave men and women who fought for your freedom and the freedoms of others. The only way I can thank you now is to show you the respect that you wholly deserve.

John 15:13
Greater love has no one than this:
to lay down one's life for one's friends.

You can see for miles from up here. We watched aircraft carriers, destroyers, and other naval vessels coming and going through the bay with the wind. We could see the marinas and the ship yards at the Naval Base on Coronado, an island connected by a massive, arched bridge from the coast, into the bay. I received another stamp as we visited the Monuments Visitor Center.

"The center had all of these Spanish Artifacts from 1542. As the park's namesake, Juan Rodriguez Cabrillo led the first European expedition to explore what is now the west coast of the United States. Cabrillo departed from the port of Navidad, Mexico, on June 27, 1542. Three months later he arrived at "a very good enclosed port," which is known today as San Diego Bay. Historians believe he anchored his flagship, the San Salvador, on Point Loma's east shore near Cabrillo National Monument. Cabrillo later died during the expedition, but his crew pushed on, possibly as far north as Oregon, before thrashing winter storms forced them to back to Mexico.

"Cabrillo National Monument, established in 1913, commemorates Juan Rodriguez Cabrillo's voyage of discovery. A heroic statue of Cabrillo looks out over the bay that he first sailed into on September 28, 1542. At the Visitor Center, the film, "In Search of Cabrillo" and an exhibit hall present Cabrillo's life and times. Ranger-led programs about Cabrillo are usually available on weekends and on many weekdays during summer months."[28]

"The southern end of Cabrillo is one of the best-protected and easily accessible rocky intertidal areas in southern California. The word "intertidal" refers to the unique ecosystem that lies between the high and low tides along the shore. Tidepools are depressions where water is trapped during low tides, forming small pools that provide habitat for numerous plants, invertebrates, and fish. These depressions are formed over geologic time through a combination of biological, physical, and chemical processes.

Although the whole rocky intertidal is often referred to as the "tidepool area," it is important to note that shelves and boulder fields surround the pools, and these also provide a great habitat for the multitude of organisms that call this zone home. For many people, visiting the tidepools is the only direct experience they have with marine ecosystems.

"Cabrillo National Monument is an extremely popular destination for tourists, and it is estimated that more than 215,000

---

[28] nps.gov/cabr/learn/historyculture/juan-rodriguez-cabrillo.htm

people visit the tidepools annually. Compared to sandy beaches, the diversity of life in the rocky intertidal is impressive. People go to the beach to swim, sunbathe, or surf, but they come to the tidepools to explore, experience, and learn."[29]

It was another beautiful day of seeing and learning something new. Thank you, Lord.

NOVEMBER 24

Today was Thanksgiving. A day to give thanks. And oh, did we have so much to be grateful for. Just one year ago on this date, things were so different. My neck was in a brace, I had just completed my first full day back to work, and the pain had been unbearable. Those days had been so miserable. If you had told me then where I would be today, I wouldn't have believed you at all. God is so good.

For the past several years, we had been enjoying Thanksgiving dinner with Larry's Mom and sister, Lisa at California Dreaming in North Myrtle Beach. As Mom's gotten older, it had fallen upon me to cook for such events. Back when I was still working full-time, Mom had mercy on me and suggested we go to a restaurant near her condo.

California Dreaming has one offering on Thanksgiving, and it's everything you could possibly want: oven roasted turkey breast, sugar cured ham, sweet potato casserole, green beans, honey-butter glazed carrots, mashed potatoes, homemade giblet gravy, southern herb stuffing, cranberry relish, and cornbread muffins. You have your choice of drink and choice of pecan or pumpkin pie. One price,

[29] nps.gov/cabr/learn/nature/tidepools.htm

one plate. Every bite was delicious, and you couldn't possibly eat everything. Then you got up, took the leftovers (if any), left the dirty dishes, and drove home. You just couldn't beat it. But today would be the first time in many, many years that we would be separated from all family.

When we checked into the campground, we'd been told that there would be a Thanksgiving Dinner. The campground would supply the turkeys and stuffing, and everyone attending was to bring pot luck. I chose to make a delicious 7-layer salad to share (my version of the recipe is in the back of the book.)

We reported to the decorated activity room and claimed 2 seats at the long tables. I set out my salad, stirred it all up and got it ready to serve. When everyone was seated, I was grateful that a man, whom I believe was the owner of the campground, got up to say a blessing over all this good food. It was a heartfelt prayer, wonderfully done, to praise God in His abundance, to keep us all safe in our travels, to bless our families so far away, and blessings for our new President. It was a simple man's prayer, nothing flashy. It was exactly the kind of prayer that I would have prayed. I complemented him as I soon went to get my food. Well done, good and faithful servant.

And the food was spectacular! They had prepared dozens of turkeys and they were done to perfection. When I attend pot luck, my theory is to take about one tablespoon of every single thing, so that I can taste them all. The plate I'd brought just wasn't big enough, so I plopped a couple of items on Larry's plate, too. There were also abundant homemade desserts from which to choose.

Late afternoon had to include a nap, of course. That's tradition! This would be a day to remember. Not my classic

Thanksgiving, but a very special one nonetheless. And plenty of time to ponder just how blessed we truly are.

> 2 Corinthians 4:15
> All this is for your benefit, so that the grace that is reaching
> more and more people may cause thanksgiving
> to overflow to the glory of God.

NOVEMBER 25

I know this is beginning to sound redundant, but it's true—it was another beautiful day of warmth and sun. We drove around to explore San Diego, to Balboa Park, the old city, and then the San Diego Zoo. We didn't stop at the Zoo, because we had been there before. Instead, we drove to the Zoo's Safari Park up in Escondido, California, 45 minutes north. The traffic wasn't bad at all.

There are visitor tours of the 1,800-acre wildlife sanctuary with over 300 species of African and Asian animals and much more. The place is covered in exotic and local plants and trees, with each habitat designed for the animals' native environment. We really enjoyed the Safari. Larry and I walked wherever we could and took a tram tour to the back fields, where the animals are free to roam within their habitats. There were all sorts of giraffes, elephants, rhinos, flamingos, condors, eagles, and camels. There were big cats, gorillas, antelope, zebras—anything with hooves and other animals and plants I have never heard of.

Our tour guide offered up amazing statistics of how this area began simply as breeding grounds for the world-famous San Diego Zoo, then decades later became a unique tourist destination of its own. He quoted numbers of once-endangered species which have now rebound here at the Safari. We watched in awe as park employees handled snakes and a mother gorilla with her newborn. We even hiked up to the Condor cages to see the massive birds closeup, and they are massive.

Although the rolling hills of the canyon challenged our backs and legs, it was a fun-filled and educational day.

This evening was a welcoming of the boats in the Marina right next to the campground, for their annual Christmas Parade of Boats. We missed the Parade somehow, but there was a tremendously decorated fire engine offering rides throughout the campground. They had karaoke at the gazebo and we sat around, laughing at the participants. Santa was a big hit. What a crazy evening of wine, cheese, karaoke, fire engines, sirens, and Santa.

NOVEMBER 26

I didn't make any notes about what we did during the day, so it was none too special. The evening, however, was very special indeed.

We had a date with Larry's cousin, Margie. She's eight years his junior, now in her fifties. We'd made last-minute plans to meet at Brigantine Seafood Restaurant in Del Mar, California, in northern San Diego. The restaurant was located close to the Del Mar Horse Park, and had a beautiful view. The restaurant was all decked out for the holidays, with small white lights and a brightly decorated Christmas tree. You could tell there were office parties being held throughout the restaurant.

It had been a very long time since he'd seen Margie, probably 40 years ago. I remembered meeting her only twice. Larry's dad and Margie's mom were brother and sister, both of whom have passed away. When the kids were young, their families were very close and spent a lot of time together, camping and boating and Sunday afternoons. But, as families too-often do, the grownups got mad at each other and the kids never saw each other again. Such was the case of Larry and Margie. They were cousins long estranged, beyond their control. They had found each other on Facebook.

We arrived first and sat close to the front door. As she approached the paned door, she spotted me first, through the glass. A smile of recognition bloomed broadly, thank you, Facebook. When I told Larry that she was coming in, he stood to greet her. Their eyes met, and it was such a God-blessed moment. They hugged, long and hard. She backed up and looked into my eyes. She hugged me. She looked up again at Larry and hugged him some more. My eyes tear again as I remember the love they shared at that moment.

How much love had we all missed in these decades of parental anger? Joys and sorrows are always best when shared. It was all so sad that none of those moments can ever be replaced.

Margie had made the reservations and they sat us when she arrived. There was so much to catch up on! They enjoyed rehashing many of the memories they shared together. "Do you remember when…" I heard a lot of laughter and a few stories about Larry, despite 44 years of marriage, that I'd never heard before. They treaded carefully around the matters that had separated their parents. Those times were gone, irreversibly so, and there was no reason to bring them up, rehash them, or assume blame. The conversations continued, jumping from one subject to another.

We talked about her kids and the difficulties they face. We talked about Bobby and Diana. They talked about memories of grandparents long gone. They caught up on the lives of each other's siblings, their babies, and their grandbabies. Of course, we all talked about our faiths. And it was wonderful to know that Margie shared the same, deep faith and trust in the Lord as we do. Larry shared detailed experiences in mission trips and the times that God has spoken personally to him. He shared his going to heaven and returning. Margie shared how life had brought her to her knees and only then did she completely hand over her broken soul to God.

Larry guards his emotions well. I'd say, way too well. Margie had managed to bring tears of joy to his eyes and a smile to his face. I'm so grateful for this reunion. Their lives had been ripped apart by other people's feelings and this evening had glued at least some of those people back together again.

We ate our delicious meals slowly, and needing an excuse to stay longer, I ordered a dessert I certainly didn't need. None of us wanted to have to say goodbye; I think we feared we may never have this opportunity ever again. We tied up that table for a solid 3 hours. Larry left a brochure and seed packet and we had thanked the server repeatedly for his hospitality.

Thank you, Lord for an amazing gift of family reunited.

---

1 Corinthians 13:4-7
Love is patient, love is kind.
It does not envy, it does not boast, it is not proud.
[5] It does not dishonor others, it is not self-seeking,
it is not easily angered, it keeps no record of wrongs.
[6] Love does not delight in evil but rejoices with the truth.
[7] It always protects, always trusts, always hopes, always
perseveres.

NOVEMBER 27

We drove to Palm Springs, California today. We traveled northeast on the I-5, I-805, I-15, then CA79, CA371, CA74, across the Bernardino Mountains Range. We had reservations at the Sunland RV Resort, Emerald Desert, Palm Desert. California, which Larry rated a 10. It was beautifully landscaped with manicured camping sites, concrete pads, and generous patios. We're only staying a couple of days, solely to visit Joshua Tree National Park. It's not a well-known park, and we discovered it purely by accident on the National Park Service website.

It was a winding, wet road, and there were lots of switchbacks to navigate. It was slow-going. Most of the day, it was spitting rain, as we would call it back in Ohio. But, when we reached the high country, it was snowing to beat the band. Visibility was low, but there was no accumulation--yet. It was so strange to leave the sunny California coast with temperatures in the seventies and then a few hours later, be in snow! With the mist, and the sun attempting to break through, we were treated to 7 separate rainbows during the trip. Wow.

Larry did a fine job of steering the rig through the mountains. When we could finally see the spectacular view of the flatlands and valley of Palm Springs in the distance, I told Larry that I saw blue lights flashing behind us. The cruiser wasn't running with sirens, and Larry soon found a place large enough to pull over. It was California Highway Patrol. He walked up to the door on my side.

"Is there a problem, officer?" I asked when I opened the door. He virtually ignored me and spoke straight to Larry, "Do you realize there was a line of traffic behind you?" Larry replied that he did, but respectfully explained that we'd pulled over whenever we could, but there had been nowhere to pull over these last few miles.

Well, not in this officer's opinion. He had apparently been stuck back there for a little while and was none too happy about it. He returned to the cruiser and came back with a warning to be more aware. Larry and I are always aware when we cause delays of others. There was no sense arguing. We knew we were supposed to pull over if there are more than 5 vehicles backed up. I'd guess we made him late for lunch. Grumpy.

Ephesians 4:29
Do not let any unwholesome talk come out of your mouths,
but only what is helpful for building others up
according to their needs,
that it may benefit those who listen.

Palm Springs and the surrounding area was so clean. The streets are perfect—well-paved, no pot holes, manicured, beautiful, and undoubtedly expensive. After road conditions, back in LA and San Francisco, you could almost eat off these streets! We decided to stay in for supper and enjoyed sloppy joes for the first time in a while. We had seen the entire gambit of seasons today. Tomorrow will be mid-60's, but the sun is forecast to come out. I can't wait.

NOVEMBER 28

Today we drove to Joshua Tree National Park today. We took the I-10 east to exit 168 at Cotton Springs Road. We drove from the Cottonwood Visitor Center to the south all the way to the west border of the park. Even though we've been to many amazing parks, we'd not seen one like this. Each National Park has its own crowning characteristics, its own "something special" that should be protected. Joshua Tree National Park has over 800,000 acres of something really special.

"Two deserts, two large ecosystems primarily determined by elevation, come together in the park. Few areas more vividly illustrate the contrast between "high" and "low" desert. Below 3,000 feet (910 m), the Colorado Desert (part of the Sonoran Desert), occupying the eastern half of the park, is dominated by the abundant creosote bush. Adding interest to this arid land are small stands of spidery ocotillo and cholla cactus.

"The higher, slightly cooler, and wetter Mojave Desert is the special habitat of the undisciplined Joshua tree, extensive stands of which occur throughout the western half of the park. According to legend, Mormon pioneers considered the limbs of the Joshua trees to resemble the upstretched arms of Joshua leading them to the promised land. Others were not as visionary. Early explorer John Fremont described them as "...the most repulsive tree in the vegetable Kingdom."[30]

"A fascinating variety of plants and animals make their homes in a land sculpted by strong winds and occasional torrents of rain. Dark night skies, a rich cultural history, and surreal geologic features add to the wonder of this vast wilderness in southern California. These trees are only found within the boundary of the protected park and a few outside in the city of Joshua Tree."[31]

We stopped at the park visitor center, watched their park movie, and stamped my Passport. We headed through the park and stopped at quite a few pull offs. We took in the trees but also saw these weird looking cacti called Teddybear cholla. There were plenty of varieties of plants, but this one caught my eye. I just had to pick one up off the ground. Then I saw signs that it was dangerous to touch. ───────────────

[30]nps.gov/jotr/planyourvisit/desertpark.htm

[31]nps.gov/jotr/learn/nature/jtrees.htm

"Teddybear cholla, for instance, can withstand an air temperature of 138 degrees F. Most other plants would literally cook at this temperature, but Teddybear cholla often rises 59 degrees F or more above the air temperature!"[32] They have a puffy white flower, I guess you would call it a flower. There is so much in our world that you can't explain. How can there not be a God.

There were so many varieties of cactus plants, all sizes, and colors. I can't imagine what this area looks like at the times these plants are in bloom. Every time the car turned another direction, there was another beautiful view of mountains, rock formations, and desert. The change from one side of the Park to the other—the change from one ecosystem to the other—was amazing. Such vast changes in such a short distance was remarkable.

We badly needed lunch. We found a little Mexican (of course) restaurant, Castaneda's Mexican Food, at the entrance of the park on Joshua Tree road. It was delicious.

We drove CA62 back to the I-10. While we headed back to the campground, we saw the most amazing site. We thank Google once again for answering our ever-repeated question: "what in the world is that?" We quickly learned all about the San Gorgonio Pass Wind Farm, "a wind farm located on the eastern slope of the San Gorgonio Pass in Riverside County, just east of White Water, California, United States.

"Developed beginning in the 1980s, it is one of three major wind farms in California, along with those at Altamont and the Tehachapi passes. The gateway into the Coachella Valley, the San Gorgonio Pass is one of the windiest places in southern California. As of January 2008, the farm consists of 3,218 units

---

[32]nps.gov/jotr/learn/nature/cacti.htm

delivering 615 MW. A single Southern California Edison Path 46,500 kilo-volt power line crosses the pass on the northern edge of San Jacinto Peak. This line links the Los Angeles metro area with the Palo Verde Nuclear Power Plant."[33] It seems like there are miles and miles of these huge wind turbines. You can hear them swishing in the wind.

"Increasingly popular as alternative sources of energy, wind turbine generators are a type of windmill that produces electricity by harnessing the wind. Wind turbine generators are much less harmful to the environment than burning fossil fuels, but they do require average wind speeds of at least 21 km/h (13 mph). The largest of these windmills stands 150 feet tall with blades half the legend of a football field. The compartments at the top containing the generator, hub and gearbox weigh 30,000 to 45,000 pounds.

"A wind turbine's cost can range upwards to $300,000 and can produce 300 kilowatts - the amount of electricity used by a typical household in a month. Almost all of the currently installed wind electric generation capacity is in California. The high-tech megatowers are engineered in cooperation with NASA and nursed by federal and state subsidies. This wind farm on the San Gorgonio Mountain Pass in the San Bernardino Mountains contains more than 4000 separate windmills and provides enough electricity to power Palm Springs and the entire Coachella Valley."[34]

1 Timothy 4:4
For everything God created is good,
and nothing is to be rejected
if it is received with thanksgiving,

[33]en.wikipedia.org/wiki/San_Gorgonio_Pass_Wind_Farm

[34]palmsprings.com/services/wind.html

When we finally arrived back at the motorhome, I laid down to put ice on my neck, then we headed out to the cinema to see *Allied* with Brad Pitt. Good movie. It kept us on our toes until the very end.

We had heard on the news that a wildfire was burning in the Great Smoky Mountain National Park, near the Gatlinburg entrance. We had lived in Gatlinburg, within just a couple miles of that entrance from 1988 – 2005. We have lots of friends still there. We were concerned. It wasn't too bad at first, and the fire was well within the park borders, where very few people live. But something quickly changed in the wind, and suddenly the fire was burning several miles away, on the other side of town, where a lot of people live.

As the day progressed, we learned that there were mandatory evacuations for certain parts of the city. We prayed that rain would pour from the heavens and douse the fire quickly. Please, Lord.

But it was not to be.

NOVEMBER 29

We received a call very early this morning from our dear friend Bonnie in Gatlinburg. Because of the time, we immediately knew that something was wrong. She and her family had escaped the burning fires last night with literally only the clothes on their backs. Some of their precious dogs had already run away in fear, and couldn't be found in time to take them along.

She described their perilous escape, that there was fire on all sides. Larry maintains a company web site for her family, with whom we have been friends for decades. They shipped inventory from their garage, which is most likely gone now. Nevertheless, mail order on the site must be shut down for now.

She explained that her son had been watching TV upstairs. He noticed the grandfather clock making an odd sound, and he got up to investigate. When he did, he saw the fire right outside the window. He yelled for everyone to get out of the house. A few minutes later would have made the difference between life and death for them all.

Thank you, Lord for making the clock act up. We know that was You. We thank you, and praise you for sparing the precious lives of our dear friends.

Revelation 20:14
Then death and Hades were thrown into the lake of fire.
The lake of fire is the second death.

We drove the motorhome towards Phoenix, Arizona today. Our route was I-10 all the way, and it was a long 5-hour drive. There wasn't much to see, as it was all dry desert. The road was straight and simple. There were no problems, and Larry found it kinda boring.

We said bye-bye to California. I think I've had enough of California to last me the rest of my life, thank you very much. We were officially "on the way home" now. We'd be heading eastward from here on, to be back in Myrtle Beach in March. We'll be flying home for Christmas to be with family, but we'll drive the motorhome back to arrive in March.

We were actually headed to Freightliner in Chandler, Arizona to have routine maintenance completed on the motorhome. It was due to have a 11,000-mile maintenance, oil change, and lube job to keep it running smoothly. When we checked in that afternoon, they told us to give them about 4 hours. We explored, enjoyed lunch, and passed some time at the Wild Horse Pass Casino nearby. We played the slots awhile, earning enough to pay for supper tonight, and the next few nights, as well.

When we checked back in, they told us there'd been a recall on the chassis and they wouldn't be able to finish the job until the next day. The graciously allowed us to stay in our home on their lot that night, so we didn't have to pay for a hotel.

We slept well, locked safely in the lot.

NOVEMBER 30

Larry is now officially an "old man", turning 62 today. Happy Birthday! But celebrations would have to be another time. We had gotten up and showered early, figuring they would take our rig back in first thing. They didn't. It took them 4pm to finish and that was only after pestering the daylights out of them. Yay, what a birthday.

We continued on I-10 East, and arrived much later than planned at Rincon Country West RV Resort in Tucson, Arizona, which Larry rated a grand 10. The weather was sunny and warm once again, after a bout of clouds and spitting rain. We really could use a good downpour, because the car and motorhome really need baths.

The RV Resort was filled with permanent residents. They were getting prepared for the judges to award the best Christmas decorations of the park. There were trailers, motorhomes, and park models all decked out for the holidays. They were really decorating! They gave us an entire book of upcoming activities that included crafts, game clubs, bingos, aerobics in the fitness center and the pool, karaoke, day trips, dances, etc. This would be senior living at its best. There was also a train set and miniature village outside that residents work on as a hobby. There were all sorts of activities for everyone. If one retired here, you would never lack for something to do.

By the time we arrived and set up, we were both tired. I tried to convince Larry to go out, since it was his birthday, but no. He wasn't walking another step today. And I really didn't blame him. What a lousy birthday. Thank God for a microwave.

I had already called Dish to get our satellite services changed to this region, but somebody dropped the ball. I called them again.

A frustrating day, but we were here and we were safe. And we'd be here a couple of days, thank you, Lord. We slept well.

DECEMBER 1

We got up early to drive to the Biosphere 2, an earth systems science research facility located in Oracle, Arizona, a little northeast of Tucson. The tour lasted more than 2 hours and it was amazing. Some of you may even remember it, a hub of activity from September 1991 to September 1993. It was an amazing facility that completely sealed in 8 scientists for the 2-year experiment.

"Biosphere 2 was the largest completely sealed environment ever built. Its themed environments, or "biomes," include living examples of the rainforest, the ocean, tropical wetlands, savannah grasslands, and a coastal fog desert. The true goal of Biosphere 2 was to learn as much as possible about living in captivity, to learn about sustainable living, and to learn about small group dynamics. Could they grow enough food to survive? Was it possible to live in a sealed environment that long? Nobody knew for sure. The purpose of Biosphere 2 could be stated more correctly as a long-term study in sustainable living."[35]

Was the Biosphere 2 project a success or failure? After reading a great deal on this subject, the answer just depends on who you talk to. You will have to judge for yourselves.

We grabbed lunch at the complex then drove to Saguaro National Park. When we watched cartoons when we were kids, some of them took place in the desert. I remember them as expansive, desolate places with cactus plants scattered about, here and there. And there was only one type of cactus: the base was round and went straight up, with a couple of curved "arms", reaching up to the sky.

I learned today, for the very first time, that it was a Saguaro cactus, and they grow in only one place on God's green earth— Saguaro National Park. We both thought they were all over the Southwest. Wrong!

The City of Tucson splits the Park in half, an east park and a west park. We visited the west park. We went to the Visitors Center, saw the park movie, went through the educational displays, and received yet another stamp for my Passport. It was getting late, and the sky provided the plants a vast backdrop of orange, pink, and purple. It was breathtakingly beautiful.

The day had been sunny and hot, but a cooler breeze touched us then. There was an old movie studio just down the road, and we stopped for a quick walk-through.

---

[35]trevorland.com/words/biosphere-2-a-successful-failure/

"Old Tucson is a movie studio and theme park just west of Tucson, Arizona, adjacent to the Tucson Mountains and close to the western portion of Saguaro National Park. Built in 1939 for the movie *Arizona*, it has been used for the filming of several movies and television westerns since then, such as *Gunfight at the O.K. Corral*, *El Dorado*, and *Little House on the Prairie*. It was opened to the public in 1960, and historical tours are offered about the movies filmed there, along with live cast entertainment featuring stunt shows and shootouts."[36]

My heart has been so heavy all day, worrying about the wildfire in Gatlinburg. My iPhone reports that the fire continues to spread, due to extremely high winds. Those winds have carried the embers far and wide, most recently 20 miles outside the city to an area known a Cobbly Knob. Dozens more homes have been lost out there.

Diana has kept in touch by Facebook with a lot of her high school friends, many of whom still live in the area. She had busy Facebooking them all day. Her contacts included the daughter of the Mayor of Gatlinburg, so she kept well-informed. She kept relaying those updates to me, none of which were encouraging.

God. please protect all my friends. Homes and businesses can be replaced, friends cannot.

Isaiah 43:19
See, I am doing a new thing!
Now it springs up; do you not perceive it?
I am making a way in the wilderness and
streams in the wasteland.

---

[36]en.wikipedia.org/wiki/Old Tucson Studios

DECEMBER 2

My plan for this free day was to get month-end accounting done. But, as has been the case lately, I spent 2 hours on the phone with Intuit instead. Again. What a necessary waste of time.

Diana called today to rejoice in the fact that she submitted her cash down payment on the house she intends to buy, and hopes for a quick closing. She called again later, all upset because the numbers on her closing sheets were all wrong. They will have to begin again. She's been working on this deal for months, and has become so frustrated by all the changes in inspections and requirements for closing, changes in terms, now changes in how much the buyer (her) will incur in closing charges. I pray for closure in this. Or a huge brick wall, I just don't know which!

Sitting around here, checking all the updates on the fire has upset me terribly. I called Bonnie to check up on her and her family. They had returned to their property and everything had burnt to the ground. Their only happy point was that one of their beloved dogs had returned. She and her husband, Tommy had bought that house together about 30 years ago and had made a lot of memories there. We had visited there many times. Tommy passed away just a few years ago, and now their home was all gone, too. I can't imagine her heartbreak. Just a little older than us, she will begin anew.

For your information, in the end, over 2,400 homes and businesses were destroyed. Over 17,000 acres had burned. More than 14,000 souls had been evacuated, but 175 were injured, and 14 still died. This wildfire was a tragedy in every way.

But the most profound news came days later when a hiker discovered that while hiking the Chimney Tops Trail, his Go Pro camera had recorded proof that 2 teens he'd passed had been throwing matches. Laughing and having fun, throwing fire, despite the drought, despite the burn warnings. He had their faces, the date and time, and their exact location. He did the right thing—he called the law.

Arrests were made of 15- and 17-year old boys from nearby Clinton, Tennessee. It has not yet been in court. Will they be tried as adults? Will they be charged with 14 counts of murder? God will ultimately determine their fate.

Update: As I prepare final edits on this book, I can report that the minors will not be charged with the devastation of the fire. Determinations were made by professionals that, although they had proof the kids started the fire, they also determined that the National Park Service had failed to suppress the fire appropriately. Although they watch fires closely, they believe that wildfires are the circle of life for a forest, and allow them to burn naturally. So, when the winds increased suddenly, they were ill-prepared, and the fire spread rampant. I personally knew many folks who lost their homes, and one who lost his life. God bless them all.

Psalm 34:18
The LORD is close to the brokenhearted
and saves those who are crushed in spirit.

DECEMBER 3

We left Tucson for Tombstone, Arizona, heading east on I-10, south on AZ80, where we had reservations for Wells Fargo RV Park, which Larry rated a 2. It was old and small, but we just needed a place to park, so it would do. It had taken a couple of hours to get there, after a quick food stop at a Walmart on the way.

After we arrived, it was a short walk to the main street of the historic town. There was a gunfight in the center of the dirt street at high noon. Stagecoaches and horses and people dressed in period costumes were scattered throughout the town. Everything was reminiscent of how the town looked in the 1800's.

Many of you will remember the film, *Gunfight at the OK Corral*, the original as well as the remake. The actual gunfight was a 30-second shootout between lawmen and members of a loosely organized group of outlaws called the Cowboys. It took place in Tombstone, Arizona Territory, at about 3pm on Wednesday, October 26, 1881. The locals reenact the scene twice each day.

We decided that it was just too darn cold and windy to be walking the streets today, so we returned to the motorhome early. It was supposed to be sunny and warmer tomorrow, so we will spend more time in town then.

We did learn with great relief that the wildfires in Gatlinburg were finally under control. It was such a blessing to learn that the fire had gone around the city, and allowed much of the historic downtown to remain untouched. They're going to have a rough go of it, though. At least for a while.

While we owned our business in Gatlinburg, a single T-shirt shop at the corner of the Parkway and Airport Road had a fire. A couple of shops adjacent to the store had some smoke damage. Not a big deal at all. Long before cell phones, I called my sister, Beve in Cincinnati to assure her that we were okay, that the fire had been blocks away.

She said, "Thank God you called. The biggest country radio station in town is reporting that the entire city of Gatlinburg is gone, burned to the ground." I immediately called a young lady I knew at the Chamber of Commerce and told her grimly, "Boy, do you have your job cut out for you today." I explained in detail what was being broadcast to Cincinnati, which is a large market share for Gatlinburg. Before the workday was over, she was live on the radio, assuring their city that our city was just fine, thank you very much. "Come see us for yourselves!"

DECEMBER 4

Today changed history, so to speak. At least here in our little family. Larry announced that God had impressed upon him to write a book about our Motorhome Ministry and the places we have traveled. Obedient, he dove right in on the project. He was about 5 pages into his "book", when he decided he wasn't very good at it.

When he had made his original announcement to me, I'd silently wondered about that. He is the absolute king of 100-word sentences and a poor speller, never having been taught phonics in grade school. He's constantly asking me, "How do you spell "___" as he works online.

So, today he updated his announcement that the Lord wants the book written, but I'm the one with the talent to write it. A compliment? Sounded like an awful lot of work to me. But, over the years, many people have complimented me, saying that I have a "way with words." Okay, this might actually be fun. Maybe.

Perhaps God has quietly put this in the back of my mind, and I just hadn't paid attention. I *had* been keeping a diary of sorts. I had written just a few highlights for each day, things that I could reread someday and remember as the scene unfolded in my mind's eye.

I reasoned with him that I was only 6 weeks post-surgery when we left home. There were many days that pain possessed me, and my memories wouldn't be too clear. He would have to be a lot of help, too. He agreed. We would do the book together.

That matter settled, we walked back into town and had lunch at a lively, foot stompin' place called Big Nose Kate's Saloon. According to their website, "Big Nose Kate is believed to have been the first prostitute in Tombstone. However, her biggest claim to fame was the fact that she was also Doc Holliday's girlfriend."[37]

We dined on hot calzone while enjoying the stained glass and listening to an old geezer (I had written in my diary) singing crazy bar songs. His piano said, "Vigilante Justice." He was an odd character indeed, but he was really good! We were sure to leave our brochure and seeds for the Lord in this place. I'm just kidding; it was filled with families with kids. Perhaps the ghosts reported to haunt the place will read them.

Walking on the wooden raised sidewalks outside, we visited a historic newspaper office called the Tombstone Epitaph. It sure was interesting to see various ways they printed the news back then. Oh, and you couldn't help but notice the large Christmas Tree out in the middle of the street. They might shoot you dead out there, but they sure loved Christmas.

As we walked back to the campground, the air was cold and the sun was low in the sky. What a beautiful backdrop for the old western town. There wasn't anyone available to "ride off into the

---

[37]bignosekates.info/index.html

sunset", but I secretly wished there was. It was another fact- and fun-filled day.

> John 8:47
> Whoever belongs to God hears what God says.
> The reason you do not hear is that you do not belong to God.

DECEMBER 5

Diana called to tell us that she had finally signed on the bottom line and the house was now hers! She was excited but a little nervous at the same time. The house hadn't been loved on for a while, and there was much to be done. I reassured her that we'd be home in a few weeks and we were ready and willing to help in any way that we could. Congratulations were in order!

Today we set out for White Sands, New Mexico. Yes, we're back in New Mexico, but it's a big state and we're in the southern part this time. We took AZ80 south to US191 south towards the border of Mexico, then north to I-10 east into Las Cruces, New Mexico, then picked up I-70 east to White Sands. It was a long day, but traffic was light, across the barren desert flatlands.

At times, it seemed like we were the only ones on the road. It was kinda creepy—like watching those post-apocalyptic movies. Then we'd see an occasional pickup truck, or approach a randomly-placed border patrol check point. It was scary enough in the daytime, but I'd hate to encounter one of these at night!

They're built out in the middle of nowhere, and the main highway is blocked. You have no choice but to exit into the structure. There are huge lights set up, cameras taking pictures from all directions. Each time we pulled in, uniformed officers with drug-sniffing dogs asked who was onboard. Larry politely replied, "Just the two of us." Some asked for ID's, most didn't. Each asked if we were both American Citizens. "Yes, sir." Then they motioned us on.

I know that many citizens would get ticked off if these officers would ask them to step out of their motorhome, or allow them to board. They would be ticked off if they were delayed in any way. Not me. There was never a line to wait, and I thoroughly expected them to acquire a little more proof than Larry's word. After profiling 2 old farts in an RV, it probably would be a complete waste of their time, but isn't that exactly what the bad guys might try? I know we have Motorhome Ministry signs on the rig, but again, wouldn't that be a great cover? I was rather disappointed at the lack of drama, but I should probably be grateful. They might have found an illegally obtained seashell or something.

We had planned to spend the night at the Walmart in Las Cruces, but we found the lot too busy and much too small for any peace or quiet. The day had gone well and we decided to go on. We're so glad that we did. When we stopped at the White Sands Monument, we found them getting ready to close the visitors center for the night. We were there just in time for them to give us directions to the public lands site just down the highway. We could stay there for free!

The only sign the Park Ranger directed us to was a graphic "binocular" sign. We drove the 5 miles and nearly missed it, a small 12 x 12 sign with a left arrow beneath it. It was so small that we nearly missed the turn! It was a dirt driveway that directed us through a narrow but open farm gate. Larry had no idea where this road led us to, if there was room to park, or turn the rig around.

We still weren't sure that this was the right place. It was a dirt road, rustic and not heavily traveled. Larry's first reaction was to turn around, but we inched forward. We traveled slowly through the bumps and potholes for what seemed to be a long time, then suddenly around a corner, there was a lake. There was plenty of space to turn around here and leave, but this was much too pretty. We did turn the rig around, so that our front door opened out onto the lake.

We were all alone, off the highway as the sun set down over White Sands. The sands are so white that it made the scenery look snow-covered. We armed ourselves with all the cameras and captured some beautiful pictures of the sunset. The sky lit up with colors of orange, purple, and pink, with the moon showing off in all its glory.

There was definitely scat in the sand, so I knew there were critters sneaking around. Did you know there's a children's book that the National Park Service sells in its gift shops entitled, "Who Pooped in the Park?" There are 20 different versions, written for 20 different National Parks (I am not making this up), because they all have different wildlife leaving poop. I wish I had one right now. According to the Park brochure, the scat I'd discovered was too big for the local Apache Pocket Mouse, but perhaps a Black-Tailed Jackrabbit or a Coyote had been through here.

We slept well in the absolute quiet. We were all alone in the world, it seemed. It was cold, and we were off the grid, but thank God once again for the propane furnace.

DECEMBER 6

Our goal for today was to drive to Carlsbad Caverns, but we had things to do here in White Sands before we left.

First thing, we returned to visit the White Sands National Monument Visitor Center, saw the park movie and received another stamp in my Passport. "White Sands National Monument is in the northern Chihuahuan Desert in the U.S. state of New Mexico. It's known for its dramatic landscape of rare white gypsum sand dunes. Trails through the dunes include the raised Interdune Boardwalk and the Dune Life Nature Trail, dotted with interpretive exhibits on wildlife and other features. Dunes Drive is a looped road from the White Sands Visitor Center to the dune field."[38]

We took the dunes road to go into the park. Once again, it all looked as if covered in snow. It even looked cold. "There is no place on earth like this. Rising from the heart of the Tularosa Basin is one of the world's great natural wonders - the glistening white sands of New Mexico. Great wave-like dunes of gypsum sand have engulfed 275 square miles of desert, creating the world's largest gypsum dune field. White Sands National Monument preserves a major portion of this unique dune field, along with the plants and animals that live here."[39] And poop there.

The white sands have been used as a back drop for films like *Transformers* and *The Book of Eli*. It's amazing what you learn along the way on a discovery trip like this.

---

[38]google.com/search?q=whhitesands&rlz=1C1CHBD_enUS731US731&oq=whhitesands&aqs=chrome..69i57j69i59l3j69i60l2.9279j0j8&sourceid=chrome&ie=UTF-8

[39]nps.gov/whsa/index.htm

Now that our exploration here was done, we were on the road for Carlsbad Caverns. It was a long, 4-hour drive on US70 east to US82 east, then south on US285 to a campground called Carlsbad RV Park, Carlsbad, New Mexico, which Larry rated a 3. It was another old, former KOA park that needing some loving care. We were going to stay tonight, drive the rig to park at the caverns, then move on.

We had crossed an entire mountain range today, gaining then descending 6,000 feet. We saw real snow on the ground, then learned that a BIG winter storm was on its way.

We decided then that we would visit Carlsbad as early as possible, then put the pedal to the medal and hightail it south to Texas, out of the path of the storm.

I had a long call with my bestest buddy Deb, who had called seeking prayers for her grandson, Lane. He's a high school hockey player, a fantastic defenseman, I'm told. He had suffered a concussion during play recently, and things were not progressing as they should. I will most certainly pray. Our God is the Great Physician, and I pray that all will progress as He wills. There are so many folks in my world who need prayer right now. God knows each one by name.

Not long ago, I purchased an adult coloring book entitled, "Images of Hope" by Jacqui Grace. I began coloring the first one for Bonnie. I chose some words of encouragement to hang in her next home. She's a quilter and a stitcher—a crafter with amazing skills and she would appreciate any labor of love. It was taken from Isaiah 61:3: "Beauty for ashes, the oil of joy for mourning, the garment of praise for the spirit of heaviness." The entire verse is as follows:

Isaiah 61:3

> ...to bestow on them a crown of beauty instead of ashes,
> the oil of joy instead of mourning,
> and a garment of praise instead of a spirit of despair.
> They will be called oaks of righteousness,
> a planting of the LORD for the display of his splendor.

DECEMBER 7

Every time I ever write this date, my mind goes on to say, "December 7, 1941—a date which will live in infamy..." The statement by President Franklin Delano Roosevelt continues, "The United States of America was suddenly and deliberately attacked by naval and air forces of the Empire of Japan."

One day, back in the 80's, my dad drove me to a place off the beaten path of US27 in Northern Kentucky. Everything was different than it had been in 1941, of course, but he described to me in great detail where he and his girlfriend, Dixie Lee Whitehouse, had been when the radio station broke in with the news of the attack on Pearl Harbor. He said they both knew in that instant that their lives had been changed forever.

My dad had turned 18 just 2 months before. He knew without a doubt that he would be called to serve in this war. They were in love. They thought they had all the time in the world to make plans. Any playful talk they had been enjoying had turned completely serious. They had life plans to make. And they had to be made right now. December 7 indeed. A solemn day in US history.

Rested and ready to visit the Caverns, it was chilly. Time for those Alaska sweatshirts, the end of fall is finally catching up with us. These overnight lows in the 30's are really putting the furnace to task.

We parked the motorhome at the Visitors Center and, as usual, we watched the Park movie, stamped the Passport, and went off to explore. Nevada Barr had also written a book about Carlsbad. I couldn't wait to see what my mind had already imagined.

Let me drop in another tidbit of information here. Through her books, I learned that each National Park has a 4-digit codename, created with the first 2 letters of the first word and the first 2 letters of the second word. She voiced in amusement in her 1998 book, *Blind Descent* that Carlsbad Caverns is nationally referred to as CACA.

Haha.

"Carlsbad Caverns National Park is in the Chihuahuan Desert of southern New Mexico. It features more than 100 caves. The Natural Entrance is a path into the namesake Carlsbad Cavern. Stalactites cling to the roof of the Big Room, a huge underground chamber in the cavern. Walnut Canyon Desert Loop is a drive with desert views. Rattlesnake Springs, a desert wetland, attracts reptiles and hundreds of bird species."[40]

"High ancient sea ledges, deep rocky canyons, flowering cactus, and desert wildlife - treasures above the ground in the Chihuahuan Desert. Hidden beneath the surface are more than 119 known caves - all formed when sulfuric acid dissolved the surrounding limestone leaving behind caverns of all sizes."[41]

[40]google.com/search?q=Las+Cruces&rlz=1C1CHBD_enUS731US731&oq=Las+Cruces&aqs=chrome..69i57.1889j0j8&sourceid=chrome&ie=UTF-8#q=carlsbad+caverns

[41] nps.gov/cave/index.htm

In lieu of taking the natural trail, we chose to take an elevator straight down into the cavern, several stories down. This time of year, there weren't many visitors here, but I would bet, in the heat of the summer, folks flock to his 56-degree constant.

When the elevator doors opened, it was as though we'd been transported to another world. It was a wide-open space, with a gift shop right in the middle. Restrooms were right around the corner. The walk was self-guided, and even though we were in a hurry, we did take the time to enjoy this amazing place. With few others there, there were great stretches that we appeared to be the only ones here. What a fantastic visit!

The Big Room is the largest single-cave chamber by volume in North America. The 1.25-mile trail is relatively flat and will take an average of 1.5 hours to walk it. Actor and comedian Will Rogers called the cavern, "The Grand Canyon with a roof over it." You will be rewarded with spectacular views, cave formations of all shapes and sizes, and a rope ladder used by explorers in 1924.

We noted that many sections of the Big Room were wheelchair accessible. My only advice to folks considering this tour: take a powerful flashlight with you. The lighting is very low and I'd wished many times to get a closer look at water, texture, stalagmites, and stalactites. Even some of the signs were difficult to read in the limited light. Oh, if I could only walk it again with a flashlight!

After an awesome but exhausting walk through the Caverns, we took the elevator back up to the surface and returned to the rig. We turned on the generator long enough to zap some lunch before hightailing it toward Texas.

We took US62 south to US285 south to Fort Stockton, Texas. The highways in this part of the state were so bumpy! And the wind was blowing without restraint across the flat Texas landscape. The motorhome was rocking in the wind and it was difficult for Larry to keep the rig in the lane. We could see oil wells in every direction we looked, and orange flames of the refineries dotted the horizon. There were lots of trucks coming and going from this area. There weren't many cars, but lots of trucks, and the roads just got worse.

We drove right past a museum for Judge Roy Bean, an eccentric saloon keeper and Justice of the Peace in Val Verde County, Texas. He called himself, "The Law West of the Pecos." I remember his name from a western movie. We didn't stop, because we had to stay ahead of the incoming storm.

Larry drove as far as he could, and we decided to boondoggle at another Walmart. This store closed at 10pm, then things were blissfully quiet. We were beat, and slept well.

DECEMBER 8

It was bitterly cold, in the 20's, when we awoke early to set out for Big Bend National Park. Larry was definitely in a hurry, but I was skeptical of heading directly into a posted winter storm warning. I argued there could be black ice anywhere with it so cold. Eventually, we debated even going to Big Bend at all. It's on the southern border of Texas and requires a long drive.

But we knew we would never be this way again, and it was surely out of the way of the storm, so once we got there, we'd be fine. But, exactly as I'd feared, the storm caught up with us. The sleet was freezing on the windshield, which is so large that the defrosters just weren't very effective. The wipers froze and it was hard for Larry to see to drive. Luckily, the further south we went, the warmer it got and we were finally south of the storm. The windshield melted and the drizzling rain cleaned up the windshield. But if we had just waited a couple more hours, would it have been better or worse?

We took US385 south all the way into the Park, then into the campground, Rio Grande Village, Texas. The land is flat and barren. We seemed to be the only ones on the highway to the park, as we went for miles without seeing anyone at all. We checked into the campground as the sun was beginning to set, and the colors were beautiful. The mountains in the distance were in Mexico. We received our site assignment from a man in the tiny Village Store. It was a small campground, just a parking lot with utilities. There are about a dozen of us camped here and have all 800,000 acres to ourselves. It's an absolutely beautiful park with mountains, plains, desert, rivers, and so much more.

"There is a place in Far West Texas where night skies are dark as coal and rivers carve temple-like canyons in ancient limestone. Here, at the end of the road, hundreds of bird species take refuge in a solitary mountain range surrounded by weather-beaten desert. Tenacious cactus bloom in sublime southwestern sun, and diversity of species is the best in the country.

This magical place is Big Bend."[42]

| Deuteronomy 1:8 |
| See, I have given you this land. |
| Go in and take possession of the land the LORD swore |

[42] nps.gov/bibe/index.htm

> he would give to your fathers—
> to Abraham, Isaac, and Jacob—
> and to their descendants after them."

We agreed to stay in the rest of the day, due to the cold. I was delighted to have all afternoon to color with my pencils. I finished Bonnie's gift, then colored one for Diana's new house, start to finish.

Thank you, Lord for bringing us safely through the bad weather, as so much could have gone wrong. We are here. We are safe. We are blessed.

DECEMBER 9

I had an early morning dilemma: where in the world was my computer mouse? And where was my journal? I looked everywhere. I always put them on the seat where I write. I had even crawled under the kitchen table, looking in every nook and cranny. Unlike my husband, I already knew that it couldn't have just disappeared.

I was trying to recreate the scenario of the bumpy roads we drove yesterday, then remembered that we stow our trash can beneath the table while traveling. Both items were right there, in the trash can. I am so grateful that we hadn't put anything messy in the can, nor had the need to dispose of it. Thank you, Lord.

That crisis averted, we spent today exploring the park. Big Bend National Park encompasses the entire Chicos mountain range and a large swath of the Chihuahuan Desert. The Ross Maxwell Scenic Drive leads to the ruins of Sam Nail Ranch, now home to desert wildlife. The Santa Elena Canyon, carved by the Rio Grande, features steep limestone cliffs.

We eventually parked to explore the Langford Hot Springs, on the Mexican border. We learned the history of the Hot Springs, explored the foundations of the old bathhouse, and marveled at the huge palm tree planted here long ago. It was said to be quite an oasis in its heyday.

J. O. Langford built the bathhouse in 1909. He was a sickly man who had heard that hot springs could do amazing things. Langford claimed the springs had cured him of all his medical problems, and as word spread, people from all over the country came to enjoy the benefits, as well. He was a marketing genius in this time.

As we drove the car to this place, I noted that the access road even today is barely fit for man or beast, so it amazed me that this was a busy place a century ago. The drive is on a narrow dirt path, and if you don't pay close attention, it would be really easy to drive right off the path into the small canyons. It's obvious that the area is prone to flash flooding and flooding from the river itself.

We walked right up to the Rio Grande. Larry and I were both expecting something, well, "grand," but there wasn't anything grand about it at all. It was mostly hidden in stands of what appeared to be sugar cane, shallow, and not very wide at all. The Rio Grande serves as "The Wall" separating the US and Mexico here, but it's a poor excuse for one. Anyone could cross here, anytime they wanted, and I'm sure they do.

As we followed another dirt track along the river, we came to a place where the hot spring bubbled up within the foundation of the old bath house—the foundation being all that was left. There were a few folks already bathing in the moss-filled foundation. The water was Jacuzzi-hot, probably about 100 degrees. The hot spring bubbles out of the ground right alongside the Rio Grande. We had no plans to get in, and hadn't dressed for the occasion at all.

> Isaiah 12:3
> With joy, you will draw water from the wells of salvation.

And right over there—a good stone's throw away—was Mexico. No fence, no wall, just the shallow water between us and them. We continued our walk up the path and discovered a colorful display of Mexican crafts. They were all priced for sale, with a sign that explained their honor system, and a can to leave your money in. There were walking canes, beautifully carved and brightly painted for $10, children's dolls, and small creatures made out of colorful wire and beads. I'm just guessing here, but I would venture to say that someone was crossing that river every day to collect their money, and set out new crafts. They came and went as they pleased.

Continuing our exploration in the hot desert, we went to 2 visitor centers, one at Panther Junction and the other at the Rio Grande Village. They offered different movies, so we enjoyed both. And I received different stamps at each center, too.

At one point, we were driving along and spotted a bird standing by the side of the road. It was a roadrunner! He ran quickly along the side of the road, then crossed in front of us. I was surprised at how small they were, not much bigger than a crow. That's what I get for watching cartoons; here I thought they were 2 feet tall.

We enjoyed ribs and corn on the cob for supper. Yummy. The weather forecast promises a warmup tomorrow. We can only hope.

DECEMBER 10

Today is our last day to enjoy Big Ben. I will say that it's been kinda nice to not have cell service these past 3 days. Larry lives with his face in his phone, gleaning news and information, but not this week. Diana and friends should be moving her things out of the storage area to her new home today. I'll check on her tomorrow, when we drive back into cell service.

I've been coloring like a woman on a mission. I finished a lovely page for my bestest buddy Deb's birthday, and even crafted her a Christmas present. God is good.

We headed out to get a good last look at the park. On the way, a coyote crossed the road in front of us. Larry wondered out loud where that roadrunner was. "Meep, meep," he says. We purchased gas from the only station in the park before continuing up into the mountain to what they call the "Window." What an amazing view from up here. And there was still snow on the mountain top nearby.

Up the road from the campground we saw a dirt road running off to the side, with a large metal gate. We learned that the gate is unlocked every Saturday, from sunrise to sunset. Folks can drive through, then cross the Rio Grande by way of a local makeshift ferry. The small town of Boquillas del Carmen is nearby. I assure you, we stayed on our side of the border!

A little further down the road on the US side, there is the Boquillas Overlook, which overlooks the snaking Rio Grande and the small aforementioned village. We were certainly not alone. There was a half-dozen folks on the overlook with us, as well as a group of Mexicans in a small park on the other side. The Mexicans had a roaring campfire and were yelling and whooping up at us.

From the vantage point of the overlook, we spotted a man riding horseback charge noisily into the Rio Grande from our far left. He had appeared out of nowhere on the US side, rode a few hundred feet right down the center of the river, then disappeared into a stand of trees on the Mexican side. He looked like someone out of a western movie. He knew exactly where he was going, as if he'd done it a hundred times before—and he probably had.

We stayed long enough to be blessed by a beautiful sunset, and watched as the folks on the other side packed up their stuff and went home. We were so glad we had driven so far to come here. It's a park of exceptional beauty.

As we drove back to the campground, we spotted the coyote on the road again, twice in the same place. This must be his territory, so we left him alone in his world. And what a beautiful world it was.

Isaiah 58:11
The LORD will guide you always;
he will satisfy your needs in a sun-scorched land
and will strengthen your frame.
You will be like a well-watered garden,
like a spring whose waters never fail.

DECEMBER 11

We started out early for the long drive toward San Antonio, Texas. We began on the only road in and out of Big Bend, US385 northeast, then US90 along the Rio Grande. We try to break up travel days to no more than 4 hours, but we'd left so early and made such good time, that Larry decided to travel on.

We talked to Diana for the first time in days, to learn that she was moving today. We kept the conversation short, because there was so much for her to do; we would talk later.

After the fiasco with the sleet storm and the bad wiper blades, I convinced Larry to stop at an auto parts store to buy new ones. I wanted them mounted as soon as possible, before another storm could come. The clerk tried his best to remove the old ones, but the screws were so corroded, he feared he would break the wiper mounts. Then Larry tried his best, but it was late and he was getting cranky and impatient. That "hangry" mood is why I don't like long days. One of the screws did break, and there was no consoling him. Look, there's a Home Depot nearby, let's just go buy what we need.

We parked the motorhome at the Home Depot and quickly found some hardware that could be rigged into working. He fixed the wipers right there in the parking lot. Then we drove on to Walmart. We would boondoggle tonight, right here. We walked in long enough to get my hair cut and rent a movie from the Red Box. We took a short walk to a nearby Applebees and were surprised by their amazing service and quality of food. Our Applebees back in Myrtle Beach, quite frankly, aren't known for either.

We enjoyed watching *Tarzan*, then collapsed into bed. We would return the Red Box in the morning.

DECEMBER 12

We drove the rest of the way into San Antonio, Texas, following TX1604 right to the Blazing Star RV Resort. Larry rated it an 8, but said he would have rated it higher if they'd only had a hot tub. We do love hot tubs to soak these old, weary bones. Along the way we stopped at a truck wash to wash off the motorhome it was a dirty mess, carrying all the dust in from west Texas. We had a few things we wanted to do in San Antonio, but they would have to wait. The weather is still chilly, and those 2 long days of travel from Big Bend have really kicked our butts.

I did some housecleaning and caught up on laundry. The campground internet won't work and I wound up on the phone 3 times, trying to diagnose the problem. The guy said it should be just fine tomorrow. Yeah, we'll see about that.

And Larry's all over me about writing a book. I know my husband well enough that once he gets something in his mind, it will be a race under pressure to get it done. I need to get with the program. I did color some this afternoon, then started writing once Larry went to bed. Things were finally quiet (no FOX News) and I got a good start. I wrote later than I should have, but when I tried to sleep, I couldn't. My brain just wanted my fingers to keep writing. Geesh.

DECEMBER 13

We left the motorhome under clear, sunny, and blue Texas skies. We drove the car into the city, parked in a downtown garage, then began walking toward the Riverwalk. On the way, we passed the famous Alamo. It wasn't at all as either one of us had imagined. It was right here, in the historic downtown area, with a hotel off to both sides. The streets are tightly packed with businesses. We figured it would have been out in the middle of nowhere, sticking straight up in the middle of the desert, like in the movies. Who knew? We would come back here later, once we were done at the Riverwalk.

How we ended up there, I really couldn't say. We were just following the walking route on Google Maps. This was a truly amazing place! The San Antonio River Walk runs along the San Antonio River downtown. There are paved pathways that sit a story below the city streets. They're beautifully landscaped with cypress trees and flowers, among dozens of shops and cafes.

As you walk, you can see arched stone bridges for the streets above. We thought the best way to see the whole thing was to take a water taxi through the entire route, then walk back to anything of special interest. We really enjoyed the tour, and we could see there were millions of lights running through the trees for this Christmas season.

We agreed to come back this evening, to enjoy the Walk at night.

We ate lunch in the food court of the mall, then headed back to the Alamo.

The Alamo was originally known as Mission San Antonio de Valero, which dates to 1718. This simple stone building was the center of the bloody battle for Texas's independence from Mexico in 1836, and it was fascinating to learn of its history.

One of the tour guides told us a grim story that his father had told him. One of their ancestors had come to the Alamo as a small boy, years after the battle. They planned to use the mission building after years of neglect, but the blood left behind had to be scrubbed off the walls and the floors. He was told it was a gruesome sight, indeed.

I had heard many of the names before: Travis, Bowie, Crockett, Esparza—the defenders of the fortress. History books say that between 182 and 257 men died for Texas and upwards of 600 Mexicans perished or were wounded in the bloody battle. Only 11 people—wives and children of the defenders as well as a slave of Travis—lived.

Larry had seen the 1960's movie *The Alamo* with John Wayne, and we'd both seen the 2004 remake of the same name with Dennis Quaid, Billy Bob Thornton, and Jason Patric. It was produced by Ron Howard and Brian Grazer. I'm grateful for the Hollywood men who feel the need to bring these important historic events to life.

As the Alamo is a historic landmark, it is maintained by the National Park Service. We watched the park movie, got my stamp, and lingered among the informative displays. Sam Houston's cry, "Remember the Alamo" has certainly come to life here.

We turn down offers to take a horse-drawn buggy ride through the city streets. The buggies are mostly white, and they and the horses have been creatively decorated in flowers. They are beautiful, though, and quite busy, even without us. The horses seemed to ignore the tourists as they walked by. They have seen it all before.

We had all afternoon to kill before our return to the Riverwalk after dark, so we decided to catch a movie at the mall. I made no note of the movie, I just wrote in my journal that it was "creepy." I think it was *Passengers*. We walked in, bought our tickets and our snacks, expecting to just walk a few more feet down the hall to our movie. Isn't that the way we always do it? Oh, no. Not here.

The movie we were going to see was several floors above us, through a maze of elevators and hallways. Picture this: we're carrying our large bucket of popcorn and our large drink through the mall, up the elevators and down the halls, looking for the cinema. We stopped twice to ask for better directions. It took literally fifteen minutes to get to where we needed to be! The movie was worth the confusion, but why does it have to be so hard?

When we returned to the Riverwalk, it was packed with people enjoying the evening. The paved path was crowded with tables full of diners and wait staff balancing large trays of food and drinks. You had to pay attention or you would wind up in the river! But the lights were breathtaking! Millions of lights, white lights, colored lights, some steady and others blinking. The cypress trees were full of long strands of lights hanging down, nearly to the water. Christmas music played in the background. The day had been perfect.

With the Riverwalk restaurants so crowded, we decided to grab McDonald's on the way back to the campground. The wifi was still not working, so I wasted some more time on the phone with them. I think, there is no hope. We called it quits and headed for bed.

DECEMBER 14

We spent a lot of time in the car and on the road today, for good reason. On this chilly and cloudy day, it took us 1 ½ hours to drive to the Lyndon Baines Johnson Presidential Library in Austin, Texas.

Larry nor I had much preconceived opinion of LBJ, as he was commonly known, as we were barely 10 when John F. Kennedy was assassinated and Johnson became our nation's 36th president. We didn't understand what was going on in the world , nor really cared to, at that age. When we'd seen him on the news, he just looked grumpy.

We learned today that LBJ had been a teacher for a short time. Really? We just couldn't connect that grumpy face to teaching school kids. Then he became a Navy man, who fought in the Pacific, before he got into politics. We learned that he and his wife, known as Lady Bird Johnson, were immeasurably kind to Jackie Kennedy following her husband's assassination. More importantly, we also learned he had worked his way up through the government, experiencing it at each executive level: US Representative, US Senate, Vice President, and finally President. He was only 1 of 4 people who have ever served in such a way.

Our Pass once again paid for itself, as we entered into another Presidential Library for no charge. We quickly learned that LBJ was a man of simple origins, with a reputation of being a story-teller and jokester, and a gentle man at heart. When we toured a display of his Air Force One later that day, we were shown which seat LBJ had sat in, with his wife on one side of him and Jackie Kennedy on the other, still dressed in the outfit stained with the blood of her husband. The coffin holding the body of JFK rode there with them, as well; they did not put him into the cargo hold.

We were privy to read a hand-written, multi-paged note penned by Mrs. Kennedy, thanking LBJ for his kindness, thoughts, and prayers following the assassination. To witness those personal jotted thoughts was sobering.

Going through the museum, we encountered an animatronic exhibit where LBJ came to life, all with the press of a button. He repeated jokes and stories he'd told at various gatherings at the White House. The gestures he made with his lips, eyes, hands, and arms were life-like. Some were quite funny, coming from the

President of the free world. The Presidential limousine was also there.

There is an entire section that displays just a few of the amazing gifts they received from world leaders during his presidency. There's also a section dedicated to the First Lady, displaying the dresses and accessories worn to various special events. She was also passionate about social causes, one of them, the Head Start Program, which continues today.

Her office was preserved as it had been during the term. She had chosen a solid orange couch with tan stripped pillows, a wooden end table that in no way matched the wooden desk that now overlooks the University of Texas stadium. I certainly wouldn't have chosen this setting, even back in the late sixties, but then again, I wasn't the First Lady.

Upstairs is the massive library itself, preserved for generations to come. LBJ is quoted to have said, "I want to be the President who helped to end war among the brothers of this earth." He inherited a country invested waist-deep in Vietnam, and the civil rights movement was rising up. True to his word, LBJ did what he could to activate legislature for the general welfare of Americans. He also continued to support President Kennedy's venture into space.

The traffic on the trip back to San Antonio was horrific. It was nearly impossible to get back to where we'd come from. I begged Larry to let me drive, because stuff like that just doesn't bother me the way it bothers him. He was in a terrible mood, the traffic upset him so badly, and his legs hurt so bad from the stop-and-go. I just hate to see him so upset. It reminded him of trying to drive in Los Angeles.

It was a great day of discovery, but I think we're in need of a simple day of rest. Perhaps tomorrow?

DECEMBER 15

I needed some fresh air, all by myself today. I announced that I was going to nearby Hobby Lobby for the frames I needed to finish the Christmas and birthday gifts I'd colored. I'm a crafter of many things, but I just don't get to do much of it nowadays. But that doesn't keep me from marveling at all the craft opportunities in a place like Hobby Lobby. Left to my own resources, I have gotten lost in craft stores for hours. I happened upon the nicest woman back in the framing department to help me with the 4 coloring sheets I had completed. She did help me find 4 stock frames, which lowered the cost, but I wanted mats in them, too. And I needed to get them shipped right away. She said she wasn't busy just then, and was more than willing to cut the mats for me, right there on the spot.

When that was done, I headed over to CVS to ask questions about insulin changes coming to my insurance in the coming year. That was fun.

Errands completed, I returned to the motorhome to a quiet husband, finally taking a break from the pressures of the world. The rest of the day continued to be quiet. I spent a little time packing little things for our upcoming trip home. I can't believe it's only 4 days until we see Diana again.

I've pondered that it just doesn't feel like Christmas this year. Last year hit me hard, too. I have always been in Christmas concerts, cantatas, or dramas, and the pain of my broken neck just made it too difficult to even try. But this year, I have no music to learn, no drama to rehearse, no choir rehearsals, or performances.

And the weather outside the rig isn't helping much, either. Sunny and warm in Texas sure isn't like growing up in Ohio and praying for it to snow on Christmas. Perhaps when we get back to Myrtle Beach with Diana and Zoe, Mom and Lisa, my friends at church...perhaps then it will finally feel like Christmas—and the real Reason for the Season.

DECEMBER 16

It was time to ship the few presents I've prepared for folks that I won't see. I headed to the UPS store and had them pad and pack and ship 3 of the gifts. They were a crazy size and required a lot of packing material, so by the time you added the UPS charges, WOW! I think the next time I want to give a framed gift, I'll roll up the artwork and include cash to have it done themselves locally. Double wow.

We returned home and nuked some P.F. Chang's for supper. It's always a great choice.

I watched a Christmas movie *Christmas Shoes* on DVD, then Larry joined me to watch American Sniper. Excellent movie with such a very sad ending.

---

1 Corinthians 13:4-8
Love is patient, love is kind.
It does not envy, it does not boast, it is not proud.
[5] It does not dishonor others, it is not self-seeking,
it is not easily angered, it keeps no record of wrongs.
[6] Love does not delight in evil but rejoices with the truth.
[7] It always protects, always trusts, always hopes,

> always perseveres.
> [8] Love never fails. But where there are prophecies,
> they will cease; where there are tongues, they will be stilled;
> where there is knowledge, it will pass away.

DECEMBER 17

We stayed at the campground all day, which made for a quiet day overall. I did plenty of laundry, washing towels and bedclothes so they'd be fresh when we returned.

In my first book, I explained how my friend Marcella had given me a prayer shawl right after my surgeries. It provided a great deal of comfort during those months of painful recovery. I felt that it was time to pass it on to someone else who needed to be covered in prayer.

I have a friend, Dana, who was recently diagnosed with ALS, more commonly known as Lou Gehrig's Disease. I took some quiet time to compose a letter of encouragement to her, explaining the origin of the shawl and how much it had been prayed upon. Especially, I described how much it had comforted me over the past year. I planned to give it to her at church. Afterwards, I wrote a similar letter to Marcella to explain to whom and why I had passed the blanket on to someone else, to ask her to pray for Dana, as well.

That afternoon, Larry washed all the windows outside, while I worked inside. I listened to the movie *Mooseport* on DVD while I cleaned. It's an utterly ridiculous movie with Gene Hackman, Ray Romano, and Laura Tierney. It's always great for a good laugh.

We still had some stuffed salmon from Costco in the freezer, and we fixed it for dinner. We buy cheap, but we do eat well.

It made it to 77 degrees today, but tomorrow is forecast to rise only to 41 degrees. There's something blowing in for sure—this place is really rockin'.

DECEMBER 18

We definitely stayed in all day today. After washing windows outside yesterday, it's barely above freezing out there now!

I negotiated with Larry early in the day that if he would keep the TV turned off, I would write. I knew he wanted me to write, but how badly did he want it? Bad enough to give up FOX News for a whole day? Apparently so, because I wrote the entire day.

By 11pm, I had completely written, edited, and inserted corrected headers all the way up to page 89. And that, my dear Larry, is how this girl rolls.

Good night.

DECEMBER 19

We arrived early for a factory tour at SAS. I've known of SAS shoes for decades, but never gave a minute's thought as to what that acronym stood for: San Antonio Shoemakers! The factory is in an area that is primarily industrial, although there were plenty of Mexican restaurants and tiendas. We were there for the first tour of this frigid day. Even I resigned to wear a heavy coat against the chill.

The tour was amazing. I knew their shoes were on the expensive side, but now I see why—they are completely and totally made by hand! Per their website, "Today, we continue to handcraft our shoes from only the softest, highest quality leather. Just one pair of shoes may go through up to 100 different steps. There are 14 primary operations that take place in our factories like leather selection, die-making, cutting, lasting, and more. Within those operations, approximately 80 different skilled pairs of hands are carefully constructing and inspecting each shoe to make sure the SAS shoes you choose are the best made pair of footwear in your closet."[43]

"SAS shoemakers create footwear one shoe at a time with the highest attention to detail and standard of comfort. You can see the journey the shoes take with this tour of one of the few remaining shoe factories in the U.S. We were amazed to see the tireless dedication of the shoemakers and the interesting tools and machines they use for their trade."[44]

One thing we noticed was a lot of pleasant, hard-working people, proud of what they were making. Made in America, for sure! We saw plenty of friendly gestures, smiles, and waves as we walked the aisles of the factory. Some were hand-stitching the shoes. We asked one woman, how many shoes she could hand stitch in an hour. Our guide asked her in Spanish, and interpreted her answer back into English for us: 4. If she can stitch 4 shoes an hour, that is 32 shoes a day, 160 shoes during a work week, and she had worked there for 30 years, that's a lot of shoes! We monitored the entire process, while we enjoyed the pleasant scents of leather and glue.

"SAS takes great pride in their dedicated employees. Their website claims that, "many of our team have been with SAS for

---

[43]sasshoes.com/history

[44]sasshoes.com/factory-store-tours

upwards of 10, 20, even 30 years. In fact, 42% of SAS's workforce has been on the job for over 15 years..."[45]

Factory tours have become a highlight of our adventures, because learning how things are made gives you a whole new appreciation for those things made in America.

Attached to the factory is a nostalgic store with vintage automobiles parked inside and outside. The owner of SAS shoes was a collector of cars. Back in their huge retail store, I found some shoes discounted more than 60% off retail. I found a wonderful pair of pink leather active shoes that fit me perfectly. I think I paid like $50 for them in the clearance section of the store. As I write this, their website shows they were originally listed for $171 and currently on sale for $109.99. I was truly blessed!

Then I remembered that my mother-in-law, Lois is always complaining that she can never find good shoes that fit, because her feet are so narrow. They had a simple, slip-on moc-style that I knew she would love, and they were $133, marked down to $35 a pair. I called her from the parking lot and she said, "Yes, yes, get them for me. I need new shoes so bad!" So, I bought her 2 pair. I couldn't wait for her to try them on at Christmas.

We scooted back to the motorhome after the tour, with much to do before our morning flight to South Carolina. I packed everything up, so that all we had to do was get our persons ready in the morning. We were both so excited to see Diana and to see what this new house was all about. And to see Mom and Lisa. Family. It's always all about family.

Psalm 127:3-5

---

[45]sasshoes.com/history

> Children are a heritage from the LORD,
> offspring a reward from him.
> [4] Like arrows in the hands of a warrior are
> children born in one's youth.
> [5] Blessed is the man whose quiver is full of them.
> They will not be put to shame when they
> contend with their opponents in court.

DECEMBER 20

Today, we flew home to Myrtle Beach, South Carolina for Christmas. We left the campground, drove the crazy city spaghetti junctions, took the wrong exit the first time, found the correct exit, then drove right into the Budget Park and Fly at the San Antonio Airport. We had it all worked out ahead of time. We discovered that the lot was already pretty full, but we found a long space along the fence to park the rig.

Inside, we went through our mental checklists: the propane furnace turned down to 50 degrees, refrigerator on gas, the inverter off, water pump off. Check, check, and check. Appropriate jackets in hand? Check. We were parked so close to the fence, that we battled with a large bush to get the door open and pull the large suitcase out. We walked up to the office and explained where we had parked.

They gave us a free ride on the courtesy bus to the airport and we had the opportunity to share our Motorhome Ministry with the driver. He was a Christian and said a blessing for us. On the ride, he got a call on the radio to bring us back to the lot. They had moved a van, and wanted us to move the motorhome up to take its place.

We finally arrived at the airport. We were there plenty early, so there was no rushing, and I hate to rush. I managed to get a terrific large, hot, sweet, and light coffee and that really helped. We caught our flight to Atlanta, Georgia, then home to Myrtle Beach, South Carolina. We were conscious of the fact that we had just flown over the states we will visit in the months ahead.

We'll pick this story back up when we return from our trip. Meanwhile, may each and every one of you enjoy the peace of the promise of hope God gave us in his son, the Christ, Jesus.

Merry Christmas!

Luke 2:1-7   Jesus is Born

In those days, a decree went out from Caesar Augustus
that the whole empire should be registered.
² This first registration took place while Quirinius was
governing Syria.
³ So everyone went to be registered, each to his own town.
⁴ And Joseph also went up from the town of Nazareth
in Galilee,
to Judea, to the city of David, which is called Bethlehem,
because he was of the house and family line of David,
⁵ to be registered along with Mary,
who was engaged to him and was pregnant.
⁶ While they were there, the time came for her to give birth.
⁷ Then she gave birth to her firstborn Son,
and she wrapped Him snugly in cloth
and laid Him in a feeding trough—
because there was no room for them at the lodging place.

Luke 2:8-20   The Shepherds and the Angels

In the same region, shepherds were staying out in the fields
and keeping watch at night over their flock.
[9] Then an angel of the Lord stood before them,
and the glory of the Lord shone around them,
and they were terrified.
[10] But the angel said to them, "Don't be afraid,
for look, I proclaim to you good news of great joy
that will be for all the people:
[11] Today a Savior, who is Messiah the Lord,
was born for you in the city of David.
[12] This will be the sign for you: You will find a baby wrapped
snugly in cloth and lying in a feeding trough."
[13] Suddenly there was a multitude of the heavenly host with
the angel, praising God and saying:
[14] Glory to God in the highest heaven,
and peace on earth to people He favors!
[15] When the angels had left them and returned to heaven,
the shepherds said to one another, "Let's go straight to
Bethlehem and see what has happened,
which the Lord has made known to us."
[16] They hurried off and found both Mary and Joseph,
and the baby who was lying in the feeding trough.
[17] After seeing them, they reported the message
they were told about this child,
[18] and all who heard it were amazed at what
the shepherds said to them.
[19] But Mary was treasuring up all these things
in her heart and meditating on them.
[20] The shepherds returned, glorifying, and praising God
for all they had seen and heard, just as they had been told.

CHRISTMAS WEEK 2016

Our Christmas trip home had been wonderful. We stayed at Diana's new home, which was land-locked with storage bin stuff. We worked on organization and made lots of trips to Goodwill. I washed dozens of loads of stuff before storing them away in closets. Larry did some Zoe-proofing and other repairs. We slept on a mismatched mattress set, while Diana camped on her couch. Much to Diana's dismay, her snuggle-dog Zoe found the couch too small for them both, and wound up plopping her not-so-little butt right in between us most every night. What a bed-hogging sweet, spoiled-rotten spirit.

We attended our home church, Langston Baptist, on Christmas Sunday morning and I stocked up on Smiles of Recognition and heartfelt hugs from my Sunday School and church friends.

I gave Dana the blanket, along with my note of encouragement before church started. I assured her that I would continue to pray for her and the progression of her ALS, as God wills.

Church was fantastic! I was blessed to watch Pastor Jonathan lead my choir friends sing something that I didn't know, and they were wonderful, as always. Larry and I sat in our "spot" and made sure to exchange handshakes and hugs with everyone around. As I listened to Dr. Drum's message, my heart was so full of love, it felt as if it would burst. Now, THIS is what Christmas is all about!

Lisa had a commitment to sing at her home church, Chapel by the Sea, this morning, where Mom is Church Secretary and counts the offering. We met up later to spend the rest of Christmas

Day together, and it was a quiet but wonderful day. Mom did a noble job of hiding that she was upset deep inside, because she always managed to spend Christmas in Cincinnati, staying at Sherri's home and visiting all her grandkids, their spouses, and their kids. This year, it simply could not be, and it was just the 5 of us. Zoe's cute, but she's no replacement for 5 grandkids, 3 and one-on-the-way great-grandkids, and the chaos of their crazy dog.

But, little did any of us know at the time, this would be Mom's last Christmas.

DECEMBER 29 through DECEMBER 31

The plane ride back to San Antonio was uneventful; we were both quiet and solemn. We had missed everyone so much and it had been great to visit. The good-byes were hard, but we'll be back in Myrtle Beach in April, when we finish our first year on the road.

There was so much more to be done at Diana's and quite frankly, we missed our own church. But we truly felt that God wasn't finished with this Motorhome Ministry just yet. We had joy in our hearts and are at peace with His will for us.

We knew what we would do. We would drive on.

We landed safely in San Antonio, and quickly caught the bus to the Budget Park and Ride, where had parked the rig. Everything was exactly how we'd left it. The food in the fridge was cold, everything else untouched. Thank you again, Lord, for that amazing hedge of protection.

We were eager to hit the road, but we had one piece of unfinished business to take care of. Mom's shoes had turned out to be too skinny, which never happens, so we headed over to SAS factory to make some quick exchanges before leaving the city.

We headed down I-37 south, then US77 (69E) south to South Padre Island, in the very southern point of Texas. The 4-hour drive took us over flat desert and lots of grassy grazing lands. The scenery was a curious mix of deciduous trees, conifers, palm trees, cacti, dirt, sand, and grass. There weren't nearly as many oil pumping stations as we had seen in other parts of Texas.

South Padre is a sub-tropical island on the Gulf of Mexico, and only a few miles from Mexico itself. Although this Island is a resort, there is an uninhabited barrier island just to its east. There were plenty of pelicans having a great day, and of course, there were gulls. We finally arrived at Isla Blanca Park Campground, which Larry rated a 3. It was an older, city-owned campground on the Gulf, but it was a lot cheaper than the KOA right up the street.

Our site was under some high palm trees, just a few rows from the beach. The water was in the 50's, so there would be no swimmers this time of year. Water has to be well into the 80's to get me to swim!

It was quiet here, and a bit chilly. After all the busy running around we've done this past week, we will be spending the next few days catching up on laundry, bookwork, and sleep.

New Year's Eve comes every year, and the anniversary of Bobby's death, and it always lays heavy on our hearts. We acknowledge it, try not to dwell on its details, and do our best to "delight" in what was God's will for our son. He's accomplished great things through the death of that small child, and we do rejoice in that.

No parties, no drinking, just a usual evening, early to bed for these old folks.

We are now Winter Texans.

JANUARY 1, 2017

HAPPY NEW YEAR!

Matthew 5:16
In the same way, let your light shine before others,
that they may see your good deeds
and glorify your Father in heaven.

To celebrate the New Year, I stayed in bed late. Some of the time was spent sleeping, some was in prayer for the new year and some was reading Facebook. Snuggled up and quiet, listening to the air conditioning run. Fox News was only a mumble coming through the bedroom door. Life is so good.

We are healthy and God has provided everything that we need. Abundantly.

Philippians 3:13-14
Brothers and sisters,
I do not consider myself yet to have taken hold of it.
But one thing I do: Forgetting what is behind
and straining toward what is ahead,
[14] I press on toward the goal to win the prize for which
God has called me heavenward in Christ Jesus.

I called my best friend Deb, to find out she's got the Crud again this year for the holidays. She sounded terrible. So, we cut the conversation shorter than usual, and she went back to bed.

The rest of my day was spent in writing this book. Larry spent the day on his computer, about eight feet away, planning the next phase of the Odyssey. He called me over occasionally to show me the plan. He even made some reservations for next winter.

We nuked something simple for supper (those Stouffer's meals are great) and tried desperately to find something to watch on the satellite, but failed. He went to bed early, since he'd been up since 5am anyway.

Left to my own resources, I popped in the Kendrick Brothers' *Courageous* DVD. I love every one of their movies! I have watched them repeatedly. This one especially hits home because they suffer the loss of a young child. The characters seem to validate many of the feelings I struggled with as a Christian when Bobby was taken so suddenly. Larry can't stand to watch it, as it brings up just too many emotions for him. The movie ended late and it was time for bed.

What a splendid beginning to the New Year.

Revelation 21:4
He will wipe every tear from their eyes.
There will be no more death or mourning or crying or pain,
for the old order of things has passed away."

JANUARY 2

Another late start to the day, then straight to the computer to write. The sun has finally decided to shine! Between the clouds the past several days and being socked-in with fog last night, we were beginning to wonder if the sun ever shined in Texas. It was mostly cloudy when we stayed in San Antonio, and cloudy most of the time we were in Myrtle Beach. Finally! SUN!

Ecclesiastes 11:7 Remember Your Creator While Young, Light is sweet, and it pleases the eyes to see the sun.

We drove to the mainland to make a Walmart run for groceries. The drive over the causeway was beautiful, with the sun shining, blue skies, and the water along the island a Caribbean blue. Dolphin tour boats filled with tourists were cruising in all directions on the open waters of the bay.

Their Red Box didn't have any movies Larry was interested in, so we found a single Red Box at the CVS on the Island. We spent the evening watching *Free State of Jones*, starring Matthew McConoughey. It was an excellent production, telling a side of the Civil War I could have never imagined. It seems I've learned more about American History in the past ten months than I ever knew.

It was another evening of fog. Geesh.

JANUARY 3

I think I had a bug. I wasn't really sick or anything, but I just couldn't wake up. I did get up once for a bowl of cereal about noon, but slept hard again until 4:30.

What a wasted day. But Larry told me that no day is wasted! God gives each of us His plan for us every day. I will assume then, that God wanted me to rest.

And Larry was having all sorts of problems with his computer. He attempted to work on the book website when he concluded that a great number of photographs he had uploaded to iCloud were now missing. He was beside himself.

And the day outside was just as ugly. The fog had totally socked us in before the sun went down (well, I assume it went down).

While fixing a delicious Marie Callender's entrée for supper, I suggested he try to see if any of the photos were on his Carbonite backups. As the evening progressed (and we were back to watching FOX news), he did find some of them on the backups and was doubly glad to see many of them saved on his Facebook timeline. One thing is truly apparent: if anyone ever comes up with an idea or invention that brings efficient wifi to RV'ers at a reasonable price, they will become a billionaire.

But recovering them must wait until tomorrow.

JANUARY 4

I really messed up my sleep cycle by sleeping so much yesterday. My body still wanted to sleep, but my mind was wide awake. I laid in bed about an hour, then decided to get up and write.

It was wonderfully quiet and cool in the motorhome. The words seemed to flow effortlessly from my fingers. At 3:45 am, I decided to try sleep again. By 4:30 am, I got up again to take something to sleep. Wow.

But I was up for the day by 10:30 am, roaring to go. Whatever put me down yesterday is gone.

The sun is shining today, but it's windy. The palm trees throughout the campground are making soothing swooshing sounds all around us. The motorhome was rocking and rolling and not for the reason you with "dirty" minds are thinking, but by Mother

Nature's forces. It's only in the 60's, but some of the windows are open.

It was a beautiful day.

I ran into Port Isabel, Texas for some bargain shopping. By the time I'd returned, the sky had turned completely cloudy again.

We treated ourselves to supper out, and was delighted at the feast at Blackbeard's. We had driven past it several times and assumed the place was popular, as the parking lot was big and packed with cars.

It was 5:00pm and the snowbirds were walking in from the parking lot, from up the street, and across the street. They were coming from all directions to get into this restaurant. We knew then that we'd chosen well.

We were promptly seated and we ordered the Wednesday night special, fried shrimp for $12.99, with sides of coleslaw and baked potato. Larry ordered a bowl of clam chowder.

First, they brought the slaw. It was as much as KFC would give you as a family bucket side! Then they brought Larry's "bowl" of chowder. It was served in a bowl that must have been a full foot across, and was delicious.

Then came the main course. It was served on an oval platter and consisted of large, crispy fan-tailed shrimp and the potato. And a wheat supper roll. Without asking what sauces or toppings I wanted, she had brought cups of tartar sauce and cocktail sauce for the shrimp as well as butter, sour cream, crumbled bacon, and shredded cheese for the potato. Wow!

We ate until we could eat no more. We brought home two carryout containers of leftover chowder, as well as four shrimps, half of the potato with the trimmings, and plenty of slaw.

Sounds like lunch tomorrow. Yum

Found Alaskan Bush People on satellite and enjoyed a couple of episodes. It took us a bit, but we figured out that we've visited the Alaskan town where their "going to town" trips led. Maybe that's the reason we were attracted to it. We've been there! Then on to bed.

What a blessed day.

JANUARY 5

It was finally a beautiful sunny and warm day in South Padre Island, TX. We had a great day.

I decided to dig my heels into year-end bookkeeping. With Larry watching FOX news, I quickly reconciled both checking accounts. Yay! I'm far from done, but it's a great beginning.

Larry mumbled something about the bad weather forecast for tomorrow and that "we should go out on our bikes but you probably don't want to go." The last time I tried to ride my bike in San Francisco, it was a fiasco. I'm still terrified of wiping out and after being confined in my cervical collar for so long, I tire so easily.

But I replied that it sounded like a fine idea, so long as we go at my speed. He quickly agreed.

I was a wonderful idea! The sun was spectacular, the temperature perfect. The sea breeze kept us cool and my safari hat kept the sun out of my eyes. We pedaled to the beach, taking our time. The beach was busy, with lots of folks soaking up the sun, beach walkers, a group playing some sort of ball-rolling game, and others flying kites. The waves were rough, due to an approaching storm from Mexico. We are only about 10 miles as the crow flies from Mexico, in the farthest point of south Texas. I took photos of the shrimpers and tourist boats looking for dolphins.

We were both winded when we returned to the motorhome. We should do that every day.

Larry had seen signs for twice-weekly Bingo earlier in the week, and tonight was the night. We are definitely OLD folks! This is as much partying as we do. We ate, cleaned up, and arrived early. It was a good thing, as the place was packed. We paid a low cost for the cards and I bought Larry a bright orange dabber of his very own (I already had a hot pink one, and was not about to share). We played ten games the old-fashioned way and even came close a couple of times. They offered free coffee, free popcorn, and fifty cent soda cans. They even had free cookies at intermission.

They played games that I have never encountered, so it kept both of us busy. I bought six chances on a beautiful quilt that one of the residents had made. I've been wanting a new bedspread, but Larry sees no need. So maybe I can get this one for free! They're not drawing it until after we leave, but they assured me that they would ship it to me.

We finally got lucky when they called raffle tickets and I won! I was presented with a variety of items from which to choose, including a brilliantly-decorated jacket (much too small for me), a laundry supply basket, a small cooler, and some gift certificates. When I returned with my choice of a $15 gift certificate, I explained to Larry that I thought it was for a restaurant, but the gentleman explained it's a little jewelry shop with all sorts of beautiful gems. I guess we'll go there tomorrow.

He had to laugh when I explained what a woman at the next table had selected for her gift: a little gift bag with cute curly ribbon bows on it. What was inside? Two black tank treatments. For you non-campers, it's scented chemical stuff you put in your toilet holding tank. He didn't believe me at first, but I confirmed that gift was indeed practical for anyone in this group. We both had to laugh. What a prize that would have been!

Larry went straight to bed when we got back.

I guess Bingo was harder work that he'd thought.

> Isaiah 24:15
> Therefore, in the east give glory to the LORD;
> exalt the name of the LORD, the God of Israel,
> in the islands of the sea.

JANUARY 6

The weather was the exact opposite of yesterday's. Even at noon, it was only 50 degrees and the wind was blowing so hard, the motorhome was rocking! It was completely cloudy and the ceiling so low that only the bottom of the cell tower nearby was visible.

Most of the day I tried to write, and I thought it was funny that my monitor kept rocking back and forth on its pedestal. The heat pumps tried their best to keep up. But, when nightfall came, it really started getting cold, we had no choice but to turn on the propane furnaces. With the windshield drapes drawn and every window double-covered, it finally began to warm up inside.

Still rocking and rolling at 9pm, I wondered if I would get any sleep tonight. Wind unnerves me. I really don't know why, but it's a fact. Send me thunder and lightning and I'm just fine. Wind is a whole other matter, perhaps because you can't see it. It had been a great day to stay indoors.

JANUARY 7

Larry was awake at 2am because the wind was rocking the rig so badly. He decided to retract all three slides of the motorhome. Considering their toppers are made of fabric, he feared that the wind would damage them.

We had wind chill, freeze, wind, and surf warnings posted for the area, and they continued the entire day. We did not expect a 16-degree wind chill here! The wind gusted to thirty knots and the waves from the Gulf of Mexico were cresting at twelve feet. It is so strange to see palm trees all around us, yet this cold outside.

I dared to go out in the ugly weather around noon. I had that great $15 gift certificate I'd won at Bingo and we were leaving in the morning. I had called ahead yesterday to be sure they'd be open today. Yes. Absolutely. 10am to 5pm.

But when I arrived, the shop was as dark as the open sign. Someone had printed a sign that said, "We are closed today. We will reopen tomorrow." Well dang it anyway. We need to be on the road early, because we have so far to go. Larry suggested I give it to the woman next door. Yes, that would be nice.

Despite the cold, I explained that I was craving pizza badly, so we bundled up and headed for Pizza Hut here in South Padre. I wonder if their heat was out, as it was terribly cold in there. But the service was good as was the Pepperoni Lovers Pizza with a pretzel crust. Yum. Craving satisfied.

We hurried back to the campground and drove the car up on the tow dolly. The straps will have to wait until morning...if indeed it is any warmer or less windy then.

I did get a lot of research and writing done, so it wasn't a wasted day. I can't wait until the sun shines again!

JANUARY 8

We woke up to the sun shining! It was still bitterly cold, but the wind had finally died down and the sun was out.

When we were ready to pull out, I did knock on the neighbor's door and gave her the gift certificate I won at Bingo. At least someone gets to enjoy the win.

It was a travel day north again on US77 north and then south on I-37 through Corpus Christi, TX to get us to Mustang Island State Park in Port Aransas, Texas, which Larry rated a 5. A small campground, it's basically a large paved area with campsites around of the perimeter. We have electric and water here. It was well-maintained, with a little covered area built over the picnic table at each site. There's no view, except for the highway, but the lights from the nearby city after dark were beautiful. The island is 5 miles of beach and surf. It was named for the wild horses that roamed the island, a long time ago.

Larry has signed us up for a trial basis on yet another app for road navigation. I guess it wasn't exciting enough that Frick and Frack would argue, now we have another app join the circus.

But the trip did go well. We drove most of the way today on Route 77, then off on 385 to the park. It was a level drive, and the wind was thankfully gone. The scenery was a lot of farmland, some grazing lands, and a lot of wild, untouched land.

We settled in quickly. The "low tire pressure" light came on in my car yesterday, so we thought we'd better stay put today and wait to drive to the Ford dealer on Monday. It's the only time I don't like the nitrogen in my tires—when they need to be filled.

Anyway, while we were eating supper, there was a knock on the door. A young gentleman introduced himself as Jarrett and he gave me a business card. "www.TheTouringCamper.com," it said. He also introduced his daughter, Sarah. The card further explained, "the Touring Camper is searching for adventure on and off the beaten path while reviewing places to camp and highlighting awesome places to visit." They had seen the Motorhome Ministry banner and explained that once a month, they do a report on a ministry they encounter while camping.

We invited them in and had a delightful conversation. We exchanged email information and promises to keep in touch. How very special was that?

We sent them off with three packets, one for each of their girls.

It had been another truly blessed day. This is what our ministry is all about. The God-blessed encounters of meeting people and sharing the word.

---

2 Corinthians 9:13
Because of the service by which you have proved yourselves,
others will praise God for the obedience that
accompanies your confession of the gospel of Christ,
and for your generosity in sharing with them and
with everyone else.

JANUARY 9

We set off in our car to get the low-pressure warning serviced. To make a long story short apparently, dealers can choose not to carry nitrogen for tires, and this Ford dealer did not. So, we headed to the movies, and there happened to be an independent tire dealer close by. He explained that nitrogen seemed to be a passing fad, and he recommended filling it with air. Well, that was easy—we could have done that ourselves two days ago.

Per Larry's request, we went to see the movie *Jackie*, a story of Jacqueline Kennedy's life during and right after the assassination of her husband, President John F. Kennedy. It was in tremendous detail and of course, regarding a very somber subject. I left with a sad heart. I cannot begin to imagine what she felt those days, having witnessed up close such a brutal assassination of her husband.

It was our errand day, so we went to Walmart and Sam's to stock up on groceries. Those $5 rotisserie chickens are a great deal and we had chicken and stuffing for supper. We froze the dark meat for soup on a cold day and we had enough leftover white meat for supper tomorrow, and then some. Yum.

While at Walmart, I spied the most curious thing (at least curious to me). In the fresh meat coffin cooler, there was an entire hog's head, shrink-wrapped and tagged for sale. I joked to Larry that we should take a photo and post it to Facebook. Then he did.

Oh, the discussions and remarks that followed! Eeeew. Ick. Yuck. Gross. But when Larry asked why it would be for sale, we received a tutorial from friends about Hog Head Cheese. I remember seeing that stuff in South Carolina and I had always said that I could never eat anything that looked like that. I hadn't given much thought to the "hog's head" that would be used. Yuck, indeed.

It's also a low country, Louisiana delicacy, we learned. But I'm not from around there. I like pork chops, bacon, and ham, but I draw the line at snouts and tongues and ears. Eew.

It turned out to be warmer than forecast today. The shorts will come out tomorrow.

JANUARY 10

What a beautiful day! We opened the windows all around that morning. As I sat at the computer, the wind was blowing in the window over my keyboard and the sun is shining brilliantly overhead. The air wasn't warm, but a very pleasant cool. During the afternoon, the motorhome was visited by numerous black birds that entertained me with their pleasant cries.

The day was perfect to write all day long. It was so peaceful. There's the hum of the cars on the nearby highway and an occasional small plane overhead. There was also the constant, soothing sound of the surf.

We enjoyed leftover chicken and stuffing and cream of chicken soup. We spent the evening watching *You've Got Mail.* Aren't Tom Hanks and Meg Ryan just perfect together?

Smiling, I decided that it had been a very, very good day.

JANUARY 11

Larry woke up early to view the sunrise over the Gulf of Mexico. He told me later that he'd been the lone soul on the beach. A Blue Heron stood watch over him as the sun rose in all its glory over the Gulf. He described a spectacular sunrise, the sky full of orange, pink, purple, and blue. The solitude was so peaceful, he said, "God was in His full glory this morning. He had truly witnessed that it was a new day, a new beginning.

2 Samuel 23:4
he is like the light of morning at sunrise
on a cloudless morning,
like the brightness after rain that brings grass from the earth.'

I slept through it. I have never been a morning person. But the photos were surely something to see.

> Genesis 1:5
> God called the light "day,"
> and the darkness he called "night."
> And there was evening, and there was morning—
> the first day.

I decided to take some "me" time and go into Corpus Christi for Bath & Body Works' Semi-Annual Sale. If you enjoy Bath & Body Works, or want to stock up early for birthdays and Christmas, The January & July (or is it June) sales are the times to go.

When you are with your spouse 24/7 in 350 square feet, you MUST take time to recharge the "me". For me, it is a time of quiet, to reflect what is important in life and a time for just thinking and taking care of me. It is a time for prayer and thanking Him for all my blessings. Larry's me time is at 6am in the morning when I am fast asleep. He is usually reading the Bible, catching up on Facebook, answering emails, and reading Fox news. Yes, reading it from his iPhone. He just can't get enough.

> Philippians 1:21
> For to me, to live is Christ and to die is gain.

They have a massive, beautiful mall here, the La Palmera. After paying for my bargains, I walked the entire mall. They were doing some skylight repair work, but it didn't hinder mall traffic at all. It was very nice.

But the noteworthy part of the day was my drive to and back from the Mall. It was about 15 miles each way from Mustang State Park, the sun was shining in the bright blue sky, and the view was awesome. On the way, there, the Gulf of Mexico was to my left.

The dunes rose up, protecting the length of Padre Island National Seashore. On my right, was nearby Corpus Christi Bay.

Adjacent to the road on both sides were wetlands, and there was abundant wildlife. The State Park claims home to over 400 different species of birds. Well, I can't begin to name a dozen birds, but I enjoyed many Blue Herons, pelicans, egrets, and gulls.

I soon turned the car to the right, to drive over the beautiful John F. Kennedy Causeway. The entire Corpus Christi Bay came into view. The water was blue and smooth and waterfowl were flying or roosted or swimming everywhere. There was a group of pelicans all lined up on a fence.

By the time I returned from my errand, the wind had picked up—a lot.

The flags by waterfront businesses were flapping wildly; palm trees were tugged back and forth by the wind. Whitecaps chopped the Bay on both sides of the bridge. What a calming and soothing effect the drive had had on me. I returned, ready to write again. Even a short drive can give you so much meaning when you stop the rush of life and just take in the sights, sounds, and smells of the day you are given. Every day becomes a new beginning. Every day is a blessing from God.

The afternoon passed quickly

We grilled hamburgers for supper. Trying to avoid the carbs, we cut them up and served them in a heap with sliced tomato and onion. Yum.

I could still hear the surf through the closed windows. It was a me day for the Great I am.

Exodus 3:14
God said to Moses, "I AM WHO I AM.

> This is what you are to say to the Israelites:
> 'I AM has sent me to you.'"

JANUARY 12

It was another beautiful day.

We wasted part of the afternoon, driving the area, trying to get an x-ray done. To spare you a long story, they wouldn't take an order from my South Carolina doctor. We'd had no problems when I had my neck x-ray done months ago, but apparently, in Texas, it's a big problem. I surrender to the fact that it will have to wait until I get back to South Carolina in about ten weeks.

But I also blame this on the Affordable Care Act (ACA). Since I left my employment, I have had coverage through ACA. I must first say that my coverage through ACA in 2016 was top-notch. With back-to-back neurosurgeries, my out-of-pocket was minimal.

Now that I'm retired but not old enough for Medicare, I again went through ACA for 2017. I got all signed up with a new plan, well before the first of the year. But, before 2017 even started, I received an email from the provider. It explained that they had to cut benefits in some way to keep costs reasonable, so from now on, to get coverage, services must be received in the state of South Carolina. Well, excuse me, but for those of us who travel full-time, that bites.

It seems that most services, whether through the government, the medical industry, or insurance industry, are structured to serve individuals that have stationary homes in one place. I do understand the importance of that, but it's way above my pay grade. But there should be something for the growing number of baby boomers who choose to live on the road.

JANUARY 13

I'm sounding like a broken record, but it was another gorgeous day.

I had a craving for sweets today and there just never seems to be any in the motorhome. I drove to CVS, just 4 miles away. I always show my CVS card when I go. I had $15 in free stuff coupons, from previous purchases. I received $1 more when I scanned my card, with a $2 off coupon if I bought a couple of specific bags of chocolates. I'm not too picky about my chocolate, as long as it's chocolate.

I walked out of there with four full-size candy bars (BOGO), 2 12-ounce bags of chocolates (on sale 2/$6 less the $2 coupon), one bag of orange slices, two bags of peanut butter-filled pretzels, a large bottle of Suave shampoo (the kind we like) and two ladies' razors for the whopping price of $2.32. That's enough sweets to last for a while, if Larry doesn't get into them. Another me item! CHOCOLATE!

I had a great afternoon writing, enjoying the sunshine, the breeze through the windows, and chocolate. Yum!

JANUARY 14

And yet another beautiful day.

Headed into Corpus to see *Patriot Day*, a movie about the bombing of the Boston Marathon. It was outstanding! There were lots of details in the movie that I didn't remember hearing in the news. I don't know whether those details were artistic license, or the eventual release of facts. It starred Mark Wahlberg and quite a few other recognizable stars. The officers that worked up front in that case will never be the same, permanently scarred by the event.

We treated ourselves to supper at Joe's Crab Shack by ordering a sampler that included a big crab cake, skewered grilled shrimp, fried clam strips, and fish, all of which were delicious. It came with a lot of fries that we couldn't finish. I didn't realize until we were back home that the waiter never brought us our coleslaw. Darn. I really like their slaw.

JANUARY 15

We left Mustang Island early, because we had lots of miles to cover today. We started up TX361 east, then took a ferry across the Intracoastal at Port Aransas. This was the first time we had taken the motorhome on a ferry. We had all sorts of trepidation for such a big rig and tow, but it was easy on and easy off. Then we drove up TX35, then over to the Gulf coast by way of TX332.

We used the Sygic GPS app for truckers today, for the first time. Because of Frick and Frack, Larry quickly announced that we would refer to this app as Frank. Okie dokie.

We learned quickly the difference between Frank and Frack. Frack had a time of 45 minutes faster than Frank, so we decided to go with Frack—who doesn't want to save 45 minutes?

So, we turn onto a secondary road, per Frack's instructions. A short distance down the road, there was a sign for a bridge ahead: NO TRUCKS. Bridge Weight 4 tons. OMG! What were we going to do? This was barely a 2-lane country road, with no place to turn around. And we were way over 4 tons! We can't back up with a tow dolly with the car on it. And you can't just pull into someone's yard with a 56-foot rig. OMG.

Well, as usual, God went before us. There was one small road that turned to the left before we ever arrived at the bridge. We were scared half to death to turn, but we had no other choice. While driving down that road, Larry was still carrying on loudly with a "what will we do" attack. Before we knew it, we were right back to the highway. Another crisis averted. God is so good.

Frank's "truck route" took us on a truck route, for sure. We drove for miles out in oil country. We drove past hundreds of oil wells, dozens of refineries, and fuel depots. The only other folks traveling these mud-caked highways were oil transports. We really saw the nuts and bolts of Texas Tea today.

Off TX332, we took the Bluewater Highway over the San Luis Pass, on the west end of Galveston Island. There was a toll booth at the mouth of the bridge, and it was not meant for motorhomes. We watched nearly 100 motorcycles coming through the gate from the opposite direction. The poor guy in the toll booth was busier than a one-armed paper hanger! We finally arrived at Galveston Island State Park, which Larry rated a 5. The water was beautiful.

There were birds of every size, shape, and color. I recognized the obvious mix of gulls, herons, and quite a few varieties of ducks. It was the first time I'd personally seen a roseate spoonbill, but I'd seen plenty of photographs of them, back in Myrtle Beach.

"Birds from throughout the eastern hemisphere visit during the spring and fall migration seasons. You can see wading and shore birds, mottled and mallard ducks, and more. We have recorded more than 300 bird species in the park."[46]

"The small amount of relatively pristine habitat found in Galveston Island State Park is an important resource for many bird species. The property is in the path of the migration flyway used by most of the bird species that seasonally travel between North and

[46] tpwd.texas.gov/state-parks/galveston-island/nature

South America. In the spring, many birds make their first landfall on the island after flying over the Gulf. In the fall, birds pause at Galveston Island before beginning their long overwater journey. There are also many birds that either make their home within the park or regularly use the Gulf, prairie, and salt marsh habitats to forage.[47]

After setting up, we fixed something simple for supper, then watched a bit of TV. But it had been a long day, so we went to bed early. It sure doesn't take a whole lot to wear out these old farts nowadays, does it?

JANUARY 16

Today was a memorable day. We drove to Johnson Space Center (JSC) in Houston, Texas. Remember the infamous words, "Houston, we have a problem?" We wound up spending nearly six hours there. It was amazing.

We went on Martin Luther King, Jr.'s day. You could easily tell that schools were out for the day because there were plenty of kids at the JSC. But I marveled to Larry many times that I couldn't imagine what the place would be like in the summer, with hundreds of hot, cranky, and screaming kids here!

It was a great day to come. It was partly sunny, with low but gusty winds leading in the approaching storms. We purchased our senior tickets and the greeter recommended that we take the tram rides first. It was a smart move, because the crowd increased by the hour.

They drove us through the streets of the huge complex. The first things we saw had <u>nothing to do with NASA, but</u> definitely with

---

[47] galvestonislandstatepark.org/nature/galveston-island-bird-watching.html

Texas: longhorns. They were amazing animals, the first longhorns we had ever seen closeup. It was to clearly illustrate that before NASA arrived, this was simply grazing land, hundreds of acres of it.

We learned so much that day. We learned about all the phases leading up to space travel. We learned about the development of the International Space Station. We walked inside the space shuttle Independence, and viewed a simulator that was designed for training the astronauts. We walked inside the NASA plane that carried the space shuttle. We enjoyed dozens of interactive displays and games. It was totally, completely awesome!

We sat in the same seats in which the wives and dignitaries had sat in Mission Control. They had watched through the glass of the operation center, as each mission unfolded before them. It was overwhelming to imagine the tension and excitement in this room at certain moments in history.

It was amazing to consider what those faded and worn seats have witnessed. Folks had been sitting there, listening to "The Right Stuff" men like Alan Shepherd and John Glenn speak. The Mercury missions. The first flights into space. The Gemini space walks. The grand day, on July 21, 1969 when Neil Armstrong first set foot on the moon during the Apollo 11 mission. Or when Jim Apollo 13 radioed, "Houston, we have a problem."

Those faded seats even had built-in ash trays in the arm rests.

Ecclesiastes 1:13
I applied my mind to study and to explore by wisdom
all that is done under the heavens.
What a heavy burden God has laid on mankind!

While we were still there, Larry received a FOX News alert that Gene Cernan, the last man to walk on the moon had died that very day. You could hear an increase in chatter while the news passed through the Center, and was finally announced over the loud speakers. The 6pm news was alive with his biography. He was 82.

We ate supper at a nice little Mexican place in Galveston named Salsa's. When we walked inside, we realized that this was the same restaurant we had eaten at several years ago, when we worked a wholesale show for our business Oyster & Pearls at the convention center right up the street. The food was again great and the view of the ocean crashing up against the seawall was a sight to see.

I remembered that I had a couple of prescriptions to get filled, so we drove a few miles to a CVS. When we parked, we were amazed at the enormous number of birds gathered on the utility lines above. I asked one of the employees inside if the birds did this often. I mean there were probably a million of them on the electrical lines for blocks in every direction, just a wing's space apart! Remember the movie, *The Birds*? This was the remake.

Anyway, the lady told me that they do this every single night. And that they stay there all-night long. What a fascinating phenomenon. The birds of Galveston…

JANUARY 17

We drove to the historical part of Galveston, TX and along the docks. We visited The Ocean Star Offshore Oil Rig & Museum, a museum dedicated to the offshore oil and gas industry. It's a retired rig that offers 3 floors of models & interactive displays, plus education programs & a gift shop. It was fascinating.

"The Ocean Star was built in 1969 in Beaumont, Texas by Bethlehem Shipbuilding Corporation for the Ocean Drilling and Exploration Company (ODECO) fleet. She worked in the Gulf of Mexico throughout the Texas and Louisiana Gulf Coast and drilled approximately 200 wells during her active life. The museum, sponsored by the Offshore Energy Center (OEC), is a non-profit organization funded through private donations, admissions, and corporate donations. The OEC acquired the Ocean Star and spent 2 years converting her into the museum. The museum opened to the public on April 27, 1997.[48]

Walking through a real oil rig was interesting. We learned more than we'd known about the Deepwater Horizon accident and those who died. We were surprised to learn that George H.W. Bush (Bush 41) was part of the oil rig pioneers of the industry.

There were pelicans everywhere waiting for the fisherman to come in with their catch. We stopped at one of the fish markets on the docks, bought some fresh shrimp, and got a quick lesson on how to prepare them. They had all kinds of fish, eel, and shrimp—as well as other local seafood—displayed in crushed ice for people to buy. We cooked our purchase in a shrimp boil, then deveined them, according to the instructions from the fish market staff. We set them in the fridge to chill for a huge helping of shrimp tomorrow.

Leviticus 11:10
But all creatures in the seas or streams
that do not have fins and scales—whether among all the
swarming things or among all the other living creatures in the
water—you are to regard as unclean.

JANUARY 18

Today was a day to stay in. Rain was predicted all day, but it came and went. It was overcast and cool, in the low 60's.

---

[48]en.wikipedia.org/wiki/Ocean_Star_Offshore_Drilling_Rig_%26_Museum

I decided that it was a perfect day to write a book!

The highlight of today was supper. We had boiled our fresh shrimp last evening and they were ready to throw on the grill tonight. But, grilling was cancelled due to weather and we enjoyed great chilled shrimp cocktails with bowls of hot clam chowder.

JANUARY 19

It was yet another dreary, rainy day here in Texas.

Politics have never been a big thing in my life, but both of us were busy watching FOX news this morning. Tomorrow we will swear in a new President of these United States of America. Yes, we voted for Donald Trump and we truly believe that he will *Make America Great Again.*

Larry and I have both said for many years that this nation needs to be run like a business. Someone really needs to seriously look at the bottom line and realize that the government cannot continue to operate with Billions of dollars in deficits. It cannot afford to allow huge overruns without challenges. It cannot continue to fund ridiculous matters that benefit no one. It cannot continue to police the entire world at our own expense.

There are still so many people sitting around asking, "How did this happen?" The Reverend Franklin Graham has now publicly and repeatedly said what many of us already knew, "God Showed Up."

In 2016, he visited every state, stood on the capitol grounds, and led thousands upon thousands of people in prayer. We are visiting nearly every state for Him as well (sorry, Hawaii). They prayed for our country, our leaders, they confessed their own personal sins and asked God's forgiveness for allowing Him to be pushed aside. He prayed that God would bless this great country.

For that entire year, Reverend Graham encouraged through every means possible that people pray about the election. Even if only for the future of the Supreme Court, he encouraged Christians to show up to vote, to make our desires known.

It was with great admiration that I learned only yesterday that Mike Pence, our Vice President elect, plans to open the Bible to one particular verse that I have mentioned before, as he is sworn in:

> 2 Chronicles 7:14
> If my people, who are called by my name,
> will humble themselves and pray
> and seek my face and turn from their wicked ways,
> then I will hear from heaven, and I will forgive their sin
> and will heal their land.

I believe that God has abandoned us in recent years because America first abandoned Him. If one person screams they are offended, they get their way. We have allowed those "one persons" to take away so very much from this godly nation that our forefathers set us up to be. And I hope it is now the time to reclaim as much.

That was as political as I will ever get. God Bless America.

We decided to take in a movie today, so we chose *Hidden Figures*. It was outstanding. It was based on a true story of three gifted black women in the early space program. They were close friends and worked together at NASA in Virginia. Each was brilliant and eventually contributed in varied monumental ways to John Glenn's successful first orbit of the earth.

I found it very interesting that the brilliant mathematicians behind the scenes were titled computers, because they computed. They do introduce the IBM computer in the movie, although it was nothing compared to the brilliant minds of the women.

They had made a huge difference, despite the social prejudice and segregation at the time. I rate it a Must See. It was of special interest to us and king of ironic, that John Glenn passed away just a month ago, and that we had just visited Johnson Space Center.

JANUARY 20

Oh, what a spectacular day this was!

I will downplay the fact that today was Donald J. Trump's inauguration as President of the United States, which made the day spectacular day to him.

But I will tell you in great detail why this was a spectacular day to me.

On the Alaskan cruise, we met Lucy and Bob. I've told you about how we became instant friends that week at supper. One night, Lucy mentioned they had horses. I became excited and told them that I'd only "ridden" a horse once in my life. It was a trail horse in Mackinac Island, Michigan. I really wanted to ride a horse.

Just for your info, my "ride" went like this. Larry and Diana decided they wanted to go on a trail ride. Other than a pony ride when I was like 4, I had never been on the back of a horse. They said, no problem. At least I could mount the horse, after watching so many cowboy movies. I do know how to do that. So, we go on the ride.

It's one single line of horses on a trail. Larry and Diana were up ahead in the line, perhaps 3-4 horses ahead. I complained loudly about my horse wanting to wander off the trail. Larry yelled back to me, "Show the horse who's boss!" I replied loudly, "This horse has absolutely no doubt whose boss!"

The entire line laughed. I was out of my comfort zone, out of control, and didn't like the feeling one bit. But I finished the ride.

Anyway, we had exchanged promises to get together with Lucy and Bob when our travels took us closer to Dallas, with Lucy's promise to ride horses.

Well that day came today!

We left Galveston Island and drove to their home in Santa Fe, TX, just south of Houston. The sun was shining and the temps were already in the low 70's. We knew that storms would be arriving this afternoon, so we went out to see the horses early.

Lucy introduced me to Wendell. He was an old, quiet soul. Just perfect for me! She saddled and bridled him for me, and I managed to mount him by myself.

She took me to the pen, and led Wendell around for me. She explained the basics of "steering", and eventually how to get him to trot, and of course, how to make him stop. When I was comfortable riding on my own, she left us to saddle her steed.

Together, we roamed—and trotted—the pasture for more than an hour. Sometimes we stopped and talked in the shade. Then trotted some more.

At one point, we rode to the front section of the pasture fence to visit the goats next door. Wendell wanted to stay with the goats. So much, that Lucy had to ride back and lead us away. It was precious time with a precious new friend.

She repeated the name of her horse to me like ten times, but I still can't remember it. But after the guys were unsaddled and put outside the gate, Lucy said, "Watch this—it is so cute."

The horse kissed her hand. Again, and again. Then her arm, over and over. He even kissed mine, which she exclaimed he doesn't usually do for strangers.

When we went back in the house, I scolded Larry terribly for not coming out to take any pictures. I was mostly kidding, but it was such a great moment. I wanted some lasting proof, but I will always have great memories of this day.

Lucy served us a wonderful early supper of pot roast, taters, and carrots. It was delicious!

We watched some of the FOX News coverage leading up to the inauguration parade. When lightning struck outside, and thunder shook the house, that was our signal to get back on the road and back to the rig.

We hugged all around. This friendship was genuinely a "God thing." What a blessing!

---

1 Samuel 20:42
Jonathan said to David, "Go in peace, for we have sworn friendship with each other in the name of the LORD, saying, 'The LORD is witness between you and me, and between your descendants and my descendants forever.'"
Then David left, and Jonathan went back to the town.

JANUARY 21

I'd slept well because of all the fresh air yesterday. But, when the alarm went off, by body screamed in outrage over what I'd put it through the day before. The muscles in my upper legs were in pain from the famous "Horse / Saddle Seat" stretch.

I took some Tylenol and told them to shut up.

The afternoon was spent once again with our cruise friends, Lucy and Bob. We wanted to see them, considering we had no idea when our paths may cross again. We'd invited them out here to Galveston Island to visit us at the State Park. Conversation is easy with them and we chatted for a long while. Topics varied widely and changed frequently. We talked about politics, travel, foods, pets, horses, life, families. Larry told stories of what God has done in his life and how his faith has changed over the years. It was a time of sharing God's blessings and being able to share His words. Remembering the verse once again:

Matthew 18:20
For where two or three are gathered in my name,
there am I with them."

I sincerely offered to make Skyline Chili for supper, but they had to go home to feed the horses.

We were craving seafood (well, I was) so we drove to Jimmy's on the Pier at sunset over the Gulf of Mexico and ate what we could of a delicious platter of fried shrimp. The leftovers will be Larry's lunch tomorrow. It was a very nice finish to the wonderful day He had given us.

We didn't spend much time on the beach, but time here on the coast has been nice. I enjoyed writing these past few days, looking past my computer screen to watch the sun dance off the incoming surf. God is so good to us. He goes before us and always present with us.

Please keep that hedge of protection around us, Lord. Thank you for all our blessings.

JANUARY 22

Today was for traveling, and it was a very, very bad day.

Let me say first that God was good in getting us safely to where we wanted to go. For that we were grateful. But...

We knew that the weather forecasters had said it would be windy today. That was a gross understatement! A front had come through during the night, so everything was wet from the rain. The wind was already gusting over 30 mph when we left Galveston Island in the morning. Which is not all that bad and very manageable. But on the road north to College Station, Texas were 50+ mph gusts. Larry had to constantly struggle to keep the motorhome in its lane.

> Genesis 8:1
> But God remembered Noah and all the wild animals
> and the livestock that were with him in the ark,
> and he sent a wind over the earth, and the waters receded.

We headed out of Galveston on Seawall, and the waves were really kicking in the wind. We took Route 87 north to jump on I-45. From Houston, we took Route 290 northwest, then Route 6 north.

When we arrived in College Station, Texas, we pulled the rig into the parking lot at the George Herbert Walker Bush Presidential Library, also referred to as Bush 41. It was all we could do to walk into the wind to get to the Library.

Inside was nice and calm and we enjoyed our time there. We learned all about his ancestors and that he was not a Texan at birth. He was born in Connecticut. I never knew that!

Walker's Point in Kennebunkport, Maine is named after Bush's maternal grandfather, George Herbert Walker. They displayed dozens of pictures of summers at Walker's Point and how Bush 41 as well as Bush 43 spent their summers in the family home in Maine.

One of the centerpieces of his library was a large portion of a large block of cement from the Berlin wall. Bush 41 was Vice President at the time of President Ronald Reagan's famous speech, "Mr. Gorbachev, tear down this wall." The 2 sides of the wall matched the piece we'd seen at Ronald Reagan's Library: The Communist-ruled side had absolutely no marks on it, where the people with freedom had marked all sorts of graffiti on it.

What impressed Larry the most was a very simple statement that Bush 41 had made: "Faith, Family, and Friends..." The museum emphasized that everything he did in life he accomplished with those priorities. He did have his priorities in order.

Hebrews 13:7
Remember your leaders, who spoke the word of God to you.
Consider the outcome of their way of life and imitate their faith.

When we were finally back on the highway, things were just as bad and windy as before. We also needed to get propane. We stopped at a Love's Truck stop (I can't tell you where, a very remote exit) and it had yellow tape all around it with one small sign that read, "Closed". There were dumpsters and porta-potties everywhere. We weren't alone. There were truckers pulling in at a regular pace, everyone confused about the closure.

We turned around in their large lot and continued on our miserably windy way.

The next Love's down the road was close to Waco, in Hearne, Texas.

We pulled up for propane. It took about 15 long minutes for someone to come, and the man apologized that they couldn't find the keys. The guy who actually had the keys had gone on a service run. He fumbled through a dozen keys but couldn't find one that fit. Larry had reached his stress level for the day and was ready to blow. But I was probably the only one who knew. Christians do lose their temper, at least once in a while. We are still pathetically human.

I told the man it was fine. We were pulling in for the night anyway, and we could wait until morning. He was relieved.

We moved the motorhome, looking for the perfect spot, but they were all back-in spaces. There were no pull-throughs. So, Larry decided we would park by the curb out by the entrance. .

We were beat. I fixed something quick to eat and we turned on the satellite to relax. Within minutes, the train tracks just across the highway came to life, the loud engine blasting his whistle to come through the crossing, just another 100 feet up the road. And from where we were, this track was like 75 feet from us. AND this was the entrance and exit for every truck that came and went. Oh, boy.

Larry was in bed by eight. He couldn't have chosen a worse place. I stayed up another half-hour and the trains were coming every ten minutes. The trucks were constant, right outside the bedroom window. How in the world would we sleep?

I prayed. I prayed hard. I prayed for a hedge of protection in this busy place, as well as a hedge of soundproofing. I took a sleeping pill and went to bed.

Both of us slept straight thru until sunrise.

JANUARY 23

Refreshed from a surprisingly good night's sleep, we headed back to I-35 north, to I-820 east, to arrive at Grapevine, Texas, just northwest of Dallas. On the way, we made reservations at The Vineyards RV Resort, which Larry rated an 8.

The campground is located on 8,000-acre Grapevine Lake. Our site had beautiful views, both out of my dinette window as well as a view of the boat docks out the front windows. The deciduous trees are naked for the winter, with the exception of a few oaks that are hanging on to their brown leaves. It's very pretty here.

We declared it a catch-up day and I started laundry the moment Larry hooked us up. After tidying up a bit, I told Larry I needed to get some prescriptions filled at CVS and today was the best day to do that. I headed out with the car and good old Frack in my hand.

The CVS stop took well over an hour, then I headed to a local Container Store, just for fun. If you haven't experienced one of these, go check them out. They have stuff for every purpose and budget you can think of! You can spend a bunch if you choose, but I found two plastic baskets for the fridge and only spent $4.99 each. They were a perfect fit.

On to Walmart and got everything on my shopping list. At least the laundry was done when I got home, so I could start another load.

We spent a quiet evening watching satellite after supper.

It was a good day.

JANUARY 24

Today was a whirlwind kind of day, Texas style! We went everywhere!

I'd bet we put over one hundred miles on the car, driving all over the Dallas downtown and suburbs. Praise God for the invention of Google Maps. One trip we made today probably took 20 different highways, access roads, and surface streets. How would we have ever navigated that without Google Maps?

If you remember like I do, the atlas and local paper maps, searching for cross numbers and letters to pinpoint your location and then trying to determine which way was north. Then trying to follow a road from where you are to where you are going. They have vanished like the pay phones of yesteryear. Thank you, Google, Apple, and bless Steve Jobs!

We began the day by going to the George Walker Bush Presidential Library, Bush 43. The junior Bush as Texans say. Laura Bush explains in her book, *Reflections: Life after the White House* that there was initially some confusion when both men were in the same room. How to differentiate who they were talking to or about, when each of them was respectfully "President Bush?" Junior really didn't work, because he wasn't a Junior. That's when the numbering started, and it was an idea that worked—and stuck.

There is absolutely no redundancy in the Presidential libraries we have seen so far. Each one has its own personality outside and the manner in which history is presented inside is just as different.

Each Library has an introductory movie. This one was truly unique!

We were told to wait by standing in the middle of a large atrium. The floor was polished marble and about three stories above—at the top of each wall—were huge murals of the Texas countryside.

Without fanfare, the tumbleweeds on the four pictures starting to move. The "murals" disappeared and the movie began, in a huge square.

Now I understood why there were no seats. Each LED screen was showing a different picture! There were dozens of people shown in different uniforms, to illustrate what the people of Texas do in industry and commerce, education and health, arts and sciences, public service, and government. It was quite a testimony.

Then the movie took us on a flight from the Lincoln Memorial, over the Capitol and on to the Washington Monument. You could see before you, after you, and off to both sides. My neck really ached from looking up at such an angle, but it was worth the discomfort.

The rest of the museum did not disappointment. We took another picture of Larry in the Oval Office, sitting at the desk of Bush 43, answering the phone. This has become the tradition in all the libraries we have visited. I guess he imagines himself as President one day! We saw a replica of the bust of Winston Churchill that's been in the news lately, when Trump brought it back to the White House after Obama had returned it to the British embassy. We learned all about Laura Bush and her philanthropic undertakings. We had not known that Bush 43 was such a joker and usually the life of a party. Who knew?

A large area of the museum was rightly appointed to 9/11, with the twisted and broken steel beams from the collapse of the World Trade Center. I do remember that day vividly, as I know all of you do, if you were born at the time. The world was forever

changed that day. And Bush was right smack in the middle of it.
Wow.

We drove downtown to see The Sixth-Floor Museum at Dealey Plaza. The Museum is in the original former Texas School Book Depository--the place from which Lee Harvey Oswald fired the shots to assassinate President Kennedy.

It was a sunny 80 degrees, and we enjoyed the short walk across the transit rails to the Museum. We paid our admission and was issued a lanyard with an audio guide and a set of headphones. We took the elevator to the sixth floor.

We walked through a maze of exhibits with photos and printed narratives. The audio guides offered even more information. There were displays of cameras that had taken pictures that day. Everyone was listening to their headphones, so the place was eerily quiet.

We were both struck by the realization that we were standing right where Lee Harvey Oswald had plotted and eventually assassinated President Kennedy. The area by the window where the shooting took place is glassed-in for preservation, along with a replica of the rifle he used. A sign explained that the original is kept in the National Archives.

From the sixth-floor windows we could see the white X on the street, which marked the spot where the car was at the time of the first shot. Eerie. The whole place was very solemn. Memories from my childhood come racing back. This was the first major historical event of my lifetime, and it has remained embedded in my mind.

We turned in our audio equipment and were quiet as we left the building and crossed the street.

From there, we could clearly see what has come to be known as "The Grassy Knoll." What struck us then was the small perimeter of everything. From the movies and news reels we have seen over the years, we imagined a large knoll, a wide street, and a great distance to the overpass where Kennedy passed under, as he was rushed to Parkland Memorial Hospital and eventually died.

Here we could see that it was a very small knoll, smaller than my last front yard. The overpass abutted the knoll. The street is one way, three small lanes. It all looked bigger than life on TV, but it was all so small.

The jail is right on the other side of the highway. This is where Jack Ruby shot Oswald. Everything happened in such a small space in such a large city.

We spotted a Subway and went in to have lunch. Their air conditioning was out and, if it was 80 degrees outside, it must have been 95 in there. We ate quickly and walked back to the car.

It was getting late in the afternoon and Larry set Frack for "South Fork Ranch." Do you remember the TV series *Dallas?* Do you remember everyone talked about "Who shot JR" all summer long back in 1980? As we got closer to our destination, I told Larry I didn't think this could be right. We were in a very upscale neighborhood and when we arrived; Google had apparently taken us to a home office that gave tours of South Fork.

When I re-Googled South Fork Ranch, we now needed to drive thirty miles in the opposite direction, but we did finally arrive. We took lots of photos, parked out along the highway. The place is classically beautiful, just as we remembered from the TV show.

With no plans to take the tour, we walked into the gift shop anyway. There were large portraits on the wall of those characters we knew all too well.

Do you remember? Who shot J.R.?

By the time we started to head back to the campground, we were in the middle of rush hour. I began looking for some place to eat, to get us out of traffic. Larry suggested Texas BBQ, as we hadn't once in this past month in Texas had some real Texas BBQ.

We wound up in a town named Plano, Texas. The main street was busy and parking was at a premium. We got lucky and parked right in front of Lockhart's Smokehouse, our choice for supper.

When we first entered, it just looks like an old-time bar with creaky wood flooring. When I looked puzzled, the bartender sent me back to where I could order food. We ordered the ribs, macaroni and cheese, and orange cream banana pudding for dessert. My choice for ribs is to be "fall off the bone" tender and these certainly were. They wrapped them up in butcher paper—there wasn't a plate in sight. Larry chose a table by the front window and we took photos of this unique and delicious supper. I'll have plenty of mac and puddin' for lunch tomorrow.

While we were eating, I spotted a barber shop across the street and encouraged Larry to get his hair cut, as he'd been looking a bit shaggy these days. There were three still ahead of him, but it didn't take long. Much better. He was blessed to converse with the barber and some other patrons about our Motorhome Ministry, Trump's election, liberals vs. conservatives, family—even the economy.

When we finally started heading back to the campground, traffic was a bit lighter and the sunset was stupendous. Pinks and purples and blues streaked throughout the sky.

A perfect end to a wonderful day, except that I'd left the doggie bag of delicious food sitting in the barbershop.

> John 16:13
> But when he, the Spirit of truth, comes,
> he will guide you into all the truth.
> He will not speak on his own;
> he will speak only what he hears,
> and he will tell you what is yet to come.

JANUARY 25

Today was our last day in Dallas. As we will be leaving in the morning, it was important to get all the laundry caught up. That's just a background thing. The day was mostly spent in writing.

Although yesterday was in the 80's, today's high was 56. Tonight, will be literally freezing, at a low of 32 degrees. Yikes.

We had seen Larry's cousin David and his wife, Sally back in California, when we stopped in to see his Uncle Tom and Aunt Marilyn. We had made promises then to meet them again near Dallas.

They came to the campground to see our motorhome, where Sally gave me a gift. We had discussed our separate crafting talents when in California, and I'd told her that I wanted to learn to quilt. Well, she quilted me a beautiful 2-foot square that will look lovely on my kitchen table.

The centers of the nine inner squares were all camping stuff. Tents, camping trailers, folding chairs, bikes, pink flamingos, coolers, campfires, and what my daddy affectionately called "tacky lights." Areas of flowers, dots, paisleys, stripes, and weaves were all in contrasting colors of teals, peach, and green. She said she had really liked the material when she bought it, but had no idea how she would use it. It was perfect! And, it was precious. I will cherish it always.

They drove us to a restaurant called Cotton Patch Café in Grapevine, TX. They weren't overly crowded, so we didn't feel guilty in tying up a table for 2 ½ hours. We had a wonderful, wonderful visit. I ordered the chicken fried steak, broccoli and cheese rice, and fried okra. With very little help from Larry, the plate was cleaned. He ate mostly the chicken fried steak, because he doesn't eat cooked broccoli or fried okra. I had done everything but lick the plate. I joked with the waitress when she cleaned up, "Gee, I didn't care for that at all. Can't you tell?" She laughed, as well.

It was so easy to talk with David and Sally. We talked about our travels, we shared much about our faiths, how we share it with others, by just talking. We don't judge others or quote scripture by the pound. We explain what we do in service for Him. We want others to feel the peace we have in our salvation and desire that peace for themselves. David and Sally have that peace, too. My desire is that my books will help other have that peace, as well.

We didn't want the evening to end, but the restaurant was ready to close. We chatted on the way back to the campground, wondering how we might arrange a way to meet once again.

What a wonderful last day in Texas. On to Oklahoma!

Psalm 122:8
For the sake of my family and friends, I will say,
"Peace be within you."

JANUARY 26

What a fun-filled, amazing day.

David and Sally had told us over supper last night that they take one special weekend a month and drive up from Dallas to the WinStar Casino just across the border into Oklahoma. They had a bunch of coupons they gave us and encouraged us to go, just for fun.

We decided to do just that. The WinStar Casino is in Thackerville, Oklahoma, not far from the Oklahoma-Texas state line, on I-35. The whole place is beyond ginormous! It has eight connected and themed gaming plazas like Paris, Beijing, Rome, Madrid, London, Vienna, Cairo, and New York City. Over 600,000 square feet!

I went to check in at their campground. I asked for a pull-through—they all were. I asked for full hookups—they all have them. I asked for one long enough that I wouldn't have to take the car off the tow dolly—will an 80' site do? Well, yeah. She proceeded to ask if I planned to go to the casino? Of course, why? She explained that if I applied for a Player's Club Card (at no charge), then my campsite will be free. Huh? Well, we were only staying the one night, I explained.

No matter, it would be free. This was too good to be true!

They have been a Good Sam Top Rated Park from 2013 – 2016. Rated 10/10*/10. Larry rated it a 10, too.

We set up quickly and walked to the nearby shuttle stop. When we told the free shuttle driver that we wanted to go to the casino, he asked us which one. He could tell we were confused, then explained that the casino complex was 1 ½ MILES long!

Well, then pick one with a Player's Club Desk nearby.

We quickly signed up for two Player's Club Cards. The nice lady gave us each a lanyard and a large chocolate bar as bonuses. This is getting better and better!

I love to play video slot machines. I don't play them to "win big," I play them for entertainment. The only problem is, if you're not winning, then you're losing…and that does cost money. I budget ahead and budget very small.

We wanted to enjoy the day there, but God knew we are not wasteful people. We walked the entire length of the complex, then found a row of some kind of goldfish games that looked interesting. Larry was sitting at the machine next to me, mumbling some nonsense like, "I never win. This is just a waste of money. Blah, blah, blah." What a grump.

I'm winning and a little up, when he scores a bonus round on his machine. He touches the screen to pick an object, and he wins. He picks another, and wins--bigger. Over and over again. He doesn't understand what's happening, as the machine goes wild, counting up numbers. I lean over and calmly say, "If I read that right, your last pick won you over $450." His eyes met mine and he quietly asked, "Are you kidding me?"

I was not.

By the time the machine quieted, he had won nearly $600 on that bonus round. Then, after playing a bit longer, our Player's Club cards had given each of us a $25 bonus to play, as well.

We had enough "fun money" to play the entire afternoon, on lots of different machines. We lost some, then gained it back.

When supper time came, we had delicious fried catfish, jalapeno corn bread, Cowboy Beans, and fries at Toby Keith's Bar & Grill. Delish!

By the time we boarded a shuttle at 7:30pm, we were down about the price of a movie with concessions. Not a bad price to pay for eight hours of complete, detached, delightful, lights-n-sirens, all the bells and whistles fun.

We don't condone addictive behavior. We would never spend money that should go to bills. We would never play and take food off the table. With that in mind, Christians can have fun, too!

We slept well.

JANUARY 27

The devil must have been upset that we'd had such a good time yesterday, because he sure reared his ugly head at us this morning.

We pulled over to get some diesel. We pulled in behind a trucker, who was just starting to pump, then he looked confused, then went inside the truck stop store, then returned to pump some more, then, who knows where he went? We waited patiently, then it was way too long.

We never did see him finish pumping, he had just disappeared. We pulled out of line and around the truck stop lot to into another line. Finally, it's our turn at the pump! Larry starts to pump, and the debt card's magnetic strip wasn't reading correctly, declined! Then a different debt card was declined! What? We had just crossed state lines and security didn't like that the card was being used in two different states. After numerous calls to the banks and trying to get one of them to work we pumped out $100 worth and left. It still needed 25 or so more gallons.

We saw a good price on more diesel down the road and thought we would pull in to get it topped off. We pulled in through traffic and waiting to turn only to find out the lane we pulled into the pumps had bags on the nozzles. Geesh. We drove back out of the small lot and into traffic. We had enough for now.

I have always been fascinated by weather. I had applied online for tickets for the 1pm tour of the National Weather Center in Norman, Oklahoma, located on the University of Oklahoma campus.

We arrived early, then met Charles, who would take us on our tour. He was a good tour guide, who explained things just technically enough to impress us, but simple enough that we could understand.

I had my moment to shine by asking Charles if a particular rain map was from CoCoRaHS. He was impressed that I even knew about CoCoRaHS and went on to explain to the group about the Community Collaborative Rain, Hail & Snow Network. If you're basically a homebody, and could check a rain gauge every day, you should become a volunteer. I was, for nearly three years. It takes literally about three minutes a day to read and input your data. It was fascinating to observe the wide variances between local gauges, and to discuss the differences on Facebook with other local volunteers. Check out www.CoCoRaHS.org.

We could watch the folks who work for both the NWS Norman and the National Severe Storms Predictions Center. It was a very calm weather day nationwide, so all was quiet. I would never wish for severe weather, but I sure would love to be a bug on the wall in this place when it did.

> Matthew 16:2
> He replied, "When evening comes, you say,
> 'It will be fair weather, for the sky is red,'

Our next destination would be Hot Springs, Arkansas, but it was already 2pm when we left the National Weather Center. One thing we did notice were many of the cars in the parking lot were pock-marked with hail dents. I had not seen one car on this entire trip with such marks, and here in Oklahoma, there were everywhere you looked! We were right in the heart of Tornado Alley, and hail is very often a prelude to tornados. Wow.

After we left the weather center there was another GREAT price on diesel off the expressway before getting into Arkansas. We pulled off to fill it up only to find out that this Great price was for cash only. We paid the six cents higher a gallon for the fuel and filled it up. The Loves truck stops throughout OK were fifty cents higher than this place which means fifty dollars more on a fill up of hundred gallons. No brainer, let's fill it up!

We traveled a couple hours on I-40, then pulled in to boondoggle at a Walmart in Sallisaw, Oklahoma. We were tucked in between two semis, and the trains tonight were much further away. We enjoyed Arby's for the first time in a long time. Yum.

Sweet, sweet sleep.

JANUARY 28

Our travels today brought us to Gulpha Gorge Campground in Hot Springs National Park, Hot Springs, Arkansas, which Larry rated an 8. That's high for a National Park campground. All the sites are cement pads and ours had full utilities, which is unheard of in the National Park System. The park is nice and tidy, and we managed to select a long, paved campsite, backed up to the little babbling creek. With Larry's national Access Pass, we qualified for $15 a night. The utilities were quite a surprise because our greatest hopes were for water and electric. Now I can have a long, hot shower every day and keep the laundry caught up, as well.

"Hot Springs National Park is the smallest and oldest of the parks in the National Park System. It dates back to 1832 when

Congress established (40 years ahead of Yellowstone) the first federally protected area in the nation's history...it was created to protect the 47 naturally flowing thermal springs on the southwestern slope of Hot Springs Mountain."[49] The springs have an average flow rate of 700,000 gallons per day.

We headed into the small metropolis of Hot Springs.

We were fortunate to find a parking space on busy Central Avenue, considering it was Saturday afternoon. It was a chilly day, but there were lots of folks out and about on the well-manicured street.

We had parked directly across from the Bathhouse Row.

There are eight bathhouse buildings there, all constructed between 1892 and 1923. One has been converted to the National Park Service Visitor Center and another to its Cultural Center. One is a restaurant and brewery, one was closed for renovation, and the others all seemed to be doing a bustling business today.

After we crossed the street, we came across a steaming fountain. Of course, we just had to stick our hands in it. I had read that the average temperature of the springs' waters was 143 degrees, so I was careful. Yes, it was HOT! You could only stick your fingers in the fountain for a couple of seconds before pulling away.

We first entered Quapaw Baths & Spa, which opened in 1922. It's the longest on Bathhouse Row, occupying two city sites. We took the free walking tour through the historic part of the Bathhouse. There were large, deep tubs in there, each in a small, private room. There were showers with like 30 heads in them, angled from every direction. There were steam booths to sit in, with

[49] arkansas.com

only your head sticking out. There were preparation rooms as well as cooling rooms. We witnessed how folks 100 years ago, enjoyed bathing in the therapeutic thermal water. The floors and walls still had all its original 1920's mosaic tiles throughout, and beautiful stained glass, as well.

We also visited Buckstaff, just a few doors down. It too, was beautifully decorated inside. Bathhouse Row was designated as a National Historic Landmark District in 1987.

There was a public park with a sign that paid tribute to being the hometown of Bill Clinton, although I'd have to say it was a terrible rendering of him. Maybe it was supposed to be "young" Bill. In the same park is a public fountain from which you can fill all the jugs you want with hot spring water, said to be quite therapeutic. Shops nearby sold empty gallon jugs. The fountain was busy all afternoon.

No trip to Hot Springs would be complete without a dunk in the springs. The private services are too costly for us and much too short (20 minutes), so we'll take an unlimited dip in the common healing waters tomorrow afternoon.

There on the main street, we ate at a nice little Italian restaurant named Angel's and enjoyed the cheesiest lasagna we've ever had. We left a ministry brochure on the table; you just never know how something so small will affect someone's life.

We took a detour and drove up to the highest peak in the park, the Mountain Tower. There's a small charge for riding up to the top, but they were closing in a few minutes, so we couldn't go. Maybe we'll go back another day. Maybe not.

Isaiah 58:11
The LORD will guide you always;
he will satisfy your needs in a sun-scorched land and

> will strengthen your frame.
> You will be like a well-watered garden,
> like a spring whose waters never fail.

Back to the campground for a little satellite TV, but not much.

Good night.

JANUARY 29

From noon to 2pm, we soaked it all up at the Quapaw Baths and Spa. We spent time in all four of the historic pools, which ranged from a comfortable 95 degrees to the lobster boil of 104 degrees. My favorite was the 98-degree pool; even the 102 degrees was too hot for me.

The attendants kept our cups filled with chilled mineral water, which was quite tasty. They also had a mop in one hand always mopping the water up on the floor from the patrons going from pool to pool.

We're not huge believers of the medicinal powers of water, but if God created it, then who am I to doubt? You could actually see the minerals in the clear water. It also had a salty taste to it. So, we relaxed and enjoyed people-watching, which never disappoints.

We indulged in a chicken salad sandwich lunch next to the pools, prepared by their Café. It did seem tastier, perhaps after soaking in the hot spring pools?

While we were eating, we watched a young man bring a typical 5-gallon water dispenser bottle to a spigot on the wall. When it was full, he scooted it aside, and taking a full bottle from a shelf up above.

I asked Larry if he thought that was hot spring water coming out of the wall. We waited until he left and I went over to touch the bottle. Yep, it was really hot. We concluded that the shelf was for allowing the water to achieve room temperature, and that's what they'd been serving us in the pools, iced down.

I always try to say something nice to people in servient jobs. I had spoken to Sandy several times during our visit. When it was time to go, I thanked her once again for all she had done for us that day. She asked me where I was from and explained that she's been in Hot Springs all her life. She wished me well, then insisted we exchange hugs before I left. I happily complied. I hope my words blessed Sandy as much as her actions blessed me.

Back to business, what makes the water hot?

"Water that falls as rain in the recharge or watershed area sinks about a mile deep through faults and fractures. As it goes deep into the earth, it becomes heated by the natural heat gradient of the earth and compression. The hot water then rises quickly through a fault at the base of Hot Springs Mountain. (Our campsite was on the other side of this mountain.)

What's in the Hot Spring hot spring water?

Silica (SiO_2)	53.0
Bicarbonate (HCO_3)	130.00
Calcium (Ca)	47.00
Sulfate (SO_4)	7.8
Magnesium (Mg)	4.9
Sodium (Na)	4.0
Chloride (CI)	2.2

Fluoride (F)	0.26
Potassium (K)	1.4
Oxygen (O2)	4.5
Free Carbon Dioxide (CO2)	9.7

"Radon gas emanation amounts to 43.3 picocuries per liter. This low level of radioactivity is well within safety limits. Exposure to air allows further dissipation of the gas."[50]

> Psalm 104:10
> He makes springs pour water into the ravines;
> it flows between the mountains.

We spent the rest of the afternoon back at the motorhome. I decided to take my presently peaceful self and lay down awhile. Larry finished the book's web site, HisRoadTrip.com picture gallery, and all the social feeds for marketing and communicating with our soon-to-be readers and followers. Maybe you're reading this book because of God's will and Larry's marketing efforts.

We can only hope.

JANUARY 30

Today, I wrote more of the book. Nine nice, quiet hours to write the book. I pray for fluid and productive days like this one. The words came easily and I knew that God was supplying them to me.

I asked Larry to make a Walmart run, and that would get him out of the motorhome for a while. It's not like living in a house with a room dedicated to writing, where you can close the door and

[50]nps.gov/hosp/planyourvisit/frequently-asked-questions-the-hot-spring-water.htm

concentrate. My writing area is the kitchen table, and its right smack in the center of the motorhome—the furthest he can go in here in about ten feet away!

While working on the book, I saw a young lady approach the motorhome, curious about the banner and the packets. She explained that she runs a home for homeless women here in town. She had a lady coming in that very day who had two children, a 4- and a 10-year old. She had one packet in her hand but I insisted she take another, so each child would have their own.

We'll never meet that other woman or her kids, but God arranged for everyone to be in place for this delivery to happen. We pray that God would bless those packets and those lives.

We had meatloaf and mashed potatoes he'd picked up from Sam's Club and a fresh ear of corn. It's out of season, but it was tasty.

When FOX news came on, I simply opened the White Noise app on my iPhone and cranked it up through the earphones. I wrote some more.

It was yet another truly blessed day.

| James 1:19 |
| My dear brothers and sisters, take note of this: |
| Everyone should be quick to listen, slow to speak and |
| slow to become angry |

JANUARY 31

We both got up at 6:15 this morning. The race is on to secure online campground reservations for next January. Yep, eleven months from now. We want to stay in a state park in Key West, Florida because the private parks are, of course, very pricey.

We had no luck today. We'll set the alarms for another early morning tomorrow, to try again, and again, until we secure one.

It was a beautiful day today. The sun was shining and it was near 70 degrees. I spent the day here at the computer, writing and remembering all the amazing things we've seen and done to date.

Once again, I find myself on Google. What an amazing tool, when I've forgotten a specific campground or failed to take photos somewhere. All I do is Google it and poof, there is more information than I will ever need or use. What did we ever do without it?

The windows were open all day and I enjoyed the light breeze that arrived in the afternoon. I did walk outside a couple of times to enjoy the quiet waterway that streams behind us, and again when Larry grilled the rest of the fresh shrimp that we'd bought at the dock in Galveston. Yum.

I cannot believe they preempted NCIS to look at the *Greatest Super Bowl Commercials*. It was cute, but it just wasn't NCIS.

Another beautiful day. Thank you, Jesus.

FEBRUARY 1

Well, the countdown begins—only 2 months left until we see Myrtle Beach again. We were again up early to try to make reservations in Key West, but the result was the same. We will try again tomorrow.

I wrote all day again today. These days were very productive, but I think I'm beginning to suffer from cabin fever. Perhaps I will whine to go out somewhere tomorrow.

Larry's really complaining about his arm today, and I can't wait to get him back to Myrtle Beach to talk to a doctor about it. This has gone on way too long. Maybe some physical therapy would help? And the least little chill makes it hurt worse.

FEBRUARY 2

Yes, Larry agreed that we needed to get out for the day, but it really didn't start out well. We went to the McDonald's in town to have breakfast, but they messed up. Everybody messes up, and having been on the back side of a service counter for much of my life, I'm very patient when someone messes up on me. But the guy behind the counter today wasn't nice at all. In fact, he was just plain rude.

But I wasn't about to let such an uncouth person ruin my day. I would have to pray for him.

After driving past the vast water of the Ouachita River, we went to the Cinema to see *Gold* with Matthew McConaughey. He is an exceptional actor with exceptional range. The movie was very detailed, and it certainly kept my interest.

We had a delightful supper at Olive Garden. I didn't make a note of what we had, but no matter what it was, I know it was delicious. Olive Garden is a favorite with my family. Did you know they offer a low-fat Italian dressing, if you request it? I order it all the time, not because it's low-fat, but because it's not as tangy as the regular stuff. It's great. You should try it.

We were in no hurry to return to the rig, so we went to Walmart, took our time strolling about, and purchased quite a few movies on DVD. They'll come in quite handy when streaming is poor. And from their $3 and $5 bins, they're at least cheaper than buying movie tickets out somewhere.

It had been a well-deserved day away from the motorhome, away from the computer screens. Thank you, Lord. For every day.

FEBRUARY 3

Today was a travel day. A looooong travel day. We started out on US270 southeast to I-30 west to I-49 south, then took some back roads through Alexandria, Louisiana, then on LA1 southeast to Paragon RV Resort and Casino. Larry had chosen this campground because it seemed to be in a nice stopover point while heading south to the Gulf coast, and had an Excellent rating by Good Sam, a 10/10/10.

Larry had a destination in mind, but there was no rush to get there. It was over five hours from Point A to Point B and we could easily take two full drive days to get there.

We'd gotten up at 6:30am again to try to get reservations in Key West, to no avail. We were already up, so we might as well get going. We'd hit the half-way mark well before noon, so we decided to stop to nuke something for lunch, then keep going.

The change of scenery again was quite obvious. We'd come further south today and spring is already in evidence. The azaleas are beginning to bloom and if you look hard, the deciduous trees that line the interstate have started to bud.

We finally arrived at Paragon Casino and RV Resort in Marksville, Louisiana, which Larry rated a 9. We were disappointed to learn that the pool was outside and not heated. And they didn't have a hot tub. That's why we rated it a 9—what good is a pool when you can't swim in it?

Even though it's only in the 50's today, we can pretty much do a hot tub in any kind of weather. We had one at the house and went out there plenty of times when it was 40 degrees outside. We just made sure to keep the towels close and dashed right back inside. But they reassured us that if we wanted to use the pool inside the hotel, we could pay a small daily fee to do so. No, thanks.

But you couldn't beat the price. I had checked some reviews online before we arrived, and the nightly fees that were listed were between $16 and $28. Really? One of the reviews said the resort took Passport America, so I asked specifically when I registered.

That Passport America card saved me fifty percent on this five-day stay. I paid $80—like $16 a day. And the place is beautiful. For the price, we decided to stay here a total of 5 nights, since we had some time before our next reservations.

Although they have 24/7 shuttle service at your door, we chose to drive our car over to the casino after we set up. It was Friday night, and the place was hopping. Larry had established a strict small budget for today's slot machines and with the $15 free credit the casino gave us for signing up for a Player's Card, it took us about an hour to polish it off. Slot machines are always great entertainment.

But before we settled on playing a machine, we walked the entire floor, past the restaurants and over to the hotel.

As we were walking past the first restaurant, Big Daddy E's, I noticed a large platter of crayfish on display by their entrance. I knew what they were, but neither of us had ever eaten them. Growing up, we had crawdads that would burrow muddy holes in the backyard. I wondered if they were the same creatures.

A man was walking away from the display, and I called him back. His nametag read Chris. I think he was a manager. I explained that we were raised on Ohio and lived the past twenty years in South Carolina. We had never had crayfish before. Would he please explain how they're eaten?

He picked one up and showed us right then and there how to eat them. Larry asked how they taste (lobster) and how they're prepared (in a spicy shrimp boil).

I explained we had just arrived and promised to return.

Well, we wandered over to the hotel, where we learned they had alligators. Sure enough, there was a whole collection of them. Most were dried off and laying on large lighted rocks; some were floating in the water. We had read they have a feeding for the public on Saturdays. I wonder what time? We finally went back to the casino and played the machines.

And, we did indeed go back to Big Daddy E's and ordered crayfish for supper. They brought us a platter piled high, identical to the display we'd seen. They were red in color with ugly little heads, legs, pinchers, a mini lobster-type body and tail, and 2 beady little black eyes staring back at us. The tails did taste like lobster and were a little on the hot and spicy side. We concluded that the shrimp boil they use is spicier than the one I use to make Frogmore Stew. We were told that crayfish are sometimes called freshwater lobsters.

They were also served with a small loaf of delicious bread, two boiled potatoes, and a small ear of corn. We ate it all. For the record, when I posted pics of our dinner on Facebook, my friends asked if we'd sucked the heads. No, we did not, nor will we ever suck the heads. There will be no further discussion of sucking heads.

We signaled Chris back to the table when we'd finished and thanked him for explaining things so well earlier. I would have never tried them, if he hadn't been so kind in explaining them.

Upon questioning, he explained that crayfish are very popular in French cooking where they're called écrevisses. In the US, harvest comes from the waters of the Mississippi basin, and many Louisianans call their state the "crayfish capital of the world".

Crayfish can be prepared in most manners appropriate for lobster and, like lobster, turn bright red when cooked. They're usually eaten with the fingers, and the sweet, succulent meat must be picked or sucked out of the tiny shells. He also said they are grown on plantations in rice fields as a second crop. Being a freshwater animal and digging themselves into the mud during the summer months, they come out in the colder months, making them a seasonal food.

Larry left our brochure and seed packet for the waitress in the hopes she reads it and it affects her life in a big way.

When we got back to the motorhome, we discovered two letters left for us. We thought, who could these be from? They had been written by two little girls and left on our motorhome steps. By the way, those steps have been working just fine since we replaced the motor back in Zion National Park.

Sophia said she was 9 years old. She and her friend, Lauralee had each written a letter, using all different crayon colors. They wanted to tell us how happy they were in getting the "Jesus" gifts, and thanked us for giving them. They had helped themselves to the free packets, hanging off the front mirror. They wrote that they hoped that God would bless us. Their innocence brought tears to our eyes.

This is why we do what we do. We usually never know who has taken our kids packets or what it meant to them. Now we know that these 2 have certainly blessed Sophia and Lauralee.

FEBRUARY 4

We were up again at 6:30am to attempt to reserve campsites in Key West for next year. In the blink of an eye, they were gone again. I went back to bed.

Getting up at a much more reasonable hour, I spent the rest of the day writing. It was cool outside and we had the heat pumps on all day. We hope it will warm up tomorrow.

Not much other news to report today, but we got some neighbors last night. My writing "window" offers me a full view of their comings and goings. They sure don't sit still, let me say that. Between a large dog and a tiny little dog, their golf cart, and their diesel dually, someone is always coming or going.

I did watch with interest as they returned from an errand in the truck, and began covering their picnic table with a large trash bag, then a bunch of smaller, carryout bags. Finally, they brought a large carryout bag from their fifth-wheel and dumped its contents on the bagged table. Crayfish! If Larry and I had shared three pounds at dinner the other night, they had at least twice that much! It took them a good hour to finish them off. They picked up the corners of the large trash bag and zero cleanup. What a great idea! That just might come in handy someday.

We ate Stouffers and watched a DVD we'd bought, Will Smith in *Focus*. I'd never seen it before. It was a "just which con is conning which con" thief movie. You had to pay attention; it was pretty good.

After Larry went to bed, I continued to work on the book. I'm getting to the final edits for parts of the first book, with my gifted niece Jana giving priceless assistance to her old aunt. I sure don't have many connections in my life, but I thank God for the ones I have.

I'm finally allowing myself to get excited about this!

FEBRUARY 5

We were up again at 6:30am. Same drill, same results. at 6:59:59 EST, "The date you have selected cannot be reserved at this time. Please try again later at 8:00 AM Feb 9 EST." Literally one second later it says, "Inventory is not available. Site cannot be booked." We'll be up again tomorrow, to try again. Sigh.

All went well until about noon, when Larry came to the horrible conclusion that his computer had died—again—after an automatic update for Windows 10.

It had taken him days back in April to get everything loaded back in. But now he had all 8,000 photos of the trip, the book website—so much more was at risk of being lost forever. He was on my computer as well as the laptop, trying to get assistance; to see if there was any other way than starting over from scratch. It was hours later, but the final diagnosis was grim. Wipe it clean and start over.

It was a grueling day for Larry. And considering our computers are only like eight feet away from each other, my day was pretty grueling, too. I helped when I could, but that was very little. All that computer mumbo jumbo is way out of my league. My duty as a wife was to stay out of the way. And that, I did.

To get everything back on track, we would require decent wifi, just like before. We were here in a campground in central Louisiana, and had been here since Friday. The internet has not been that great. But God had once again gone before us, so that when much of the crowd left Sunday and Monday, the wifi became much speedier. Could we indeed complete everything with their Wifi?

By late afternoon and a few more phone calls, he was on the road to recovery. Praise the Lord that everything had been safely updated to Carbonite within hours prior to the crash. He began the Restore. It would take perhaps days to complete, but at least it was downloading.

I nuked a Stouffers stuffed green peppers and mashed potatoes for supper. Another A+ for Stouffers.

By supper, he was in so much pain. I do concur that stress exacerbates myositis pain, and his left "frozen shoulder" was killing him from being at the computer all day. We started a movie, but he lasted about fifteen minutes before he took a sleeping pill and went to bed.

That left me up alone to listen to the crowd at a nearby cabin howling loudly for the Super Bowl. Sorry, but if the Bengals aren't playing, I really don't much care who wins.

I wish my duty as a wife could also include taking away pain. Larry has prayed and asked God to remove this pain, but the Scripture explains that there is reason for pain:

FEBRUARY 6

We were up again at 6:30, and our efforts bore the same pathetic results. This is so frustrating. There must be thousands of people trying to secure reservations at these prime campgrounds during the winter months. It just by the luck of which computer the server picks as the winners of today's sites.

Today was my step-mom's birthday; she would have been 91 glorious years old. I miss you mom…I really do.

Today was a much better day. It was sunny and well into the 70's outside, so today we had the air conditioners running all day. It would have been a great day to ride bikes, but there was so much work to be done.

Larry's computer is still slowly downloading, and for that I am so grateful. There has been no interruption in service, so things are progressing well.

Since he's able to work on many of his programs already, that allows me to work on the book. In the quiet, with no drama going on around me. He told me that since we've been cooped up for days, we'll probably go out somewhere tomorrow, and eat dinner out. So, I edited and edited some more, then wrote.

It turned out to be a much better day than I'd originally feared. Thank you, Lord.

FEBRUARY 7

This 6:30am stuff has got to end sometime. I am just not a morning person! But we still have no reservations, so we will be up again early tomorrow.

I did go back to sleep, but Larry woke me up an hour later, loudly asking me if I knew where the camera software disc was. I told him where it should be. No, he'd looked there. I reluctantly got up, knowing there would be no peace until it was found. I found it, of course—exactly where I had said it would be. He was looking for the box it came in, not the disk that I took out of it.

Since I was up, I checked my phone to discover that we were under a tornado watch. I guess it's time to put new batteries in the weather alert radio, huh? There were indeed multiple tornadoes that passed through the next hour, but thankfully they passed east and south of us. I learned later that New Orleans was hit exceptionally hard by other tornados. I praised God that no one died. Thanks for that hedge of protection again, Lord.

Yesterday, Larry had promised a day away from the motorhome. It hit 4pm and we were both still working tediously on our computers. I Googled for "restaurants nearby" and found one of particular interest. I couldn't pronounce it, but it was called "Fresh Catch Bistreaux / Broken Wheel Brewery. (bistro?) The reviews were good, it was only a couple of miles away, so off we went.

We chose a seafood plate with fried shrimp and crayfish. It was served atop a plateful of big waffle fries and coleslaw. We were pleasantly surprised when it came, because the crayfish had already been tailed and the tails had been breaded and deep-fried. Little fried tidbits of spicy crayfish that you could just pop in your mouth. Now that was a whole lot less work!

Everything was delicious. Louisiana does know how to spice up food.

FEBRUARY 8

We were up again at 6:30am. Still a no-go on Florida winter reservations. Sigh.

I took my arthritis pills and laid down for another thirty minutes, but then it was time to get up and get this show on the road. We had a three-hour trip to our next stop.

I've explained that we now have three navigation devices. This newest one is designed to assist high-profile vehicles, like our motorhome. After much discussion about Frick and Frack, Larry suggested we name this one Frank. I agreed.

We assumed Frank would keep us mostly on interstates but mostly on I-49 south. Well, today's trip was an exercise in doing quite the opposite. I didn't keep track, but I could safely bet that our trip today took us on at least FIFTY road changes. One mile on this road, turn left for three miles on this road, I think we drove seven miles on one—this went on and on. It was ridiculous, and many of the roads were not suited at all for the big rigs. Some of Louisiana's roads are in badly need of repair, as was the case in California and Arizona, lots of pot holes and bumps from former road patch jobs. Larry drove down the middle of the road some of the time to miss the crumbling berms. Before we move day after tomorrow, we really need to check the settings for selecting routes.

It was a lovely day for travel. The big storms that flew through yesterday washed the air clean and everything seemed so much brighter today. The land here is so flat, but fertile. Many fields were tilled, and some were already planted with crops I didn't recognize, but were already a foot high.

We will eventually wind up in New Orleans by Mardi Gras. We have visited the city once before, for only a few hours. One thing we did see then were the downtown cemeteries. Well, we passed many cemeteries today, far out in the rural areas. Even though we knew why they must be above ground in New Orleans, we didn't realize there would be so many crypts and above-ground vaults this far upstate. But then again, checking Frank, we were only a foot or two above sea level. They were really something to see.

It was clear that spring has sprung here. There were all sorts of brilliant yellow wildflowers along the roads. Many trees not only had buds on them, some even had new leaves. The trees were showing their spring green color as leaves had begun to come out from the dead of winter. The tulip trees, daffodils, and azaleas are all in bloom. There was color everywhere.

We saw all sorts of new things, including hundreds of acres of rice paddies. The paddies were flooded with water, of course, and nearly all of them had little crayfish traps bobbing in straight rows. The man who had taught us how to eat the little "mud bugs" the other night had told us about these dual-purpose rice fields. By late afternoon, we saw flatboats in the paddies, with folks pulling up the traps for the day's catch.

We did have just a moment of trouble. We had stopped at a Walmart on the route to get supplies. When we came back, we decided to eat lunch before getting back on the road. Larry started the generator, but instead of the microwave coming to life, we heard a loud clicking noise coming from the back of the rig. It was the transfer switch again, that Rex had fixed for us a few months earlier when we had all the electrical problems outside of Grand Canyon. Larry went outside to check it out, reset it, then came back inside. We shut down the generator and waited. Several minutes later, we cranked it up and everything worked as it should. Hmmm. Hope this isn't another problem, rearing its ugly head.

We finally arrived at Palmetto Island State Park, in Abbeville, Louisiana, that Larry rated a 7. The sites are large, with water and electric. Our handicap site was twice as wide as the other campsites and perfectly leveled concrete. The entire park is well-maintained, and they've allowed enough natural landscape—mostly palmettos—that the sites were nicely separated, some even secluded. They have nice bathrooms and showers, a free laundromat, as well as multiple picnic pavilions, canoe and boat launches, tent pads, and cabins. They even had a splash water park for the kids (in warmer weather). It was quite an exceptional state park.

Exodus 15:27

[27] Then they came to Elim,
where there were twelve springs and seventy palm trees,
and they camped there near the water.

The first thing I simply had to do when we arrived was to defrost the freezer. It was full and I had to remove everything, so it was scattered all over my little kitchen. It takes about a half-hour with my hair dryer, and it was done. By then, my neck and back were hurting, so I celebrated my accomplishment with an ice pack, lying down on the bed. It's such a pity to get old!

I made homemade potato soup with a new recipe for supper tonight. It called for a Crock Pot, but I only have room to store a little, tiny one. I only made a half-batch, and made it on the stove.

Larry complimented it twice, which means he *really* liked it. I apologize that I cannot give credit to the source of the recipe, but I found it on Facebook. I included it in the back of the book.

We drove around the park for a little bit, just to see what was here. They have signs for "don't feed the alligators" and "look out for bears", but there was no wildlife to be seen today. Maybe in the morning…

Larry had been up since 4am, worried about the backup for his computer. With hours of driving today, he was beat and went to bed extra early. I enjoyed the quiet, listened to the air conditioners run, and got some more writing done.

It's been a truly wonderful day.

FEBRUARY 9

We were up again at 6:30am. Same request, same response. Back to bed for me.

By 9am, we were walking out the door, headed for the Tabasco Factory Tour. We stopped at the office to see if anyone had cancelled their reservations for Friday and Saturday, because there were none available when we checked in. "You're in luck!" the state park lady told me. Site 23 is now available for both nights. I told her that I would take it.

She and the other lady told me that they couldn't reserve the site for me for tomorrow, I would have to do it online. Politely, I reminded them I knew they could make reservations here, as I just walked in myself yesterday.

The said, "No, that's because you arrived here on the same day that you wanted to reserve. We can do that. Well, you can wait until tomorrow morning to reserve it here, but it will probably be gone."

Geesh. This state park reservation stuff is getting to be for the birds. But wait, it gets better.

They found a site that had cancelled for tonight, AND for Friday and Saturday. They could move today's registration to 23, then we'd be in for the whole weekend. Great. So, I paid for the next two nights, then walked outside to tell Larry all about the change of plans.

We drove the car back to site 45, driving right past site 23. Wait, there's someone in it. That's not unusual at 9:30am, considering checkout isn't until 1pm. I drove back to the office to explain that we were planning on being gone all afternoon. We couldn't move now, because there were still people there, and I knew we couldn't leave the rig on 45 until we got back, in case they needed to check someone else into it.

So, she finally understood and suggested we park the rig at the nature center. Fine. We went back to our original campsite, brought in everything and was ready to move. Now keep in mind that moving 100 feet requires the same preparation as moving 100 miles. We moved it to the nature center and finally left for the tour.

It was another day of goofy navigation for Frack. It took us through probably twenty-five changes of back roads. One included a U-turn because of a three-way intersection and another U-turn because the road was closed. As in permanently closed.

We finally arrived at Avery Island, Louisiana. You all know the brand Tabasco. It's a fifth-generation company that's been making pepper sauce since 1868—right here in Avery Island. It's distributed around the world. We saw a display of bottles in about forty different languages.

We paid our over-55 rate, given a couple of stickers to put on our shirts and a receipt. "When you finish the tour, take the receipt to the Gift Shop and they'll give you each a free gift." The grounds are clean, well-manicured, and well-maintained. In fact, it almost looks like the whole place is brand new. There were seven stops on the self-tour and they were well marked.

We got to see a sampling of pepper plants in the greenhouse first. Next were displays and videos to get an idea of how pepper mash is made, barreled, then aged for three years. We could see the aging barrels, hundreds of them. We saw the vats where the pepper mash is strained and mixed with vinegar. Then we watched in amazement how the clear bottles begin on the fill line, then automatically filled, capped, labeled, shrink-sealed, and run off the line. Absolutely amazing. I studied closely at a picture they had hanging on the wall in the bottling facility: It was taken decades ago, and showed a man and a woman on the line, their entire jobs were screwing on little red caps. That was before carpel tunnel syndrome became an official work hazard.

We went to the Gift Shop when we were finished, to claim our "gifts", which turned out to be six itsy-bitsy bottles of three flavors of Tabasco Sauce. The shop was filled with candies, mugs, T-shirts and hoodies, tableware and so much more, all bearing the Tabasco brand.

We had never in our lives tried the hot sauce, assuming it was way too hot for us. They had a tasting bar of everything they made: sauces, jellies, steak sauce, mustards and catsup, salsas, even pickles and olives. We were pleasant surprised, and even purchased a bottle of their newest flavor "Sweet & Spicy" Pepper Sauce. It's the first sauce designed to "dip". Try some, you'll be surprised.

It was lunch time, so we went into their 1868 restaurant right next door. The menu was filled with all sorts of things, but I like samplers—a little bit of this and that. We ordered the Pierogi Sampler with a Diet Coke. It included three items: shrimp etouffee, red beans and rice, and chicken and sausage gumbo. It was all delicious, and Larry tried each one with Tabasco Sauce, as well.

Frack decided that there would be only three route changes on our return trip. Why it didn't take that route to get there, I will never know. Only Frack knows.

A Cajun supermarket was on the way back, so we went inside to see what other goodies there were inside. They had way more stuff than I could list here, but I decided to purchase two new things: a Pork Boudin and some Pork Syrup Patties. I'll let you Google those. We grilled some of both for dinner later and they were both very good. Larry liked them even better with Tabasco! I think he will be adding Tabasco to everything he eats now.

Genesis 9:3
Everything that lives and moves about will be food for you.
Just as I gave you the green plants,
I now give you everything.

Well, we were in for another surprise when we returned to the campground. We stopped at the nature center to get the rig and drove it straight to site 23. And the same people are still in it. It was well after 2pm and checkout was at 1pm. I called out as I approached the trailer from my car, and with their dog barking ferociously, a woman came out. I asked politely, "are you leaving today?" And she answered no. I politely responded that we had a problem then, because the office had assigned the site to us. She explained that she had come in late the evening before, after the office was closed. A campground host had taken her information and put her on site 23 for the night, and gave her instructions to register with the office and pay her fee this morning, which she failed to do.

I heard her telling the office on the phone that it would take her at least 2 ½ hours to move, that there was a baby, and her son was doing homework, blah, blah. I think she wanted the office to redirect us instead.

To make a long story kinda short, we were instructed to pull in a nearby site and wait. We didn't get settled until about 3:30.

Then, Larry couldn't get the rooftop satellite dish to get a signal through the trees, so, he brings out the freestanding satellite. It's a two-man job—one inside, one outside—that we worked on for the next hour. After all that, he determines there will be no satellite for the next three days. It's a good thing that we had bought more DVD's on our last trip to Walmart.

While Larry was still outside with the satellite, the little boy from the trespassing trailer (who is now two doors down), approached Larry from behind. He was probably eight or nine. He was holding his arms to his chest, and I thought he'd been hurt. I hollered and motioned to Larry, who finally saw the boy. I went outside to see what was wrong. He was telling Larry that his mother had gone on an errand and said she'd be back in fifteen minutes. She still hadn't returned. He was all alone and trembling like a leaf. He admitted to me that he was scared.

He was scared but he had felt safe to come to us, having met us earlier in the day. There were other campers closer, but he knew just where to find us. See, God did have a plan in all this confusion.

We assured him that I would stay with him until his mother returned, which I did. I grabbed a Kid's Packet, and as we walked back to his site to wait, I learned his name was Hunter and he was from Colorado.

When we sat down at his picnic table, he excitedly tore into the Packet. He unashamedly proclaimed that he loved God and had learned about Him every day in Bible camp. We talked all about Operation Christmas Child. He was an excellent reader and I told him so. He knew all about the stories on the coloring sheets, and explained in detail the story of Peter walking on water with Jesus. He was so excited that he forgot he was afraid, until his mother finally returned.

God bless Hunter. Now who received the bigger blessing? Hunter or me?

> Matthew 14:28-32
>
> "Lord, if it's you," Peter replied, "tell me to come to you on the water." 29 "Come," he said.
> Then Peter got down out of the boat,
> walked on the water and came toward Jesus.
> 30 But when he saw the wind,
> he was afraid and, beginning to sink, cried out,
> "Lord, save me!"
> 31 Immediately Jesus reached out his hand and caught him.
> "You of little faith," he said, "why did you doubt?"
> 32 And when they climbed into the boat, the wind died down.

After dinner, I tried to use my FoodSaver to package the rest of the syrup patties for the freezer. Larry spent an hour, even taking it apart, trying to coax it to work. I guess we'll call customer service tomorrow.

In addition to all our adventures today, we watched an entire Denzel Washington movie, *Inside Man.* It also had Clive Owen and Jodie Foster in it. I certainly held my attention.

But now, I am so ready for bed. Gotta get up early. You know the drill.

FEBRUARY 10

God bless Larry—he allowed me to sleep through the reservation moment this morning. I guess he assumed it was so futile, there was no reason for both of us to be up at that hour. He was right, same results.

He went ahead and made reservations in other Florida State Parks for next winter, as allowed. They only allow a year reservation window. Even then, with winter snowbirds they fill up fast. He also made reservations for the upcoming summer while we are in northeastern USA and Canada. It's best to have reservations in place anytime school is out, or you may not get to stay where you want. He'll try again later for the Key West area for winter 2018.

I called the Food Saver folks this morning and they were very nice. The CSR (Customer Service Representative) looked up some little number that was stamped on the plug prong (of all places), then told me how to return it for a replacement. She asked me where I bought it, but didn't ask me when. Good deal.

No satellite reception is turning out to be a blessing. Larry did find some local channels with the regular antenna, but it's all daytime silly stuff. This quite peace is so nice, we're both at separate computers, just working away.

I warmed up leftover potato soup from the other night. I added a little milk, then nuked it. I think it was even better than the first time.

The campground is getting busy. The campground staff had told me at check in that there's a Dutch Oven Club that comes the second weekend of every month. They fill up the place to camp, then on Saturday morning, they take over Pavilion One, show their Dutch Ovens to everyone, then feed everyone—for free. We had three big fifth-wheels set up right across from us. I can't wait to see what they'll be cooking.

---

2 Samuel 17:29
honey and curds, sheep, and cheese from cows' milk
for David and his people to eat.
For they said, "The people have become exhausted
and hungry and thirsty in the wilderness."

FEBRUARY 11

When we looked outside this morning, kids were riding bikes everywhere. The warm day had a sky mixed with clouds and sunshine, with a slight breeze. It was warm, considering it was only February. We hadn't seen this many kids since Christmas break and before that, last summer. We hope and pray they clean us out of packets.

We got in the car about 10am and drove to the Pavilion area to see what the Dutch Oven folks were all about. It turns out that it was the second-Saturday-of-every-month gathering of the Latanier Cookers Dutch Oven Club, a member of the Louisiana Dutch Oven Club. Before we arrived, neither of us had even known for sure just what a Dutch Oven was.

There were over a dozen cookers scattered over the area. Each cooking team had tables, some had tents, all were cooking something, some even three or four things. We walked up to the cooker closest to where we parked and introduced ourselves, "We're not from anywhere around here. Would you please explain all of this to us?"

The man explained that each person here was preparing something different, to be served at noon today to everyone who attended. He lifted the lid of his cast-iron Dutch Oven and showed us where he had cooked a whole chicken to such tenderness, that when he'd tried to get it out, it had fallen apart. This is going to be good.

We moved only a few feet away and encountered a couple dressed up for Mardi Gras, complete with masks, and giving out strings of beads. He was trying to give us the official colors of Mardi Gras. I didn't know what those colors were, and he admitted to me he was color-blind, so I didn't know to question when he gave us each a set of green, gold, and pink.

The official colors are actually purple, green, and gold, which represent respectively, justice, faith, and power.

We walked entirely around the area, speaking to each cooker. There were amazing things at each one: shrimp gumbo, red beans and rice, dirty rice, spaghetti, penne, yeast rolls, vegetables, pineapple upside-down cake, cherry pie, peach cobbler, berry cobbler, and lots of other things I just can't remember! All of this was prepared in these Dutch Ovens with hot coals. When noon came, someone said a blessing. My heart swelled as I stood with this group, praying as one to lift up praise to the Lord, and to ask His blessing on everything we were about to eat. Everything was homemade and prepared just that morning.

I took a spoonful of just about everything and ate every crumb. The guy cooking the Shrimp Gumbo was using a 30-gallon Dutch Oven Pot, and telling us in his French accent "that his recipe was for 200 people". The culture of the people in Louisiana is loving food and being friendly. And, being friendly with food! We have met the friendliest folks in this state. We have tasted and loved their foods. I just love hearing their French accent; it is so different from other parts of the country.

Deuteronomy 12:7
There, in the presence of the LORD your God,
you and your families shall eat and shall rejoice
in everything you have put your hand to,
because the LORD your God has blessed you.

There was an alligator in the swampy pond next to the pavilion. He was enjoying the sun, as he kept a close eye on all the commotion around him. They had been selling raffle tickets all morning, but when they called all the numbers after lunch, Larry and I didn't win a thing. Oh, well.

We drove back to the cool motorhome and I wrote for a little while, while Larry took a nap on the couch. Here we were in the deep South, Louisiana Bayou country with the AC working hard to keep us cool. We had been enjoying a picnic in shorts! The poor north is recovering from a winter blizzard. I think I like this weather a whole lot better, wouldn't you?

Larry finally got up, but I decided it was time for me to take a nap, too. More writing, then a quick dinner of Stouffers Chicken Rice Bake. We can't get satellite reception here, but we did manage to find three local channels on our "normal" antenna. The TV show *COPS* was showing on one, and we watched for a while. I cannot believe what this world is coming to!

It's so very sad what folks do to themselves, and allow others to do to them. The world is a very scary place, especially when people you come in contact with don't know Him. It is a completely different world from ours. The violence, the crime, the abuse, the drugs…if they only knew Him, and lived among others who knew Him, their lives would be so much better.

Ecclesiastes 8:12
Although a wicked person who commits a hundred crimes may live a long time, I know that it will go better with those who fear God, who are reverent before him.

Once we had finished supper, and when we had seen quite enough TV, we went outside and Larry built a camp fire out of wood others had left behind. Lightning bugs graced the night swamp area as well as mosquitoes. We haven't seen mosquitoes for months, and I failed to use any spray. Oh, my goodness, they ate me alive, those little blood suckers! When I came in, I headed straight for a peppermint shower, lots of Sea & Ski, and a whole, entire Benadryl. I should sleep well tonight.

We settled down to watch a Will Smith movie, *Hitch*. We had seen it before, but it was a long time ago. It was cute to see it again, and we had a good time laughing.

As I sat and wrote some more before bedtime, I could hear the happy campers in a deep Louisianan French accent, just across from us. They were gathered around their campfire and having a great time. They had this huge TV screen attached to their camper with a projection on it of a Basketball game. They were having a great time watching the game, laughing and talking. *COPS* made me so sad, but this campground stuff makes me happy. This had been another awesomely, wonderfully, blessed day.

FEBRUARY 12

Larry was up early as usual. He is a morning person. So were the kids in the campground. They were all riding their bikes by 8am.

Today would be a travel day to Gibson, Louisiana to the Hideaway Ponds Recreational Resort, which Larry rated a 2. There was no interstate to take today. We had no alternative but to take back roads from the campground to LA82 north to LA14 south, then back on US90 south.

Driving the long stretch of US 90 was absolutely terrible. Perhaps a car would ride it better, but in the motorhome, it was awful. It's poured concrete, and concrete is usually better than asphalt, because it's not going to be full of potholes. But concrete is laid in sections. And every single time we drove across a seam in the concrete—like every second—we bumped, we tipped a bit, and the motorhome creaked and groaned in protest. The bridges were the only things that were smooth-going. We were both sure ready to get off that road! Note to Louisiana, Fix the road!

We finally arrived at Hideaway Ponds, deep into the Bayou.

We had used Coast to Coast points to enable us to prepay a $10 daily rate. We've participated in this program before, and some of the campgrounds have been really nice for that price. But others have been mediocre, at best. This one was definitely mediocre. We had already paid for the campsite, so we were expecting only a small bill to pay for cable and sales tax. But wait.

I told her that we preferred a pull through site. Oh, that will be $5 a day extra. The cable fee was $3 a day extra, and you can't opt out. I emphasized that I had to have 50 amps (to do laundry and run heat at the same time). Oh, that will be $5 extra. And then the wifi-Fi, for which I had to pay $25 for two computers for a week. To stay five days, I paid a total of $138 (plus points) for a gravel site, so-so wifi and poor snowy cable. Oh, well. I already know we won't be back to this part of Louisiana again and most definitely, not this campground.

We leave our reviews on campgrounds on social media and in Allstays, our campground app. Larry even wrote Coast to Coast, customer service about this one. People watched Larry put up our banner and kid packets. They were openly curious, and many stopped on their golf carts to get some free packets. I sure hope they did some good here.

I started with the bedsheets and ran that poor washer all day long. I got some more writing done and fixed supper.

We were parked in trees, so we couldn't get satellite, and settled for cable. It had FOX news, but the reception was terrible. And, what is it with golf carts? People were riding them all around the campground—and this place wasn't all that big.

There was this one guy riding around with a boom box blaring music from the rear. Around and around in circles he drove, all day long. Up this lane then down the next. Perhaps it was his self-appointed job to provide background music for the place. Or perhaps he was the Neighborhood Watch, I just don't know.

Larry went to bed early, because his shoulder was hurting him so bad. I wrote a bit, then played a couple of video games. I really need to pack my NCIS first eleven seasons when we get back home. Then I'll have something to watch every night, at least for a while.

FEBRUARY 13

Today was spent inside. Larry has a schedule in his mind for the book, so the book takes precedence over everything else right now. I knew this would happen. I did get a lot of writing done.

I wanted a break in the afternoon, and Frack informed me that there was a Dollar General only six miles away. I told Larry I was going there, without discussion. It was a quiet drive, hardly passing anyone else on the roads. It was a nice store, where I stocked up on impulse foods that diabetics shouldn't be eating. As long as I don't eat them all at once, I'll be just fine.

After dinner, there was a knock on the door. A lady was asking Larry about Motorhome Ministry, as she had taken three packets for family members. She was very nice and appreciated the packets. Larry explained what we did. He shared several stories of Him in his life. He could tell that she was a Christian but wanted to know more.   She asked questions in the French accent of the Louisiana Bayou.

1 Corinthians 6:19
Do you not know that your bodies are temples
of the Holy Spirit, who is in you,
whom you have received from God?
You are not your own

Larry checked the packet hook to realize that they were almost all gone now, and we spent the next hour making more. At least God proved a purpose for our being in this little, sad campground.

We watched the crummy cable until Bill O'Reilly was over, then Larry headed to bed. I began to edit and write some more until I realized it was nearly midnight, so I headed to bed, too.

FEBRUARY 14

I hadn't gotten to sleep until 3am, when I finally took a sleeping pill. I'd had way too much caffeine yesterday, me thinks. I had left Larry a note as to why I'd be sleeping late, but he hadn't seen it and came crashing in to tell me that I was sleeping my life away. I was sure wide awake then!

Happy Valentine's Day! Over the years, we have mutually agreed that using hard-earned money for a card that takes us thirty seconds to read or flower that will die, is just foolish for us. We just bank the money and use it for other pleasures on other days.

John 13:34-35
"A new command I give you: Love one another.
As I have loved you, so you must love one another.
35 By this everyone will know that you are my disciples,
if you love one another."

Today was also an anniversary, of sorts. Exactly one year ago today, I had my second surgery on my neck. At that time, it would have been impossible to imagine where we would be today. God is so good!

We headed to the nearest town, Thibodaux, Louisiana, to ship the Food Saver for a replacement. It was a pleasant little town, with lots of fast food restaurants. Frack took us directly to a handy little place called Ship N Geaux, (get it? Ship N Go) and the nice lady quickly took care of my request. With no more business to tend to, we headed to the local Walmart to stock up.

Easy Ship is back in business and Larry tried to do a shop while I shopped my list. I had nearly everything on my list when he caught up with me. He needed my assistance for the mindless task of holding open each and every door of the ice cream section so he could take a picture. This store had like thirty doors of ice cream.

By the time we got everything in the car, it was threatening to let loose a deluge of rain at any moment. Larry drove at breakneck speed back to the campground, trying to beat the storm, and we did.

Frack gave us a turn on a gravel road for several miles. Why? We do not know. Frack just made up the turn, we could have stayed on the current road before the turn and arrived at the same place. The gravel road ran between two fields of crops. It did give us a closer look at the farmer's plantings. We had been wondering what was planted in the fields locally. We could now tell they were onions.

The predicted severity of the storms passed east of us, thank you, Lord. We got a little rain, but all the lightning was focused somewhere else.

After we ate, I asked Larry to go up to the indoor hot tub with me. It was in a big building with a high, unfinished metal roof, along with their indoor pool. It was dark outside and the building was poorly lit inside. Although heated, the pool was too cold for either of us, so we headed into the hot tub. It was large, and the temperature was nice. But there was gravel all in it, maybe tracked in from outside? We stayed about a half hour, then went back to the motorhome. Not a great experience, but the water sure felt good.

The place was pretty dingy looking. This place was supposed to be a resort. Not! But, God had led us here for His reasons, and the great number of packets we handed out were proof of that. Sometimes we never know why, we just do it. Let Him guide us and you.

The wifi was good enough to stream Netflix for a couple of hours. Larry found a series named *Travelers* with Eric McCormack and we watched the first couple of episodes. It was good, and we plan to watch some more.

When Larry went to bed, I did, too.

FEBRUARY 15

I woke up this morning with plans to edit and write again all day. I tentatively finished the Dedication, the Forward, and the Back of the Book. I'll read it all again tomorrow and probably change it all.

The cold front that blew in with the storm last evening took today's high down about thirty degrees from yesterday—low in the 50's today. No reason to go outside, anyway. Larry decided to dig into 2016 business and personal tax returns today. He loaded the Turbo Tax software for each and then came the tedious calculations and input. He keeps detailed records during the year, but returns still take a lot of time.

I sure wish they would do away with all this deduction for this, tax for that. We're all in favor of a simple federal sales tax. If you buy something big, you pay the percentage tax on it. If you buy something small, you pay the same percentage tax on it. But that's just my simple-minded opinion. So, Larry spent the afternoon doing our personal return. I still have to review business books before he can even begin that one.

Romans 13:7

> Give to everyone what you owe them:
> If you owe taxes, pay taxes; if revenue, then revenue;
> if respect, then respect; if honor, then honor.

I put a new little recipe in the mini Crock Pot today. It was kinda like meatloaf with garlic, sliced tomatoes and potatoes. I enjoyed it. Larry's brutally honest when it comes to trying new things, and even he liked it.

Nothing much exciting happening today.

We watched a $3 DVD I'd picked up, *The Numbers Station* with John Cusack. I'd never heard of it, but I like most everything with John in it. It was a fast-moving, and realistic thriller. How did I miss that one the first time around?

FEBRUARY 16

Today was maintenance day for Larry. I was sick in bed not feeling well and Larry is outside fixing all sorts of things. A few days ago, he'd noticed the license plate light was out. So, he went to replace the bulb which was ok. It turned out to be the wire, as it had somehow been cut in half. Then, he discovered the license plate itself was very loose, ready to fall off. The wind had gotten up in behind the plate and pulled at the nuts holding it through the body of the motorhome. He just needed to find two nuts with bolts to replace them.

After going through every tool box (and there are quite a few of those), he finally found some nuts left over from the satellite repair last summer. The exhaust pipe was in the way if he tried to install them from the bottom, so he finally had to open the engine door above to reach them—with his bad left arm and shoulder. He said it was hurting really bad, when he finally came in.

Some things just can't be simple. And, stretching his bad arm is never easy.

Supper was just a large salad topped with chicken and crab meat. Yum.

> Job 6:10
> Then I would still have this consolation—
> my joy in unrelenting pain—
> that I had not denied the words of the Holy One.

We were finally able to get some more Netflix streaming, and watched two more episodes of *Travelers*. It's already starting to get complicated. Good.

FEBRUARY 17

Larry drove the motorhome two hours today, way down into the Louisiana Bayou country. This stretch of US 90 South was much better than the last; it was asphalt instead of that terribly bumpy concrete. Frank led us to Route 1, then all the way to the end of the road at Grand Isle. We had reservations at the Grand Isle State Park, Grand Isle, Louisiana, which Larry rated a 6.

The drive went quickly, and the details to the scenery changed often. Most of the general trip was a four-lane divided highway, with wetlands and high grasses on both sides. We saw lots of egrets. pelicans, and other waterfowl flying and looking for food in the water. Out in the far distance of the Gulf of Mexico, were massive oil rigs as in the movie, *Deep Water Horizon.*

Occasionally, we passed through small towns. At one point, we traveled quite a few miles on an elevated causeway, and other causeways branched out in different directions from it—it looked like a giant octopus. We have seen dozens of boats, shrimpers, fishers, tugs, barges, and other vessels on the waterways, in all colors, shapes, and sizes.

It was gently raining most of the journey, but cleared long enough for Larry to set up outside without him getting drenched. He hooked up to the water and electric, then rigged the banner and put out the kids packets. It started to rain again, just as he was taking the car off the tow dolly. It rained the rest of the evening. It was another cool day again, only crawling to 58 degrees, which will be our nighttime low. It's supposed to be 70 degrees and partly sunny tomorrow. It will be a much better day for exploring the area.

We had a small supper and watched *Hancock*, with Will Smith, Jason Bateman, and Charlize Theron. We'd seen it before, but it hit me a lot funnier this time.

Larry went off to bed, but I stayed up to listen to the nice sound of rain on the roof. Eventually, it started to lightning and thunder, but it kept a few miles away. I have always loved to watch lightning, then count until the thunder arrives.

Then I was off to sleep, as the pleasant sound of the rain continued to dance on the roof. Thank you, Lord, for another wonderful day.

FEBRUARY 18

We woke up to a sunny morning and warm blue skies. The air seemed cleaner, washed by last night's rain, and puddles were everywhere. Larry unpacked his long-unused metal detector and headed for the beach to find treasure. I took that as a terrific quiet time to write. Our tented next-door neighbors are splitting wood for a fire, and it's a pleasant sound. Now if only the other neighbors' dogs would quit barking incessantly.

When Larry returned, he said he'd found only a couple of soda cans covered in tar, probably from the deep-water rigs offshore. I sure wish he'd find a long-lost doubloon or a big diamond ring or something. He asked if I had gotten the books for year-end done, so that he could work on our taxes. I said no, because I'd been working on the book. But if that's what he wanted me to do... And it was.

While I spent the rest of the afternoon making sure that everything was correctly expensed, he decided to take the rear-view monitor apart. It had been flickering on the trip here, and sure enough, some of the contact wires had been jarred loose. Thank you, Lord, that it was a simple fix.

When I confirmed that everything in the books looked good, he began the taxes. I couldn't write anymore, because the TurboTax is on my computer, so I sat down to knit. He just about had them done, when he noticed something: why was our cost of goods (COG) so low? I went back through the entire system to determine why nothing had posted to COG, save three entries that I had posted directly, instead of through my Accounts Payable system. I looked until I was blue in the face, and everything was coded correctly, so why didn't it post correctly? I finally resigned myself to spending the next hour on the phone with Intuit.

After waiting more than 45 minutes on hold, listening to their horrible hold music, I finally got to speak with someone who really had no clue how to fix my problem in the beginning. A half-hour later, he finally asked me a key question and therein lay the whole answer. I have been using QuickBooks since 2008 and never had a problem with this. There's really no need to explain it here, but everything Larry had already downloaded to TurboTax was wrong. He had to start all over again.

But he already knew all the answers this time, and the job went quickly, praise the Lord.

Tonight, was early to bed for both of us. We were beat.

FEBRUARY19

I was still sound asleep when Larry snuck quietly out of the motorhome in the dark. It would be sunrise soon, and he loves sunrises. When I got up much later, he showed me all the pictures he'd taken. One was particularly perfect: the sun was coming up over the horizon, an egret was posed on the beach, directly in the path of the sun, and a half-dozen pelicans flew by. He captured it all. It was a "wow" photo, indeed.

2 Samuel 23:4
he is like the light of morning at sunrise
on a cloudless morning,
like the brightness after rain
that brings grass from the earth.'

I got ready and we drove to the nearby pier. They had a tower there which I had no desire to climb, so Larry went up alone. I watched all the activity offshore, and enjoyed the day's beauty. When he returned, we walked to the end of the long pier. There were quite a few fishermen (and fisherwomen) there at the end, but I didn't see anyone's catch.

To give them the benefit of the doubt, one woman had a cooler that could have held a catch, and there were a few heavy lines down to the water that could have held nets with a catch. The Mexicans were keeping to themselves on the right end of the pier; I think they were enjoying their cans of Modelo more than their fishing. Well, as long as they were happy; they weren't bothering another soul.

What we did see were dozens of dolphins. It was beautiful! They were coming up all over the bay, first to the left, then the right, you never knew where they would surface next. Larry did get one good picture of five dolphins cresting at the same time. What a spectacular sighting!

We drove over to the marina, which was pretty basic. We didn't even bother to get out of the car. We did take some pictures of one pretty sight, though. There were hundreds of seagulls covering several grassy mounds nearby. They knew sunset would come shortly, and they were there early to claim their spot for the night.

We'd been inside for a couple of days and decided we should go out to eat. Pickings were slim. Being off-season, there are very few places out here open for business. The Starfish Restaurant was nearby, so we decided to go there. Our waitress was friendly and chipper and our fried shrimp platter came quickly. It was nothing special, but it was good, well-prepared food. And their sweet tea was awesome. We ate all we could, but couldn't eat it all.

When we returned, the man camping in the site next to us spoke to Larry, before he came inside. Larry was shaking his head, and I asked him what was wrong. He said the man told him that our left-turn blinker was on, and had been all day yesterday, as well. How in the world did that happen, and why didn't he tell us that yesterday? Yet another mystery.

We watched some FOX News and Larry went to bed. I caught up on Facebook. With nothing else to do, I called it a day. Another wonderful day, I might add.

FEBRUARY 20
Today was a stay busy day in the motorhome. I did some cleaning, including taking everything out from under the kitchen sink.

Considering I don't do that often, because it kills my boney knees, it really needed to be done.

I have this really cute thing that I stuff plastic grocery bags into. It was a kitchen accessory that we'd carried in our retail store, years ago. It's a long tube made out of cloth, a pretty print of starfish and seashells. It hangs from the top (if I had a place to hang it) and you stuff your bags in through the opening at the top. Then, when you need a bag, you pull them out of the bottom. It's really handy, but since it's not hung, but laying under my sink, you have to stop and take a moment to put bags into it.

The reason I'm explaining this, is because I must have removed fifty different wads of grocery bags from under that sink! Plus, those cute little (and big) paper bags you get from specialty stores—I must have had twenty of those down there, too! There was also the plastic holder for our liquid cleaning supplies. Something had leaked all over the bottom, and it was a mess! I took it outside to an unoccupied site and hosed it down. It took three trips to the trash to get rid of all that stuff.

Another job was to tidy up the dinette. It's a catch-all for so much, including trinkets from our travels. Our beautiful daughter told us before we left, that she wanted to make us scrapbooks for our journeys. I was to keep brochures, campground info, tickets, postcards, etc. and send them to her. In between mailings, I have a cloth holder, like you can put files in, where I pitch everything to keep it altogether. Well, that holder was a disaster as well, spewing out its contents onto the dinette sea. I went through every piece and tried to group stuff together.

Well, in addition to the paper mementoes, I had kept part of bag of Community Coffee, *Mardi Gras King Cake Flavor* to send to her. I'd seen on TV that it's a family-owned coffee company in

Baton Rouge, Louisiana. I wound up buying two bags, to replenish my coffee supply. I knew Diana would enjoy it, too.

Also in the holder were three small bags of potato chips. Although Zappo's Potato Chips is located in Hanover, PA, they definitely get into the Mardi Gras spirit. I had bought a bag of *Spicy Cajun Crawtators* for myself, and they're hot, but good. I also dipped into a bag of their C*ajun Dill Gator Tators* and, as much as I love dill, they were way too hot for this wuss to eat.

There's a funny bag called *Voodoo,* that has colorful little voodoo dolls with stick-pins in them as well as *Voodoo Heat*, whose skeleton face on the cover has X's as eyes, and long, red hair sticking out in all directions. I won't even open them! I'm sure Diana will enjoy every one of them. If not, she will surely enjoy passing them around to her co-workers.

I mentioned before that I had some *Mardi Gras King Cake Flavor* coffee. I should explain these King Cakes. I had never heard of them before the Dutch Oven luncheon, as they had some on the prize table. According to Randazzo King Cake's web site, "The Mardi Gras or Carnival season officially begins on January 6th or the 'Twelfth Night,' also known to Christians as the 'Epiphany.' Epiphany comes from a Greek word that means 'to show.' Jesus first showed himself to the three wise men and to the world on this day. As a symbol of this Holy Day, a tiny plastic baby is placed inside each King Cake.

"The King Cake tradition is thought to have been brought to New Orleans from France in 1870. A King Cake is an oval-shaped bakery delicacy, crossed between a coffee cake and a French pastry that is as rich in history as it is in flavor. It's decorated in royal colors of PURPLE, which signifies 'Justice,', GREEN for 'Faith,' and GOLD for 'Power.' These colors were chosen to resemble a jeweled crown honoring the Wise Men who visited the Christ Child on Epiphany. In the past such things as coins, beans, pecans, or peas were also hidden in each King Cake.

"Today, a tiny plastic baby is the common prize. At the party, the King Cake is sliced and served. Each person looks to see if their piece contains the 'baby.' If so, then that person is named 'King' for a day and bound by custom to host the next party and provide the King Cake.

"Mardi Gras Day has a moveable date and may occur on any Tuesday from February 3rd to March 9th. It is always the day before Ash Wednesday, and always falls 46 days before Easter."[51]

And all this time, I always assumed Mardi Gras was simply an excuse for Catholics to party hearty before giving up meat and/or other indulgences for Lent. I never, ever knew.

The remainder of the day was restful. Larry headed to the beach for a while, while I chose to knit some wash cloths for Operation Christmas Child. I'd been making knit caps or years, and decided on something different for 2017.

Since we have no cable, I got out Season One of *Rizzoli and Isles,* and thoroughly enjoyed watching those episodes again. The characters are named and based on a whole series of Tess Gerritsen's books. They're based on a Boston detective (Rizzoli) and the coroner (Isles) as they address serious crimes with seriously funny friend and family complications.

After a supper of grilled pork chops, Larry decided, with the incoming storms, we should empty the grey water tank, so we don't have to do it in the rain tomorrow. There is no sewer connection at this campground, so we have to hold all the waste water. The industry terms that "being self-contained." We can go three days on

[51] randazzokingcake.com

the grey tank and six to seven days on the black before emptying it. Grey is shower and sink water. Black is the stuff you don't want to talk about. We packed up in a hurry and got that job done.

When we set back up, Larry managed to find the remote first and watched FOX News 'til bedtime. It was a great day. Again.

FEBRUARY 21

Today was a beautiful day. After the storms passed through last night, everything was once again brighter and cleaner. It was 65 degrees and sunny. I must confess a small envy for the lady staying in the site across from us. She stayed under her awning all day long, in the sunshine, reclined in a comfortable-looking bright blue chair, reading a book. That would define my dream day. But instead, my day was spent writing, here at the kitchen table, with my salt candle burning and a light breeze blowing in from the window at arm's length. I will admit that my day too, was a dream day.

We have a hard drive attached to our satellite so we can record shows through the dish called a DVR, (Digital Video Recorder) but it's been acting stupid of late. Larry wiped it clean yesterday and it seemed to work for a little while. But today he declared it dead, so we'll be replacing that on the way to New Orleans later this week.

The TV in front is mounted up above the dashboard, set into an overhead cabinet. Our big excitement of the day was when Larry pulled the TV out on its arm to put back the hard drive, it came right off the arm. OMG! The screws had worked their way out of the arm frame. I rushed to hold it up (and it was heavy!), while Larry searched for the screws. No damage done, but we'll be sure to keep checking those screws from now on! I don't want to think about how that scene would have unfolded, had we been driving!

Otherwise, Larry's bored today. He finished the business taxes in one fell swoop and now, there's just no pressing business to fret over. With his arm hurting badly, and that he cracked his head on an open cabinet door while fixing the TV, I convinced him to go take a nap. I know he's feeling poorly when he agrees to nap.

Believe it or not, I had my very first Hot Pocket today. Or, if I've ever had one before, I apologize, because I do not remember it. I had spied a new Limited-Edition Chicken Pot Pie at the grocery and decided to try it. It came with a dandy little crisper sleeve that you heated it in. It was really good! The insides were tasty and it was crispy, something that doesn't occur often, when you live out of a microwave. Well done, Hot Pockets. I'll have to get more of those.

We had little bits of this and that for supper tonight. The freezer was getting full of little bags of leftovers and it was time to up tidy things. Although very untraditional, we enjoyed it and were filled. Waste not, want not. Thank you, Lord.

We watched FOX News until O'Reilly was through, then I resumed *Rizzoli & Isles* where I'd left off the night before.

FEBRUARY 22

I awoke to yet another beautiful day. My goal was to finish my last edits on the last section of my first book. By noon, I'd emailed them all to my editor—my niece, Jana—so everything is in her hands now. We wait for her revisions and she will review my final review, and it will be ready to publish...or something like that.

The woman across the street is having another most enviable day. She's back out in that recliner, with her book. She's moved around a lot today, though. She started under their awning, but a palm tree caused her to be in the shade. She moved the chair out in front of their camper, but a different palm tree caused another shadow. She's moved way over in front of the camper now, out into the direct sun, still reading that book. It must be a great book. If I'd been sitting out in that sun, I'd be all warm and fuzzy, and sound asleep.

Larry's been slowly picking away at personal tax returns today. One of his standard intolerances is when he goes to use a piece of familiar software, and everything's been changed since the last time he used it. "Those yuppies or millennials or whatever you call the twenty- and thirty-year-olds—they just can't leave anything alone. You just get used to something and then they change everything."

According to Larry, it's a conspiracy against us Baby Boomers, I tell ya. Them durn yuppies are an enemy of the state. He says every year that the taxes get more complicated. He's a pretty smart guy when it comes to taxes and finance. He understands how the numbers work and how they all come together.

The last few years he is having trouble understanding it all. How can the average "Joe" do their taxes, he asks? It is simply ridiculous! He wonders who makes this stuff up? Take this number and subtract this number and divide by this number if that number is this or add this to the total if that number is less than the first number. The guy who thought all this up is probably laughing all the way to the bank. His bank! Taxes need to be simpler for all. You buy something you pay a tax, simple and it's done. No forms, no IRS, no additional taxes. End of lecture.

Daniel 11:20
"His successor will send out a tax collector to maintain the royal splendor. In a few years, however, he will be destroyed, yet not in anger or in battle.

Before I explain how I spent part of my afternoon, I must explain something. Larry loves movies. If he has his way, we would watch a different one every single day. On the road, there have been many times that we haven't been able to get satellite, can't get local channels, and the campground didn't have cable. Heck, there were a lot of times we didn't even have electric, but watched the TV on the inverter. I didn't even know what that was, until we blew it once.

So, over this past year, we have purchased quite a few $3-$5 DVD's at Walmart, and they've started to pile up. I emptied the overhead cabinet one handful at a time, and listed all the movies in alphabetical order on my computer. I kept about a dozen that I love to watch repeatedly, and put all the others into a large shopping bag. We'll be back home in Myrtle Beach in another few weeks and I'll trade them out for ones we'd left in storage, or at least make room for recent releases.

Being our last day here, we already hooked up the car onto the tow dolly and Larry walked one more trip to the beach. I've enjoyed it here, it's been so nice and quiet. And once the storms passed through, the weather's been perfect.

Thank you, Lord for a beautiful stay in Grand Isle, Louisiana.

FEBRUARY 23

We woke up to a beautiful sunny day with blue skies. It was so much different than when we'd arrived in Grand Isle just a few days ago. Once the tanks had been emptied, we left the campground. We headed back north on LA1 to US90 east. We were excited to be heading to New Orleans and Mardi Gras 2017.

It was an enjoyable trip today. The water, the birds, the boats. We watched as one bird dove headfirst into the water, coming up with lunch. What a delight to see such things!

We stopped at a Walmart and spent plenty to stock up for the coming week. We never extend our slides when we're not parked to camp, but there was so much to be put away, and it proved difficult in the small space. Larry agreed and I put out the driver's side extension, which gave us much more space to work. When a guy in a pickup blew his horn at us several miles down the road, we were shocked that we'd left it out! Something terrible, irreparable could have happened! Thank you, Lord again for Your amazing hedge of protection.

We passed many drawbridges in this area, but they were of a style and design that we had never seen before. They weren't a common drawbridge—where the bridge lifts up from one stationary side—or a swing bridge like we have back home in Myrtle Beach. These are known as vertical-lift bridges. With the use of counterbalances, there's a large steel framework that draws the entire length of the bridge upward, out of the way of passing boat traffic. We were sitting at a traffic light and enjoyed watching the entire procedure, from beginning to end.

The City of New Orleans is an old city, going back as far as 1718. It is a patchwork of its growth since then. The paved streets are narrow and I'm sorry to say that the infrastructure looks old and sad. It was a challenge to maneuver the motorhome through the maze of streets, around corners not created for such lengthy beasts.

We finally arrived at Jude Travel Park, which Larry rated a 4. It was a small place, another glorified parking lot with utilities, but it had decent wifi and the folks were friendly. It was located in a poorer part of the city, and security precautions were evident. They had a nice hot tub, which we would enjoy. We were given a welcome bag of Mardi Gras information, including beads and cups.

Rates for campgrounds are always, understandably, supply and demand. Larry had secured these reservations 3 months ago and had no choice but to pay twice the normal price to be here for Mardi Gras. We didn't care that this place was a cacophony of barking dogs, traffic, train whistles, racing crotch-rockets, and emergency sirens.

We were soon going to Mardi Gras!

UH, JUST A FEW MORE THINGS...

Once again, I hope you've enjoyed this book. We have seen so many wondrous and amazing things! How can folks believe, even for one second, that this beautiful earth began with a random Big Bang? As a giggle-getter, I will tell some people that I DO believe in the Big Bang. It's not Biblical, but I can believe that God said, "Let there be a Big Bang, and there it was—The Light. And Christians know that Jesus is the Light. Always has been, always will be.

I don't report daily in this book, but we have planted the seeds of the Gospel in every single place we've visited. I thought it would be tedious to report to read that we gave out 1 packet here, 12 packets there, or 50 packets someplace else. There is no rhyme or rhythm to the number of books given out at each campground. But to date, we've had 650 kids packets quietly taken from that hook on the front of the motorhome. Larry puts up that BIG Motor Home Ministry banner wherever we set up, although there have been times that we've been told to take it right back down.

We had such an encounter with a young man named Bandon, who came one day to tell us to take down the banner, while staying in an Ontario, Canada park. Book 3 explains how God worked a miracle in that, when Bandon came back to apologize the next day.

Book 3 begins with details of our big, wild Mardi Gras adventure in New Orleans. From there, there is far less time spent in National Parks, more in urban areas. Following our route across the southeast, then up the east coast, including Washington, DC and New York City, we have adventures in some of the most unusual places. We visit museums, casinos, factory tours, the Smithsonian, and even the White House. We see President Bush 41's home (from a distance) and spend a nearly indescribable day at Niagara Falls. Then there was plenty of time spent driving through Canada.

Now that the election's over and FOX News fired all the good ones, Larry never watches it anymore. The rig gets so quiet at times.

We continue to eat local fare, and we eat plenty of lobster for weeks! Our biggest technical difficulties are behind us (knock on wood), but there's always something going on.

Frick and Frack are still on board, but one day, Larry decided to give Frank the voice of a lilting British woman. It just didn't seem right to continue to call him Frank, so now she's Frankie. But the 3 of them continue their habitual bickering. He even programmed her to say "Larry, Slow down" when he runs over the posted speed limit and, "Railroad crossing ahead, Choo-Choo" when there are railroad tracks to cross over. She can be a hoot. Other times, not so much.

As I said in my last book, my greatest hope is that, despite my humanness, you have been able to see Christ in me, well, Christ in us. And, my prayer is that you desire a personal relationship with Him yourself. Some folks have the misconception that Christians think they're better and above other people. We are most definitely not. We're sinners, just like you, but forgiven by the Grace of God.

We have confessed our sins, asked that God would forgive us, and have become new creatures in Christ. It's really very simple. You can become a new creature, too.

Romans 10:9-10
If you declare with your mouth, "Jesus is Lord,"
and believe in your heart that God
raised him from the dead,
YOU WILL BE SAVED.

> [10] For it is with your heart that you believe
> and are justified,
> and it is with your mouth that you profess
> your faith and are saved.

Billy Graham Ministries' website explains that, "Jesus Christ says that we must be born again. How do we become born again? By repenting of sin. That means we are willing to change our way of living. We say to God, "I'm a sinner, and I'm sorry." It's simple and childlike. Then, by faith we receive Jesus Christ as our Lord and Master and Savior. We are willing to follow Him in a new life of obedience, in which the Holy Spirit helps us as we read the Bible and pray and witness."[52]

> John 3:5-7
> Jesus answered, "Very truly I tell you,
> no one can enter the kingdom of God
> unless they are born of water and the Spirit.
> [6] Flesh gives birth to flesh, but the Spirit
> gives birth to spirit
> . [7] You should not be surprised at my saying,
> 'YOU MUST BE BORN AGAIN

I personally believe that, "Those who leave everything in God's hand will eventually see God's hand in everything." I see God's hand in everything, every day. I hope you can understand why, after reading my words of faith. May God bless you richly.

> 2 Peter 3:9
> [9] The Lord is not slow in keeping his promise,
> as some understand slowness.
> Instead he is patient with you,
> not wanting anyone to perish,
> but everyone to come to repentance.

---

[52] billygraham.org

By the will of God, the adventure will continue.

On to book 3!

MORE OF MY FAVORITE RECIPES

RECIPE FOR "ERIN'S CHICKEN STUFF"

Preheat oven to 350 degrees

SHOPPING LIST and some prep work:

> 1 pound of cooked chicken, shredded
>> (you can use fresh chicken or canned, drained)
>
> 1 block of cream cheese, softened
> 1 cup of mayonnaise
> 1 cup of shredded cheddar cheese (I use mild)
> 1 bag of Tostito's Scoops

Mix together the chicken, cream cheese, and mayonnaise.

Mix all ingredients well and put in a 9 X 9 bakeware, suitable for serving

Bake for 30 minutes

While still hot, cover in shredded cheese.

Each person can spoon and fill his Scoops.

Enjoy!

RECIPE FOR "CROCK POT HAWAIIAN CHICKEN"

SHOPPING LIST:

2-4 boneless chicken breasts
1 large can crushed pineapple
1 cup BBQ sauce

Mix together pineapple and BBQ sauce in a bowl

Lay chicken in bottom of Crock Pot

Cover chicken with pineapple mixture

Cook on low 5-6 hours

Eat as cooked, or throw on the grill for a little crispy!

RECIPE FOR "EASY CROCK POT POTATO SOUP"

SHOPPING LIST and some prep work:

32 oz bag	Ore Ida Frozen Shredded Hash Browns
32 box	chicken broth
10 oz can	condensed cream of chicken soup
8 oz pkg	Philadelphia Cream Cheese
1 ½ cups	shredded sharp cheddar
¾ cup	bacon, crumbled
½ tsp fresh	rosemary, minced (I left this out)
	salt & pepper to taste
	oyster crackers

Combine all ingredients except rosemary in a 6-quart Crock Pot.

Cook on HIGH 3 hours.

Garnish with rosemary, if desired.

Soup thickens as it cools. YUM!

RECIPE FOR "BIG MEXICAN CROCK POT CHICKEN"

SHOPPING LIST and some prep work:

2-3 lb bag	frozen boneless, skinless tenderloins
8 oz pkg	cream cheese (do NOT use fat free!)
can	black beans, drained and rinsed
can	whole corn, drained
can	Rotel—I look for milder, you can go hotter
bag	tortilla chips

Lay frozen chicken in Crock Pot.

The following ingredients do NOT have to be layered—just dump:

cream cheese

black beans

corn

Rotel

Cook on LOW in Crock Pot for 6-8 hours. Mix well and serve over rice or with tortilla chips.

RECIPE FOR "SEVEN-LAYER SALAD"

SHOPPING LIST and some prep work:

small bag	lettuce shred
1 each	mild green pepper, deseeded and chopped
3-4 stalks	celery, thinly sliced
small bunch	green onions, remove roots and raggedy tops. Be sure to wash thoroughly, then finely chop both white and green tops together
small bag	frozen peas—do not thaw or cook
12-16oz jar	good mayonnaise (I like Duke's)
8-oz bag	finely shredded mild cheddar cheese

DO NOT STIR UNTIL READY TO SERVE:

In a large bowl, LAYER in the following order

- lettuce shred
- sprinkle pepper pieces evenly over the shred
- sprinkle celery slices evenly over the peppers
- sprinkle green onion pieces evenly over the celery
- spread frozen peas evenly

Using a large spatula, spread the mayonnaise over the peas, as you would spread frosting on a cake. Try carefully to "seal" all of the peas under the mayonnaise.

Cover with a lid or plastic wrap (don't lay on mayo directly) and refrigerate overnight.

When ready to serve, sprinkle the entire package of cheddar on top, then mix thoroughly. Feel free to improvise with other hard veges, like shredded carrots, for color. Yum!

RECIPE FOR "EASY QUICK FUDGE"

SHOPPING LIST:

½ cup	butter
2 ¼ cups	brown sugar
½ cup	milk
¾ cup	peanut butter
1 tsp	vanilla extract
3 ½ cups	confectioner's sugar

Melt butter in a medium saucepan over medium heat.

Stir in brown sugar and milk.

Bring to a boil and boil for 2 minutes, stirring frequently.

Remove from heat.

Stir in peanut butter and vanilla.

Pour over confectioner's sugar in a large mixing bowl.

Beat until smooth; pour into an 8 X 8 dish.

Chill until firm and cut into squares.

BACK OF THE BOOK STUFF

Republished from the original His Road Trip

and we added a few more …

<u>Some folks wonder how we can possibly live full-time in about 350 square feet?</u> We downsized from a 2,300 square-foot home with a huge kitchen, 3 bathrooms and a 2-car garage for storage, so YES, there were some adjustments to be made! We had yard sales for three weekends running, sold all our furniture, and brokered our antiques. I gave dozens of books to a senior living facility and some to our county library. Some precious memories could not be parted with, and could not accompany us, so they did go into storage for a time. During the yard sales, a woman introduced herself as a worker from a local Habitat for Humanity store. Not only would they pick up furniture, she said the local store would pick up anything and everything we had left over, as long as it was all in boxes, and easy to load. When we had packed, sold, donated, and brokered everything that we could, I gave her a call. It was a tremendous service to me.

Now on the road, there are times, I must admit, that I just have to get out by myself for a while. I usually feign a need for something and take the car and Frack out on a drive to Walmart, Dollar General, or whatever's available in the area. I feel much better when I get back.

And even though Larry nibbles in little bits all day, he has finally come to understand that I like to eat out, especially to sample unique area cuisine. If I've been inside for days—because of writing, weather, or whatever—much he's better now at suggesting that we go out to shop, eat, or go to a movie.

But get used to the idea that there are going to be times that both of you want to be in exactly the same place at the exactly the same time…usually the bathroom! Just be considerate of who's whining the loudest.

Some folks wonder if we could give them some pointers?
Larry would say that planning is of the utmost importance, especially if you travel when school is out of session. At those times, you can't just roll in somewhere and expect there to be vacancy. Plan your route well, because at 8 miles to the gallon, you sure don't want to backtrack!

Larry's really great at drilling in and planning, and had all of our National Park reservations in advance of our departure, most of our State Parks, and a great deal of our private parks, as well. He put in a lot of time, while I was recovering, searching the routes, computing travel times, comparing rates and ratings of campgrounds. He had searched areas to see what attractions were there. The out-of-season weather has been our biggest surprise, but you can't control Mother Nature!

Some folks wonder if there are any apps out there, to help them on the way? Larry's phone is chuck full of helpful apps!

#1 App! ALLSTAYS is an app that every person with an RV should have. You can search campgrounds and read personal reviews, find Walmarts who allow boondoggling with reviews, truck stops, rest stops, propane, dump stations, height clearances along a route, rig maintenance and repair. Their reviews have helped us avoid poor choices on the road. We use this the most in our travels. Plus, it maps it all out for you.

GOOD SAM has an app that is good for checking campgrounds near you and if they are a member with a discount as well their rating of the campground.

ULTIMATE CG app shows where there is free camping allowed on public lands. This is how we had the opportunity to stay at White Sands.

CHIMANI is an app that gives you great information on all National Parks, national monuments, historic sites, memorials, recreational areas and more.

TRIPOSO is an app that gives you everything you need to know about the places and cities you plan to visit.

GAS BUDDY is an app for finding the cheapest fuel on your route. Members are constantly updating prices, and a recently reported drop of even a few cents on diesel can save you lots of cash on 100 gallons. TIP: if you can, always fill up away from the interstate. We have seen interstate truck plazas charge up to forty cents more than a small-town guy just off the interstate, less than a mile away. Gas Buddy will help you find those deals. But also, Google it, to be sure their lot has room for your big rig.

MY MEDICAL is an app for keeping your medical records with you, wherever you go, whether you're traveling away from home, or not.

WUNDERGROUND is an app from Weather Underground that will show you live weather from every weather station out there. When you open it, it automatically homes in on exactly where you are and what weather forecast, live radar, and any weather alerts that are active at that time. Priceless!

GOOGLE MAPS (aka Frack) is an app that everybody should have for everyday use. Frack is pretty great on the long haul, but sometimes needs some human interpretation. It also has no idea that you're a high-profile vehicle with another vehicle in tow, so it may take you somewhere you really shouldn't be.

SYGIC TRUCKERS GPS (aka Frank) is what we've just begun to use. You begin by telling the program how long you are, what height you are, and what load you are, so it keeps you away from places you shouldn't be. One important talent loudly warns you of exceeding speed limits, upcoming rest areas, and railroad crossings.

RVingVIP is a maintenance app, a desktop program to keep track of all the maintenance issues of your RV.

DISHALIGN and **DishForMyRv** are invaluable tools to assist you in manually setting your dish antenna to satellite feeds.

TOLL CALCULATOR GPS helps you determine which route costs less when traveling on toll roads with a large motorhome and a "toad" (tow vehicle). This could save you hundreds of dollars, if you plan to be in areas with multiple toll roads. Personal No-Brainer: Avoid the George Washington Bridge into NY or it will cost you BIG time!

TOLLSMART is another toll calculator app.

Find a good **LEVELING TOOL**. Every single time we pull into a new campground, we need to level. There are lots of apps out there that can assist you with this.

BANK AND INVESTMENTS apps are very important. One thing we learned years ago, the hard way. When you leave on a trip, your debit card company wants you to call ahead of time. We had lived in South Carolina for so long that, one year when we went home to Cincinnati and used our debit card, the bank declined it. They continued to decline it until I called in and asked what was going on? Their security assumed that my card has been stolen, because it was being used in an area that I never frequented—it went against my spending pattern. They made a note of where I was and for how long, and the problem was solved. Now I'm sure to notify them before I go anywhere out-of-state, to avoid surprises.

<u>**Some folks wonder what to do with their mail?**</u> If you're a member of Good Sam, they offer forwarding services. They assign you an address that you give out, they collect your mail until you ask them to forward it to you. We personally, have a PO Box back home. Diana picks up everything, opens anything unusual and screen shots us copies, in case it's something urgent.

<u>**Some folks wonder about using their computers on the road?**</u> This has been our biggest challenge and our largest expense. We initially chose Verizon for our cellular service because they had

the best coverage across America. The Verizon Jet Pack is mobile and works wherever our Verizon cell service works. AND, they have recently changed to Unlimited. This rocked our world completely! Most private and some state campgrounds advertise FREE wifi, but it's usually just a token offering, and rarely works well, except in the middle of the night. So, don't depend on what campgrounds are offering, make solid, dependable plans of your own.

Some folks wonder if there are any National Park programs they should join? If you are 65 or older, or permanently disabled, you should definitely apply for a lifetime Access Pass and pay the one-time $10 fee. Every National Park has an impact fee they charge for entering the Park. The Access Pass will have your name and photo on it, and it's good for you and anyone in your vehicle.

Larry has one, so I don't need one because I'm always with him. Some federal campgrounds even offer a 50% discount on campground fees. It's saved us hundreds of dollars this past year.

I've heard that the federal government is making changes to the current permanent pass in 2018, so if you qualify, you should scoop one up before it becomes an annual, renewable pass.

Some folks wonder if there are clubs or memberships they should consider joining? We use several camping clubs. Just for your information, the average we've spent per night on the road is around $40 for full hookups, where high-end resorts could cost you $70-$100 per night. Special events like Mardi Gras, in New Orleans, one campground (we did not stay here) was charging nearly $300 per night. National Parks and State parks average around $30. Casinos, sometimes offer a great night of camping, cheap like, $20 or less—one even let us stay for free—in the hopes they get you in their casino.

Of course, you can't beat Boondoggling, it's FREE! Here are some of our personal thoughts about each:

GOOD SAM CLUB is a great value for the annual fee. It saves us 10% each time we use it and most private campgrounds do accept it. Their website has the BEST reviews of campgrounds, and Larry based most of our reservations on those reviews. They offer supplemental programs that you can sign up for, as well: Roadside Assistance, Motorhome Insurance, Travel Assist Medical, Extended Warranty, Motorhome Financing, Coast to Coast, Discounts at Camping World, Flying J, Pilot, and others, RV Forum, Mail Forwarding Services, and much, much more.

PASSPORT AMERICA is another good value for some half-priced stays. The drawback is that there are a lot of rules regarding its use and there are many campgrounds that don't accept it. You really can't use this in prime seasons.

COAST TO COAST. We have saved money with this membership, but it's costly to join up front. Usually the campgrounds are older and off the beaten path, but for $10 a night, sometimes it's worth the trip. Before buying, I'd suggest you search the internet for discounters and other agents, and be sure there would be participating campgrounds in the area you'll be visiting. Some of them can be really nice and cheap, but we have stayed in others that have been mediocre, at best.

Your nightly fee may be $10, but then it's $5 more for 50-amp electric, $5 more for wifi, $3 more for cable (you cannot opt-out—true story). They $5 you to death, until what you pay is closer to their normal rates.

KOA VALUE KARD. Many KOA campgrounds are aging, but there are still some really nice ones out there, just be sure to check out the reviews. We pay an annual fee and receive 10% at KOA across America. They don't accept any other discounts, not even Good Sam.

RESORT PARKS INTERNATIONAL / RPI. We do have this, but haven't used it at all this past year, because we have the Coast to Coast membership. The2 programs are similar and we have it because we have Coast to Coast. We have found that the resorts they offer are not in the best of shape and most are old. We have not renewed our membership.

ENCORE is also benefit of Coast to Coast, and we have used it for a 10% discount.

THOUSAND TRAILS. We don't use this since we have Coast to Coast. Some of the participating parks are old and outdated as well as being out of the way. I think it's their way of attempting to attract folks that would not come otherwise.

ENJOY AMERICA. We have used this to save 50%, but like Passport America, there are some rules you must follow. This came with our RPI membership, as well.

Some folks wonder if we could offer any tips to making reservations? Accept the fact that reservations are a MUST for popular destinations and/or popular times. Any time kids are out of school—even for a three-day holiday—people are out and about.

Make reservations at least 60-90 days out. If you want to stay in places like Yellowstone, Yosemite or Cades Cove in the Great Smoky Mountain National Park, you must make them a YEAR in advance of your date. For example, we wanted to enjoy a White House tour in 2017. We learned that, post 9/11, you must request that reservation through your State Congressman or Senator 3 to 4 months in advance of our desired date. Research your destinations.

Print out everything you reserved, your dates, an exact address for your GPS, and any confirmation numbers. Keep them in date order, organized and ready for your arrival. We keep ours on a clip board on the dash.

We use www.Recreation.gov and www.ReserveAmerica.com, a great deal for park reservations.

We are weather wussies. We have been through multiple hurricanes and 3 blizzards. We like warm weather, so if you're in search of 70-degree weather in the winter like us, I have news: so is everybody else! Places like Key West, Florida, the Gulf State Beaches, South Padre Island and Galveston, Texas fill up fast for the winter. You should probably make those reservations a YEAR in advance, too.

In Texas, they called us Winter Texans. In Florida, they'll call you Snowbirds. We love being called names.
Some folks wonder if we could help them get organized? Organization is a must. I have only a tiny fraction of the space I had in my nice home. I brought one piece of Corning Ware and rarely use it. I have two skillets, three saucepans, again, which I rarely use, because I nuke or Crock Pot almost everything. I brought 4 plates, 4 bowls, and 2 large bowls. If we ever have company, we'll eat off paper, no problem.

BUY SMALL. When I went back to work several years ago and Larry started shopping, he would bring home huge packages of stuff from Sam's Club and Costco. Early on, we had 36 rolls of toilet paper stuck away in every cabinet, nook and cranny, under the dinette, and under the bed. "But it was cheap," he said. He has finally learned that a 12-pack of Scott is just fine.

My washer/dryer uses one tablespoon of detergent per load. I had purchased Mrs. Meyers in a bottle with 68 loads. He bought a gigantic Tide that will probably last me two years. There's just no need for that, with such precious limited space.

Larry's sense of humor often tells me, "If you can't eat it and poop it, then don't buy it." Not Funny. And then he buys 6 huge tubes of toothpaste, that we will take up precious space until he turns 70.

Buy small. You can always buy more.

Some folks wonder if we have any tips for repairs and maintenance? I would recommend first getting online to use an RV forum at www.rvforum.net or www.rv.net/forum for information regarding your specific rig and maintenance. There's a strong chance that other folks have experienced the same problem you have, so you should be able to easily find solutions to your problem.

Always carry a good set of basic tools and a drill set because, believe me, you WILL need them. Other basic needs would include: engine oil, coolant, silicone, sealant, distilled water for your batteries, Gorilla Glue, duct tape, and water filters. We have found out recently about a "duct tape" from the Gorilla Glue people that you can fix a lot with it. Larry recently fixed holes in our plastic AC shrouds with this tape and then sprayed them with black Flex Seal. They look good as new! We have Flex Seal in white, black and clear. We use them all.

Basic needs you may know, but you may not:

Always use a water regulator. Many campgrounds will warn you that they have high water pressure, so I always use a regulator, regardless. And always carry a spare—they fail without any warning whatsoever.

You should carry at least 25 feet of water hose, and a spare. Since typical hoses take up room and kink, we bought one that shrinks up when not in use for maintenance, and another rubber blue EZ coil one for our fresh water uses. Also, keep on hand a couple of 3-foot sections of regular water hose. If the campsite spigots are too low to the ground, they really come in handy.

They also make rinsing your holding tank a whole lot easier. We leave one 3-foot section connected to the black tank rinse all the time. This makes it easier to rinse the tank when its time. Don't forget those water hose washers! These go missing out of your hoses all the time. They cost only $1 for a package of a dozen or so but if you don't have one you have a leaky faucet.

You will also need 30 feet of <u>electric cable</u> (I've never needed more than that). One for 50-amp and one for 30-amp. You can always use the extra 30-amp one for an extension cord if you ever needed one. A good <u>surge protector</u> is needed as well, for your electrical connection, and <u>adapters</u> to connect to different amps offered.

After a major electric failure with costly repairs and not knowing if it was the campgrounds fault, we invested in a TRC electrical monitor for about $300. Here's a little more about these: "Portable whole-RV surge and spike protectors which now offer more than twice the rated protection of earlier models. They have easy to see LCD display uses plain, easy to understand language to keep you informed of status at a glance. Built-in intelligence lets these units reset automatically at power restoration. Each now shuts off power in the event of an open ground or thermal line/load overtemperature condition, as well as in the event of an open neutral, low (under 102 volts) and high (over 132 volts) voltage or reverse polarity to protect your RV and its electrical components from damage and fire.

"Continuously monitors for voltage and amp draw (RMS) and reverse polarity (miswired pedestal or elevated ground voltage). Built-in 128-second reset delay protects air conditioner compressors. Two-light LED backup indicators for power and faults. More compact design for easier storage. Easy pull handles on connectors for safety and convenience."

To avoid any problems, you should have FOUR 10-15-foot sections of <u>sewer hoses</u>. Carry extras because you constantly get pin holes in the hoses. We use the more expensive Rhino Extreme brand hoses. They cost more but last a lot longer than the cheaper brands.

To access <u>cable</u> connections, a good quality 25-foot coax should do.

We also use a small shopvac with an extension cord for fast clean ups.

We have small flashlights all over the place in handy storage spots for easy excess as well as plenty of AA and AAA batteries.

To help us maneuver the rig in campgrounds and tight places we use walkie talkies to help us communicate with each other. Some campgrounds have huge trees, rocks, fences in really bad places when trying to back the rig. We used to scream and yell—the radios are a so much easier and quieter way to give moment-to-moment directions.

Some folks wonder about Camping World?

We do use this RV supply store. But, they can be expensive! If you can find what you need at Walmart, buy there. But, as a last resort, you can usually find or order what you need. Amazon is also a great site to search and order from if you don't need something fast and can have it delivered to you down the road.

We usually try to get maintenance done at a Freightliner chassis dealer instead of Camping World but shop around. Another thing we have learned, all RV repair places and dealers are not the same, especially mobile operators. Some are just plain and simple rip-offs! Do your research and look at reviews before letting anyone touch your rig. You can usually fix things yourself if you think through the problem and search on line for solutions. Figure out how it works before attempting the repairs yourself and if you are physically capable of doing it.

Some folks wonder how we handle keeping up with our doctors?
We sat down with our doctors before we left our home base. We explained our plans to travel and requested that they write our prescriptions in a way that would enable us to get them filled as needed, for the next 12 months. None of our doctors had any problems in doing just that.

I can personally recommend CVS Pharmacy for this. They seem to be almost everywhere, and your refill information is right there in every computer. Walmart or Walgreens probably do this, too. As long as there were refills left, I never had a problem in getting prescriptions filled. But if you take any controlled prescriptions, the rules are different, so talk to your home pharmacy about these.

When we planned our trip, we planned to return to our home base in the spring, when the weather would be warm. We'll spend 30 days back home to take care of dentist and doctor appointments, and get those refills rewritten for another year.

Some folks wonder about all of those factory tours we took? Other than the scenery and wildlife at the National Parks, those tours were some of our best times! Each time we arrived in a new area, we Googled it. Most cities and city Chambers of Commerce have official sites to encourage travelers to visit there. All you need is the name, and you go to their official site for possible tours, times, and prices. Most have been absolutely FREE, and those that charged, the fees were minimal.

We have already been to the following:
- Jelly Belly, Fairfield, CA
- Freightliner, Gaffney, SC
- Harry & David, Medford, OR
- Gibson Guitar, Memphis, TN
- Hallmark, Kansas City, MO
- Tabasco, Avery Island, LA
- Budweiser, St. Louis, MO
- Celestial Teas, Boulder, CO
- Boeing, Everett, WA
- SAS Shoes, San Antonio, TX
- Hammonds Candies, Denver, CO
- Pendleton Blankets, Washougal, WA
- Jim Bean, Clermont, KY
- Landstrom's Black Hills Gold, Rapid City, SD

I don't know if you'd call these factory tours, but

- The US Mint in Denver, CO was amazing too.
- The Money Museum Federal Res. Bank of St. Louis
- US Bureau of Engraving & Printing, Wash. DC

In 2017, we plan to see at least the following:

- Cape Cod Potato Chips, Hyannis, MA
- Ben & Jerry's, Waterbury, VT
- Coke, Atlanta, GA
- Hershey, Hershey, PA
- The White House, Washington, DC
- The Smithsonian
- A show on Broadway, New York City
- The 9/11 memorial
- Niagara Falls
- Old Country Cheese, West Caston, WI
- Winnebago, Forest City, IA

Don't miss the Presidential Libraries ... Buy a membership if you are going to visit more than one in a year.

ODYSSEY MAPS 2016 - 2017

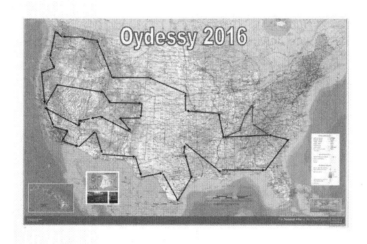

CAMPGROUND LIST 2016 - 2017

September	Moab Valley RV Resort, Moab, UT, Rating 9
September	Canyon Reef National Park, Fruita CG, UT, Rating 5
September	Ruby's Inn RV Park, Bruce Canyon, UT, Rating 4
September	Bryce Canyon NP, N. Campgr, Bryce, UT, Rating 4
September	Zion Canyon Campground, Springdale, UT, Rating 4
September	Wahweap Campground, Page, AZ, Rating 7
September	Mesa Verde NP, Morefield, Mancos, CO, Rating 3
September	Alpen Rose RV Park, Durango, CO, Rating 4
September	Santa Fe Skies RV Park, Santa Fe, NM, Rating 7
September	Trailer Ranch, Santa Fe, NM, Rating 7
September	American RV Park, Albuquerque, NM, Rating 7
October	Grand Canyon Camper Vill., Tusayan, AZ, Rating 2
October	Lake Mead RV Villa, Boulder City, NV, Rating 10
October	Las Vegas Motor Coach Rt, Las Vegas, NV, Rate 12
October	Death Valley Nat Park, Furnace Creek, CA, Rating 6
October	Hobson Beach County Park, Ventura, CA, Rating 4
October	Malibu Beach RV Park, Malibu, CA, Rating 6
November	Orangeland RV Park, Orange, CA, Rating 9
November	San Mateo CA St Park, San Clemente, CA, Rating 6
November	Chula Vista RV Resort, Chula Vista, CA, Rating 10
November	Sunland RV, Palm Desert, CA, Rating 10
December	Rincon Country W RV Resort, Tucson, AZ, Rating 10
December	Wells Fargo RV Park, Tombstone, AZ, Rating 2
December	Carlsbad RV Parks, Carlsbad, NM, Rating 3
December	Big Bend Natl Park, Rio Grande Village, TX, Rating 3
December	Blazing Star, RV Resort, San Antonio, TX, Rating 8
January	Isla Blanca Park Camgr, S Padre Isl, TX, Rating 3
January	Mustang Isl State Park, Corpus Christi, TX, Rating 5
January	Galveston Island State Park, Galveston, TX, Rating 5

January	Vineyard RV Resort, Grapevine, TX, Rating 8
January	Winstar Casino RV Pk, Thackerville, OK, Rating 10
January	Hot Spgs NP Gulpha Gorge Cgr Hot Spgs, AR, Rat 7
February	Paragon Casino, Marksville, LA, Rating 9
February	Palmetto Island State Park, Abbeville, LA, Rating 7
February	Hideaway Ponds, Gibson, LA, Rating 2
February	Grand Isle State Park, Grand Isle, LA, Rating 6
February	Jude Travel Park. New Orleans, LA, Rating 3

Proverbs 19:17

Kindness to the poor is a loan to the Lord,
and He will give a reward to the lender.

---

2 Timothy 4:6-8

For I am already being poured out like a drink offering,
and the time for my departure is near.
I have fought the good fight, I have finished the race,
I have kept the faith.

Now, there is in store for me the Crown of Righteousness,
which the Lord, the Righteous Judge,
will award to me on that day—and not only to me,
but also to all who have longed for His appearing.

Made in the USA
Middletown, DE
29 April 2021